Higher Education Through Open and Distance Learning

Open and distance learning has expanded dramatically in recent years across the world, across the spectrum of subject areas, and across educational levels. This book takes a detailed look at the state-of-the-art of open and distance learning in higher education, and presents a fascinating picture of a world and its educational culture in transition.

This edited collection contains authoritative analyses of key issues together with current accounts of practice in each region of the world. It includes:

– open and distance learning in relation to internationalisation, lifelong learning and flexible learning
– costs of distance education
– the impact of telecommunications
– applications of open and distance learning in Africa, the Americas, Asia, Europe and Oceania.

It draws together experts in the field from all over the world, and has a truly international perspective on the phenomenon of open and distance learning. Its unparalleled breadth of coverage makes it an indispensable work of reference for experts and newcomers alike.

Keith Harry was until recently Director of the International Centre for Distance Learning at the Open University, and is now a freelance adviser.

World review of distance education and open learning
A Commonwealth of Learning series
Series editor: Hilary Perraton

Editorial advisory group:

Maureen O'Neil	President, International Development Research Centre, Canada (chair)
Professor Hugh Africa	Vice-Chancellor, Vista University, South Africa
Professor Denise Bradley	Vice-Chancellor, University of South Australia, Australia
Dato' Professor Gajaraj Dhanarajan	President, Commonwealth of Learning
Sir John Daniel	Vice-Chancellor, Open University, Britain
Professor Armaity Desai	Chairperson, University Grants Commission, India
Dr Maris O'Rourke	Director, Education, Human Development Network, World Bank
Hans d'Orville	Director, Information Technology for Development Programme, Bureau for Policy and Programme Support, UNDP
Dr Hilary Perraton	Director, International Research Foundation for Open Learning, Britain (secretary)

The world review of distance education and open learning is published on behalf of the Commonwealth of Learning.

The Commonwealth of Learning is an international organisation established by Commonwealth governments in 1988. Its purpose is to create and widen opportunities for learning, through Commonwealth co-operation in distance education and open learning. It works closely with governments, colleges and universities with the overall aim of strengthening the capacities of Commonwealth member countries in developing the human resources required for their economic and social development.

Higher Education Through Open and Distance Learning

World review of distance education and open learning: Volume 1

Edited by Keith Harry

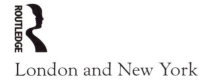

London and New York

THE COMMONWEALTH *of* LEARNING

First published 1999
by Routledge
11 New Fetter Lane, London EC4P 4EE

Simultaneously published in the USA and Canada
by Routledge
29 West 35th Street, New York, NY 10001

Selection and editorial matter © 1999 Keith Harry;
individual chapters © 1999 the contributors

Typeset in Goudy by RefineCatch Limited, Bungay, Suffolk
Printed and bound in Great Britain by
TJ International Ltd, Padstow, Cornwall

British Library Cataloguing in Publication Data
A catalogue record for this book is available from the British Library

Library of Congress Cataloging in Publication Data
Higher education through open and distance learning / [edited by]
    Keith Harry.
        p.   cm. – (World review of distance education and open
learning; v. 1)
    Includes bibliographical references and index.
    1. Distance education.   2. Education, Higher.   3. Open learning.
I. Harry, Keith.   II. Series.
LC5800.H535   1999
378.1'75 – dc21   98–31543
                         CIP

ISBN 0–415–19791–0 (hbk)
ISBN 0–415–19792–9 (pbk)

Contents

List of tables and figures

Tables

Figures

Contributors

Dr Hans-Peter Baumeister is a senior researcher in distance education at the Deutsches Institut für Fernstudienforschung, Tübingen, Germany.

Dr Denis Blight is Chief Executive, IDP Education Australia and previously worked with Australia's Department of Foreign Affairs and in the Australian Agency for International Development.

Ed Brandon is Programme Coordinator in the Office of the Board for Non-Campus Countries and Distance Education at the University of the West Indies.

Dr Fabio Chacón currently works in the Centre for International Development and Education, the Corporate University for the Venezuelan petroleum industry. For more than two decades he worked on the development of the Universidad Nacional Abierta of Venezuela.

Hung-Ju Chung is a lecturer at the Department of Social Sciences at the National Open University in Taiwan.

Sir John Daniel was knighted for services to higher education in 1994. He has been Vice Chancellor of the British Open University since 1990.

Dorothy Davis is Group General Manager, External Relations, IDP Education Australia in Sydney, with responsibility for IDP's research, consultancy, publications, communication and training programmes.

Professor Tony Dodds is Director of the Centre for External Studies at the University of Namibia and a long-time former Director of the International Extension College.

Yvonne Fung is Associate Professor in Education at the Open University of Hong Kong.

Jenny Glennie is Director of the South African Institute for Distance Education.

Patrick Guiton is Education Specialist for Higher Education at the

Commonwealth of Learning and was formerly Director of External Studies at Murdoch University, Western Australia.

Dr Keith Harry is a freelance consultant and the former Director of the International Centre for Distance Learning.

Corinne Hermant-de-Callataÿ is a Principal Administrator in the European Commission, Directorate General XXII (Education, training and youth).

Thomas Hülsmann is a research officer at the International Research Foundation for Open Learning.

Janet Jenkins is an independent international consultant in open and distance education.

Associate Professor Bruce King is Director of the Flexible Learning Centre at the University of South Australia.

Dr Robin Mason is Head of the Centre for Information Technology in Education at the British Open University.

Dr Claire Matthewson was successively Director of University Extension, University of the South Pacific, and Director, International Projects, Centre for Distance Education, Simon Fraser University, Canada.

Professor Geoffrey Mmari is the Vice Chancellor of the Open University of Tanzania and previously served as Vice Chancellor of the University of Dar Es Salaam and of Sokoine University of Agriculture.

Dr Louise Moran is a freelance consultant who formerly played a major role in the development of Deakin University's distance programme.

David Murphy is Associate Professor in Flexible Learning at the Centre for Higher Education Development at Monash University in Australia and was until recently at the Open University of Hong Kong.

Brittmarie Myringer is Industrial Liaison Officer at Mid Sweden University.

Evelyn Nonyongo is Head of the Institute for Continuing Education at the University of South Africa.

Alan Olsen is a researcher and consultant on international education who has worked in international education in Hong Kong, Australia and New Zealand.

Dr Santosh Panda is Professor of Distance Education and Director, Staff Training and Research Institute of Distance Education, Indira Gandhi National Open University, India.

Dr Hilary Perraton is Director of the International Research Foundation for Open Learning. He is a former member of the Commonwealth Secretariat.

Greville Rumble is Regional Director of the British Open University, South East Region and is a former Planning Officer of the University.

Dr Douglas Shale is an Academic Analyst in the Office of Institutional Analysis at the University of Calgary, Canada.

Dr Andras Szücs is Executive Director of the European Distance Education Network (EDEN).

Ruby Va'a is currently acting Deputy Director and Head of Distance Education, University Extension, at the University of the South Pacific.

Dr Xingfu Ding is Vice Director and Director of Distance Education Institute, and Head of Library, the CCRTVU in China.

Foreword

In 1987, forty-nine Heads of Governments of the Commonwealth of Nations made a bold decision to establish the Commonwealth of Learning (COL) as their agency to inform, assist and encourage member states to develop capacities in the design, management and growth of distance education. Political leaders came to that conclusion out of a concern for the increasing demand for more and better education from their people, coupled with the realisation that newer and more economical ways must be found if those demands were to be met without bankrupting national treasuries. Distance education appealed to them as a viable alternative. In the ten years since its founding, the COL has in a variety of ways added value to the thinking, planning, starting and managing of distance education systems across the Commonwealth. In the process, the organisation also found itself to be a primary source of information, to the Commonwealth as well as others, on many aspects of distance education and open learning.

Even in this age of near-unfettered flow of information, it is amazing how little is known about the nature, practices, successes, failures, relevance and effectiveness of training and education delivered using distance education. This unawareness is not just limited to people from developing economies or those outside the educational profession. It is widespread among people from both developed and developing economies. Also, sadly, there is as much ignorance among many in education as among those outside it, about what distance education can do and cannot do, what does and does not constitute good practice in distance education, its efficiencies and governance. Yet over the same period that the practice of distance education was growing, so too has its literature, so that the problem for those wanting to know more about the field is, where does one start?

I hope that this volume, the first in a series, will be that starting point. Overwhelmed on the one hand by the proliferation of information on distance education and concerned on the other by its inaccessibility to many who should be informed by it, my colleagues and I at the Commonwealth of Learning felt compelled to design a publication that could bring the wealth of experience in distance education in a readable and usable form to community developers, politicians, policy-makers, international development agencies and non-governmental workers among others. We wanted the experts in distance education to reach the informed as well as the uninformed. This first volume on *Higher Education* was a natural start for two reasons. First, distance education seems to have moved into the centre stage in this sector more than in any other and, second, the clamour for more higher education, especially in the developing economies, is getting louder each day even while the cost of providing it is on the increase. The use of distance education under these circumstances seems more an imperative than an option. The international experience, captured in this book, could be helpful to those with the responsibility of making the world's decisions about higher education. Subsequent volumes plan to examine other sectors and issues.

In planning and producing this volume and the series the COL was fortunate in receiving advice from a group of knowledgeable and committed internationalists, contributions from distance-education practitioners of great repute, editors with an eye for quality, and a publisher with a long reputation in the field. To all of them on behalf of the COL I express my sincere gratitude.

Gajaraj Dhanarajan
President and CEO, Commonwealth of Learning

Acknowledgements

This book exists because of an initiative by the Commonwealth of Learning which has funded its development and provided invaluable support as it has taken shape. Without this, the series, of which this is the first volume, would not have happened. Beyond that, we are grateful for the personal interest taken in the plans for the series, including this volume, by Gajaraj Dhanarajan, President of the Commonwealth of Learning. We are also glad to acknowledge the advice on its planning provided by an international editorial advisory group, chaired by Maureen O'Neil, President of the International Development Research Centre of Canada, who are guiding the Commonwealth of Learning on the development of the series.

The book has benefited from advice and comments from many friends and colleagues notably in the Commonwealth of Learning and the International Research Foundation for Open Learning. Alan Tait of the British Open University helped us in the planning stages. Thaiquan Lieu of the International Centre for Distance Learning has provided invaluable support in tracking literature for us.

Part of chapter 3, by Robin Mason, is based on material prepared for her book *Globalising education: trends and applications*, published by Routledge in 1998. The figures in chapter 3 are based on work done at the Knowledge Media Institute of the Open University by Peter Scott, Tony Seminara, Mike Wright, Mike Lewis, Andy Rix and Marc Eisenstadt and we are grateful for permission to reproduce them. We acknowledge the support of the European Commission which funded work by the International Research Foundation for Open Learning reported in chapter 6. The Open University has kindly allowed us to use material by Greville Rumble in chapter 9, some of which appeared in a different format in the journal *Open Learning*. We are indebted to the European Commission for material on its programmes included in chapter 10.

We have a particular debt to Honor Carter, Secretary to the International Research Foundation for Open Learning, who managed the whole process of putting the book together with diligence, calm, efficiency and long hours, made worse by a last rush during the school holidays.

Opinions in the text are those of the authors and do not necessarily represent the view of the Commonwealth of Learning or of the institutions on which they report. There is no political significance in the name used in the text for any country or territory.

Acronyms and abbreviations

Names of institutions, organisations and programmes

AAOU	Asian Association of Open Universities
AIOU	Allama Iqbal Open University, Pakistan
BOU	Bangladesh Open University
BRAOU	Dr B.R. Ambedkar Open University, India
CCRTVU	Chinese Central Radio and TV University, China
CIFFAD	Consortium international francophone de formation à distance
COLISA	Confederation of Open Learning Institutions of South Africa
COMETT	Community in Education, Training and Technology (European Commission programme)
DEETYA	Department of Education, Employment, Training and Youth Affairs, Australia
DELTA	Development of European Learning through Technology Advance (European Commission programme)
DES	Department of Education and Science, United Kingdom (later DfEE)
DfEE	Department for Education and Employment, United Kingdom
EADTU	European Association of Distance Teaching Universities
EDEN	European Distance Education Network
ERASMUS	European Commission programme promoting cooperation in higher education, now subsumed within SOCRATES
HEQC	Higher Education Quality Council, United Kingdom

ICDE	International Council for Open and Distance Education (previously the International Council for Distance Education)
IDP Education	Independent, not-for-profit organisation supporting international activities of Australian education institutions
IGNOU	Indira Gandhi National Open University, India
KACU	Korea Air and Correspondence University
LEONARDO DA VINCI	Action programme for the implementation of a European Union vocational training policy
LINGUA	European Commission programme promoting language learning, now subsumed within SOCRATES
NOU	National Open University, Taiwan
NTU	National Technological University, United States
OECD	Organisation for Economic Cooperation and Development
OUHK	Open University of Hong Kong
PHARE	European Union programme for the economic and social restructuring of the countries of Central and Eastern Europe
SACHED	South African Committee for Higher Education
SADC	Southern Africa Development Community (formerly SADCC – the Southern African Development Coordination Conference)
SAIDE	South African Institute for Distance Education
SICHE	Solomon Islands College of Higher Education
SOCRATES	European Union action programme for cooperation in the field of education
STOU	Sukhothai Thammathirat Open University, Thailand
TEMPUS	The trans-European cooperation scheme for higher education, part of the European Commission PHARE programme
TSA	Technikon SA, South Africa
UAJ	University of the Air, Japan
UKOU	Open University, United Kingdom
UNED	Universidad Estatal a Distancia, Costa Rica, or Universidad Nacional de Educación a Distancia, Spain

UNISA	University of South Africa
USP	University of the South Pacific (main campus in Fiji)
UT	Universitas Terbuka, Indonesia
UWI	University of the West Indies
YCMOU	Yashwantrao Chavan Maharashtra Open University, India

Terms

CAT	Credit accumulation and transfer
CMC	Computer-mediated communication
CTU	Centre de télé-enseignement universitaire (France)
CU	Conventional university
ICT	Information and communications technology
ISDN	Integrated Services Digital Network
KB	Kilobytes
Kbps	Kilobytes per second
MB	Megabytes
SLH	Student learning hours
TAFE	Technical and further education (Australia)
TMA	Tutor-marked assignment

Chapter 1

Open and distance learning for the new society

Keith Harry and Hilary Perraton

A generation ago, higher education was one of the fastest growing industries in Britain, along with electronics and newly discovered natural gas. Over the last decade, in many countries but by no means all, higher education has been growing more rapidly than ever, faster than the economies that support it. Open and distance learning has been part of that expansion; today, in industrialised and developing countries alike, enrolments at a distance form between 5 and 15 per cent of the total in many cases, over 25 per cent in a few. The purpose of this book is to report on that expansion, examining the ways in which open and distance learning for higher education has responded to the needs of the new society, and summarising the lessons of recent practice for policy-makers and educators. It is just that, a report: not a catalogue (where the International Centre for Distance Learning has a good one on-line) nor a recipe book (of which there are plenty) nor an academic critique (of which there are a few) but a review from which others can draw conclusions to guide practice.

It has been a turbulent decade, whose turbulence is reflected in its educational history. The collapse of communism brought a necessary reshaping to higher education in eastern Europe. The end of apartheid illuminated the need for South African education to catch up with the outside world, in its institutions as well as its philosophy. The new legitimacy given to private-sector activities in the 1980s is still washing over education. Changes in technology have been more rapid than we remember – few of us used faxes fifteen years ago – and may yet reshape education. Technological change and the forces of globalisation are dissolving frontiers in education, as they already have in culture. Open and distance learning has been influenced, along with the rest of society, by all these changes which are tracked, thematically in the first half of this book, and geographically in the second half.

Higher education has always had a symbiotic relationship with its host community and that community has always extended beyond the walls of the city or the nation. Dusty-footed wandering scholars were the precursors of the internationally mobile students, discussed in chapter 2, whose journeys are encouraged by international agencies like the European Commission. The 1980s saw the creation of new agencies, in both the Commonwealth and *la francophonie* to foster international cooperation through distance education. The oddity of this deserves notice. That staid institution, the Commonwealth, derided as an irrelevant imperial hangover, set up not only an international educational agency but one dedicated to a particular form of education. It did so because the techniques of distance education lent themselves to international cooperation and sharing, ideals that are of the essence of the Commonwealth. And so the themes of this book are about the responses of open and distance learning to the changing demands of society, both nationally and internationally, examining the two-way flow of ideas and influence between universities and the world society.

Definitions should help thought rather than limit discussion. We imposed none on our contributors. Happily, the *New Oxford Dictionary*, a lexicographic *tour de force* published as we go to press, has given us crisp definitions of open and distance learning: open learning is 'learning based on independent study or initiative rather than formal classroom practice' while distance education is 'a method of studying in which lectures are broadcast or conducted by correspondence, without the student needing to attend a school or college'. One more term is worth citing, though it has not yet crept into the dictionary. In chapter 5 among others we notice that the barriers are coming down between what is done on-campus and off, what is called resource-based learning and what is called open learning: Moran and Myringer, following Australian practice, talk of 'flexible learning' to cover the range of activities discussed there and elsewhere.

Remembering that, 'the examiner never asks you to write down everything you know', we have commissioned chapters in a way that is selective almost to the point of being eclectic. We report on the main trends within our general theme, but have given more prominence to the less-reported parts of the world, and to the less well-documented institutions. This overview seeks to draw out common threads from those reports, looking in turn at the international changes that have shaped open and distance learning in higher education, at national responses to them, and at institutional change.

International developments

Distance education at the end of the twentieth century reflects international economic, political and related ideological change and is shaped by technological opportunity. These changes in turn have begun to create something new, a set of formally articulated regional and international policies for education.

Economic and political change

Two economic forces, with a complex link between them, have shaped the demand for opportunities to study in non-conventional ways. In the industrialised countries, demand for education for an increasing proportion of the population has resulted in the expansion of higher education and the demand for new approaches to it. Structural unemployment has probably increased the demand for higher education, reflected in the experience of Australia and Canada. Demands for retraining have encouraged universities to seek new audiences and new styles of working (chapters 4 and 5). Meanwhile, until the Asian financial crisis that opened in 1997, demand for higher education in the newly industrialised countries has been powered by the earlier expansion of primary and secondary education and by the job opportunities offered to those with higher education. Distance education has provided a way of recruiting more students and of shifting the balance of expenditure on education away from the state and towards the learner.

The political changes that shape education are most sharply illustrated in eastern Europe and in southern Africa. As chapter 10 describes, political change in eastern Europe swept away a system of distance education, based on correspondence courses, that was associated with the former regime. Universities are reshaping themselves to work in the new Europe, sometimes remembering the structures of sixty years ago. In doing so they are trying to create a new system of distance education that can respond to national needs, but learn and borrow from the west. Changes in southern Africa are even more dramatic. The end of apartheid has brought in its turn changes to the politics of education both nationally and regionally. Within South Africa formal changes are reflected in a White Paper on education, setting out new goals and laying proper stress on quality. Ideologically, South Africa is still struggling to rid its educational thinking and practice of the so-called 'fundamental pedagogics' which attempted to rationalise apartheid (cf. Gultig and Butcher 1996: 88). Distance education is seen as one way of increasing the access to education which is a necessary part of national regeneration. In the wider region of southern Africa, there are new opportunities for cooperation: chapter 7 explores the difficulties of establishing a cooperative structure that recognises the economic realities of South Africa's domination, and the proper interests of the small population countries of the sub-region.

One ideological change has influenced open and distance learning all round the world. A generation ago, education was seen as essentially a public-sector activity. Some countries restricted or banned private schooling. The creation of the British Open University was, above all, a dramatic move to widen the gates of the university but it was also a statement about proper public involvement in distance education, until then dominated by the private sector. In the 1980s all that changed, with the private sector given a new stake and a new legitimacy, in education as in other areas of public life. In distance education, the private sector is seizing opportunities in central and eastern Europe, sometimes acting more rapidly than the public sector. In Australia, distance education is being influenced by demands from and competition with the private sector, with repercussions for the structure of higher education (chapters 4 and 11) while the government elected in 1996 had an increased 'commitment to the power of market forces in higher education' (p. 273). In western Europe, too, industry is demanding better access to courses for professional training and continuing education. One model is the joint development by partners from the public and private sectors of customised training programmes using open and distance learning (chapter 4).

Technological opportunity

Extramural and correspondence education developed, after a timelag, once railways were in place to move lecturers and support cheap post. Distance education, linking broadcasts and correspondence, grew up, after another timelag, with the coming of educational television. In chapter 3 Mason explores how telecommunications are beginning to change open and distance learning. The early experience is mainly from industrialised countries where telecommunications are allowing easier and more frequent interaction between tutors and students, and allowing universities to reach new audiences: the National Technological University in the United States exists because it has access to satellite communication.

Our crystal ball is too cloudy to forecast the pace at which the newer technologies will be available and adopted for education. From China comes a prediction that advanced technology will make inroads into traditional education both in China and worldwide. The National Open University in Taiwan is already experimenting with the use of computer-based communication. The newly established Open University of Catalonia is one of the world's first virtual universities, using computer-based technology as the main way of providing courses for its students. The planned African Virtual University may yet make teaching available to Tanzania. The regional universities of the South Pacific and the West Indies, which have made use of telecommunication links between their scattered communities since the first communication satellites, are actively exploring ways of strengthening their existing systems. Use of the Internet may help solve the problems of educational isolation in small island developing states as well as in the rich industrialised world.

And yet, the scale of all this is modest. For much of the world, print, sometimes supported by broadcasting or by the use of cassettes, dominates open and distance learning. Indeed, institutions have often reduced rather than increased their use of broadcasting over the last ten years as free or subsidised access to broadcasting has declined. The newest open universities discussed here – of Bangladesh and Tanzania – will be using print with some broadcasting support as their main teaching media. Access, in two senses, is all-important to plans for the use of media. In Bangladesh for example: adequate access to broadcasting time for the institution and access by students to radio or television constrain the choice of media (p. 169–70).

Changes in technology always mix opportunity and threat. One thread that runs through the world experience is the potential that the technologies have for changing universities, for helping them to reach new audiences, and for shifting the boundaries between what is seen as on-campus and off-campus education. Moran and Myringer (p. 59) refer to a 'three-way convergence of distance and face-to-face education and electronic technologies', made possible – inevitable perhaps – by the use of the new technologies which they see as triggering change within institutions as well as beyond them. There may be threats to existing university structure and ways of working here. But, from the standpoint of an international review, the international threats demand highlighting. Whereas, within frontiers, there are usually structures for the regulation or self-regulation of university activities, there is less regulation across frontiers and less still in cyberspace. Blight, Davis and Olsen (chapter 2) identify the problem and note that Australian vice chancellors have drawn up a code of practice for the overseas activity of their universities. (Regulatory frameworks are still in their infancy within national boundaries in eastern Europe, never mind beyond.) But it remains to be seen how far codes are followed, or enforced. We have little in the way of consumer protection for the virtual student and there is a danger of an educational Gresham's law operating. A potential student, considering enrolling on an electronic course available from a foreign country, has little way of knowing whether the provider is legitimate or bogus or of assessing the quality of what is on offer. (Hong Kong has begun to develop structures that are relevant here (p. 196).)

There is a warning from the south Pacific that the issue is one of culture as well as regulation. Materials and courses, offered through the new technologies, are culture-laden. While new networks of information may widen access to education, they can also threaten the indigenous institutions of higher education which have grown in strength, stature, and service to their host communities over the last quarter-century. It would be ironical if technology, that could provide educational resources not otherwise available to them, were at the same time to weaken the independence and local relevance of the remoter institutions of the south, and the cultures that sustain them. The second chapter, on internationalisation and its impact on open and distance learning, is an early word in a debate which needs vigorous encouragement.

Changes in technology change costs. Mason hints (chapter 3) that new technology may widen audiences and so bring down unit costs but warns that 'many practitioners have concluded that telecommunications systems do not save money in the long run' (p. 45). Hülsmann reinforces that warning with his not unexpected comment that the basic cost of preparing a text is always with us, and other technologies, whether they are used to distribute resources or to encourage interaction, have all tended to increase unit costs over the minimum needed for a text.

Regional and international policy and development

The world started creating structures for the sharing of educational experience, with the foundation of the Association of Commonwealth Universities in 1913 and the International Bureau of Education in 1925. Reports by UNESCO, policy documents from the World Bank, formal statements by regional agencies all sit so firmly on the educator's bookshelf that we forget how recent is the concern for international policy in education. Within distance education, and with the exception of the work of the Commonwealth of Learning and of CIFFAD, whose geography is governed by language not proximity, the main developments have been regional rather than international.

Europe has given a lead. There are references in chapter 2 and chapter 10 to the European Union's steadily increasing influence on the development of open and distance learning. It is seen as a means both of strengthening European integration and of supporting economic competitiveness, and is referred to specifically in the Treaty of Maastricht. The PHARE and TEMPUS projects have brought eastern Europe into the same ambit. Informal structures exist alongside the formal European ones but the activities of the European Commission, and its control of a budget for cooperative activities in open and distance learning within Europe, give it a regional presence unmatched in any other part of the world.

The two regional Commonwealth universities have formal structures for cooperation, designed to support education in states that would otherwise be too small to support national universities. In the Caribbean, one of the drivers of expanded activity in distance education has been a concern for equity between the campus and non-campus territories. In the south Pacific, with much greater distances and a more limited educational infrastructure, distance education has developed so far, and demonstrated its relevance to the educational needs of its scattered region so dramatically, that a majority of the students of the university do some or all of their degree at a distance. The ownership of the universities by their supporting territories symbolises their cooperative structure.

Elsewhere, cooperative structures are more informal. A Distance Education Association of Southern Africa, for example, goes back to the 1970s (as the Botswana, Lesotho and Swaziland Correspondence Committee) and has promoted modest cooperation between the institutions in the five countries of the region, operating somewhere below the level, and the political complexity, of formal government–government cooperation. In Latin America, regional agencies provide for cooperation between the rectors of universities using distance education, for developing television materials, and for exchanges in telematics and staff training. Within their continents the Asian Association of Open Universities and the European Association of Distance Teaching Universities have, in the same way, provided informal opportunities for exchange and cooperation.

Of course barriers to cooperation remain. Some are legal: there are difficult issues concerning intellectual property rights which are inhibiting cooperation within central and eastern Europe. In some cases there is a lack of trust between institutions in neighbouring countries. The 'not invented here' syndrome still operates and has hindered otherwise encouraging cooperative developments across frontiers in Southern Africa (p. 99). But the experience generally suggests that regional cooperation is likely to grow, driven by the search for resources, by technology, and by the developing frameworks designed to facilitate it.

National responses

Governments have invested in open and distance learning for a mixture of reasons, including educational access, equity and responding to the demands of the labour market or their expectations about economic competitiveness. The emphasis of the last decade has not so much been on the establishment of new institutions, though Bangladesh and Tanzania are important exceptions, but upon quality, upon new tasks for higher education, and upon costs and funding.

The concern for quality is double edged. Open universities, and dual-mode institutions offering flexible-learning courses, are concerned with parity of esteem between the two modes. There is still scepticism about the legitimacy of distance education in countries as different as Swaziland, China and Canada. Within Europe, open and distance learning is still struggling to gain acceptance and respect and is sometimes ignored by the conventional university system. One job to be done therefore is to establish that the quality of open and distance learning can match that of conventional university teaching. Scepticism needs also to be cut away with the other edge of the sword, aimed at inferior practice within open and distance learning. Despite the restructuring of distance education in South Africa, the educational quality of what is being offered is still the subject of severe and proper criticism (p. 103). One part of national policy is to develop measures for raising the quality of what is being offered to the public as distance education. India, for example, has designated the Indira Gandhi National Open University as an apex institution, concerned with quality throughout the distance education sector.

In many countries higher education is being asked to undertake two new tasks: to reach wider audiences and to give new emphasis to continuing education. The governments of Bangladesh, Taiwan and Tanzania have all invested in distance education principally to widen access. As noted above, the University of the West Indies is expanding its system of distance education to make better opportunities available in the eastern Antilles. In India there is concern that the open universities should in fact provide improved access to students from scheduled castes and scheduled tribes. This kind of concern has been a common thread through the debates about distance education for many years. It may no longer be the main driver, at least in some jurisdictions: it is suggested (p. 264) that Australian institutions are today moving towards flexible learning not so much in the interest of equity as of institutional viability. A task that has a new prominence is to help universities respond to a changing demography of students which is 'partly a function of the shift from elite to mass higher education, and partly a consequence of a growing demand for recurrent, lifelong education' (p. 58). Many of the institutions reported here have developed new programmes, part-time programmes, and alliances with employers in order to respond to these twin needs. The new prominence given to the concept of lifelong learning during the 1990s means that almost every university mission statement now contains a specific commitment 'to develop lifelong learners' (p. 49). Swedish universities have a specific responsibility to 'meet their obligations to serve labour market needs especially through distance education and continuing professional education' (p. 58). In chapters 4 and 5 we examine how these developments are changing the functions of universities and changing the relationship between a university and its students. The concern is universal: it affects the structure of higher education in China, the South Pacific and the Caribbean as well as in the industrialised north.

The search for new audiences, and the response to their needs, has been matched by a concern for the costs of meeting them. Hülsmann (chapter 6) pulls together evidence that suggests open and distance learning can often have costs per student lower than those of conventional education, but warns against easy assumptions about savings that might be achieved. The resolution of questions about cost-effectiveness is seen as critical to the future of the Open University in Bangladesh (chapter 9). In South Africa, the concern about quality is matched by a concern about cost-effectiveness and the danger that the apparent cost advantage of distance education may be eroded by low completion rates.

Governments have found distance education economically attractive not only because it can achieve economies in capital (fewer costly new campuses) and recurrent costs (reduced wage bills for teachers) but also because it may allow education to be funded differently. Many Asian open universities draw a larger percentage of their income from student fees than do conventional institutions; India offers one example (p. 205). In industrialised countries there is a trend to shift more of the costs of open and distance learning on to the student. There is a conflict between pressures to fund an expansion of education in this way and to seek increased equity within it. In Europe, new partnerships between employers and universities may offer a channel for funds to flow from the private into the public sector where tailor-made courses are available through open and distance learning.

Institutional change

For about twenty years the literature, partly reflecting practice, was dominated by the establishment of distance-teaching or open universities. There was one in 1969, about a dozen within ten years and double that number by 1990. New open universities are still occasionally being established: chapter 7 describes the early days of the Open University of Tanzania and chapter 8 those of the Open University of Bangladesh, seen as the only possible form in which distance education could be developed there (p. 165). The National Open University in Taiwan has recently acquired a new status in which, for the first time, it can award full degrees (p. 217). But the general pattern is for conventional institutions to introduce distance education in some form and it is the progress of these dual-mode institutions which dominates accounts of institutional change.

Jurisdictional differences are important here. In Australia, higher education is predominantly the responsibility of the individual states, not the Commonwealth government, while Canadian provinces jealously guard their sole responsibility for education. One consequence is that distance education in both countries has been dominated by dual-mode institutions. King discusses the attempts by the Commonwealth government to rationalise distance education, and to establish a new Open Learning Agency which was to operate in harmony with individual universities and with funding from both private and public sectors (p. 269–70). In eastern and central Europe, too, universities have explored the possibility of becoming dual-mode: no government has chosen the option of setting up an open university. Reviews undertaken by the Commonwealth of Learning reached the same conclusion in the South Pacific and the Commonwealth Caribbean; wise development of distance education there needed to rest, as it has, with the existing regional universities (Renwick *et al.* 1991 and 1992).

Three factors have encouraged a convergence between open and distance learning on the one hand and conventional education on the other. One is the drive for dual-mode status: if an institution is teaching both on- and off-campus there are educational and economic benefits for it to look for ways in which the two modes can reinforce each other. A second factor, already touched upon, is technology. If, for example, a university is investing in computer-based teaching material, with the heavy staff costs that this entails, it is likely to look for potential users both within its classrooms and outside. The third benefit is the need to meet the demands of new audiences:

part-time students, learners wanting to get just-in-time professional updating (pp. 51–52), companies interested in new kinds of university–industry partnerships are all likely to be sympathetic to a flexible approach to learning. And so we see convergence of this kind in China, in eastern Europe where information and communication technologies may be hastening educational change and in Canada where the distinction between face-to-face and distance education is being eroded 'with the blending of teaching methods through digitally based telecommunications technologies' (p. 160). In Australia, 'throughout the last decade, the boundary between conventional on-campus teaching and distance and open provision has markedly blurred, leading to the widely used redesignation "flexible delivery"' (p. 274). Linguistically at least, where Australia leads perhaps we will all follow.

This process of convergence is likely to affect the distance-education student and institution. Already, in many jurisdictions, it is easier for students to move between modes of study within a single institution than to carry credit from an open university to a conventional one. At the same time, even where students cannot readily move, teaching materials may do so. Tanzania provides an example where materials developed for distance education are being used within conventional institutions (p. 120). It may indeed be that there will be more profound effects on universities: Moran and Myringer suggest that 'distance education methods and systems are converging with those of face-to-face teaching, strongly influenced by new electronic technologies' and that this will transform university teaching and learning as a whole. It may, too, be accompanied by new attempts at cooperation between institutions, driven by the search for resources and enabled by flexible learning.

Universities never were ivory towers: the hard-headed city corporation of Edinburgh ran the university until 1858. Its ramparts were as impressive as those of Paris, Bologna or Oxford but it met the needs of its citizens. The policies of the open universities and dual-mode universities of the 1990s are being shaped at least as much by the exogenous pressures of international change and national policy as by these endogenous changes of policy and practice.

Coda: Where are they now

Nearly twenty years ago the new open universities were of enough interest for an overview to be published of nine of the first of them (Rumble and Harry 1982). Much has changed since then. The book discussed the different model of distance education in the Soviet Union and Eastern Europe. It predicted some future for distance education within dual-mode institutions but saw this as of less significance and appropriate only where the population did not justify the establishment of a dedicated open university. Today, Baumeister (p. 247) notices that the widespread development of dual-mode

institutions in Europe contrasts with the expectations in 1982. The earlier
book asked whether the new universities would survive, noted that 'all non-
traditional educational structures are characterised by fragility', but saw as a
good omen that they had collectively survived political changes that threatened them (Keegan and Rumble 1982: 243). The forecast was sound. All nine
(in Britain, Canada, China, Costa Rica, Germany, Israel, Pakistan, Spain and
Venezuela) have survived and have in each case become part of the normal
educational service of their countries. Survival is no longer an issue. The
idea, however, that the future lay mainly with the open universities is belied
by the changes of the last decade. Open and dual-mode universities are now
both major players.

The appraisal of their work was in terms of three main themes: their
quantitative achievements, their quality and their costs. In terms of quantity,
the total number of students using open and distance learning has grown
hugely in twenty years. Distance education is significant enough as a mode of
higher education for the UNESCO *Statistical Yearbook* to include figures that
show Thailand and Turkey, for example, with a remarkable 41 and 38 per
cent of higher education students in 1992 studying at a distance. But, in this
volume as elsewhere, we have only limited data on success rates: a previous
Commonwealth of Learning report made the point that 'if open universities
are to advocate a different funding structure or to bid for more funds they
will also need to make their case by producing fuller data than have usually
been available on completion rates and costs per graduate' (Mugridge 1994:
121).

The theme of quality runs through this book as it did in 1982. The chapters in this volume report much progress in measures to check and ensure
quality: there is an expectation that we are teaching our students better than
we were. At the least we have more formal systems that attempt to check for
quality. The earlier volume noticed that lifelong learning was among the
objectives of the distance-teaching universities but interpreted their role
much more in terms of individual access to education than of contribution
to the workforce and to human resource development, the themes of the late
1990s.

We have learned more about costs in the last twenty years and been able to
put some glosses on to the arguments about the possible cost advantages of
non-conventional study. One change since 1982 is in the context of the
debate; it is now about cost recovery as well as about cost savings.

Finally, the earlier review looked forward, as we still do, to the exploitation
of technology, hoping that in the long run the distance-teaching universities
will use 'electronic means of communication to provide individualised educational systems capable of giving rapid feedback to persons who are part of
a dispersed, heterogeneous student population' in order to respond to the
needs of learners of the twenty-first century (Keegan and Rumble 1982:
248). We still want the technology, and the responsiveness. The world's

achievements in open and distance learning, reported here, can tell us a lot about how we may yet attain them.

References

Gultig, J. and Butcher, N. (1996) *Teacher Education Offered at a Distance in South Africa*, Braamfontein: SAIDE.

Keegan, D. and Rumble, G. (1982) 'The DTUs: an appraisal', in G. Rumble and K. Harry (eds), *The Distance Teaching Universities*, London: Croom Helm.

Mugridge, I. (1994) *The Funding of Open Universities*, Vancouver: Commonwealth of Learning.

Renwick, W., King, St C. and Shale, D. (1991) *Distance Education at the University of the South Pacific*, Vancouver: Commonwealth of Learning.

Renwick, W., Shale, D. and Rao, C.R. (1992) *Distance Education at the University of the West Indies*, Vancouver: Commonwealth of Learning.

Rumble, G. and Harry, K. (eds) (1982) *The Distance Teaching Universities*, London: Croom Helm.

Part I

Themes

Chapter 2

The internationalisation of higher education

Denis Blight, Dorothy Davis and Alan Olsen

Open learning and distance education are borderless in concept. There are few boundaries on the locations of their students and, increasingly, open learning and distance education cross national borders. Some 1998 examples: the British Open University has 25,000 students taking courses outside the country (Daniel 1998); it is reported to be opening its doors for business in the US (*The Australian*, 6 May 1998); of the 79,800 international students in Australian universities 6,500 were off-campus and 15,800 at off-shore campuses (IDP Education Australia 1998: 2). Does the fact that open and distance education is delivered across national borders lead to demand for internationalisation of its content? Does internationalisation of the content of open and distance education lead to demand for its borderless delivery? And what of quality? If delivery is across borders, what control or assurance is there in terms of quality, relevance, support of students, recognition and accreditation? Does borderless delivery lead to globalisation of accreditation? Moreover, does technology change the teaching and learning delivered through open and distance education? Is technology an ally in borderless delivery but a threat in terms of intellectual imperialism?

The first section in this chapter outlines developments in the internationalisation of higher education; the second looks at international delivery of open and distance education; the third reviews the application of new technologies; and the fourth highlights issues of quality, student support, curricula, costs and concerns of internationalisation and globalisation.

Internationalisation

International higher education has traditionally involved students from one country studying on-campus at universities in another country. De Ridder-Symoens (1992) describes the impact of the mobility of students and scholars in the Middle Ages:

> The use of Latin as a common language, and a uniform programme of study and systems of examinations, enabled international students to

continue their studies in one 'studium' after another, and ensured recognition of their degrees throughout Christendom.

(De Ridder-Symoens 1992: 281)

Moving to our own time, IDP Education Australia in 1995 (Blight 1995) studied future demand for higher education. Changes in enrolments over time reflect changes in population and changes in participation rates. The IDP study modelled population change and participation rates to the year 2010, and further out to 2025. It showed that population growth over the next thirty years will not have a major impact on enrolments. Changes in participation rates will make a much greater contribution; they tend to vary with changes in per capita income so that, as incomes rise, demand for higher education places grows. The study forecast that global demand for higher education places would increase from 48 million in 1990 to an estimated 97 million in 2010 and 159 million in 2025.

International student mobility

As demand for higher education places grows, so the number of higher education students at universities outside their home countries is growing. UNESCO estimates that from 1970 to the mid-1980s the number grew from 500,000 to 1 million and by the mid-1990s to 1.5 million (UNESCO 1997: Table 3–14). This increased student mobility is a function of economic demand for higher education. The United States dominates as a host country with 30 per cent, followed by France (11 per cent), Germany (10 per cent) and the United Kingdom (9 per cent). In the mid-1990s, 46 per cent of these students were from countries in Asia and 63 per cent of these students from Asia travel to English-language destinations (UNESCO 1997: Table 3–14). IDP predicted (Blight 1995: 9) that the number of international students would rise to 1.8 million by the year 2000 and to 2.75 million by 2010. Asia was expected to demand an additional 800,000 international university places in the fifteen years 1995 to 2010. Despite any short-term impact of the Asian economic crisis of 1997, it is expected that the longer term predictions will stay firm.

Essentially, this increased student mobility is a function of economic demand for higher education. The increased mobility has been assisted and promoted by a number of national, international and regional initiatives such as NAFTA education programmes, ERASMUS (followed by SOCRATES) in Europe, and the UMAP (University Mobility in Asia and the Pacific) programme in the Asia-Pacific region.

Internationalisation of higher education institutions

International student programmes are central to the internationalisation of tertiary-education institutions. They add diversity to institutions and to their local communities. They influence the research interests of staff, and over time influence the curriculum. They may start a flow of funds to other international programmes.

The scope of internationalisation in the 1990s, however, means a lot more than an international student programme. Knight (1997: 8) suggests a process approach to internationalisation of the core functions of a university where 'internationalisation of higher education is the process of integrating an international/intercultural dimension into the teaching, research and service of the institution'.

Why do stakeholders in higher education worldwide – governments, institutions, including staff and students, and community, including business and industry – seek to integrate international and intercultural dimensions into the core teaching, research and service functions of universities? Knight (1997: 9) categorises the reasons for internationalisation into four groups: political, economic, academic and cultural/social.

First, governments of nations have political incentives, including the commitment of the nation to a global economy and society, its openness to the world, its commitment to its region and its commitment to development assistance to the world and to its region. Second, economic incentives for a nation include the value of education as a service export and, for the community also, the labour market need to train students to operate in international and intercultural contexts. At the level of the individual institution there are financial incentives through international student fees. Third, the institution and the community, including business and industry, have academic incentives for internationalisation. There is an assumption that 'by enhancing the international dimension of teaching, research and service there is value added to the quality of our higher education systems' (ibid.: 11). An international academic approach attempts to avoid parochialism. An interaction with other cultures is important in the development of students. Universities have the opportunity to increase awareness and understanding of the new and changing phenomena that affect the political, economic and cultural/multicultural developments within and among nations (Knight and de Wit 1995: 12–13). The nation's own students and the community benefit from an international curriculum. Finally, the institution and the community have cultural and social incentives for internationalisation. Internationalisation of the student population adds cultural diversity to an institution and its community, leads to a demand for international exchanges and familiarises the nation's own students with the world and with their region.

Strategies for internationalisation

The international student programme of an institution is seen as one of several strategies for internationalisation. In the Australian context, Back *et al.* (1996) carried out a comparative study of the internationalisation activities of higher education institutions, examining seven themes:

1   an organisation strategy for internationalisation;
2   international student programmes;
3   the internationalisation of teaching;
4   off-shore and distance education;
5   internationalisation in research;
6   international technical assistance and training;
7   providing international student support services.

The organisation strategy for the process of internationalisation of an institution includes the internationalisation context, culture and policy of the institution, its mission statements and corporate plans, its management and business plans, its organisation structure for internationalisation, its staff policies and its institution-wide links.

An international student programme is central to internationalisation. Considerations include the number and proportion of international students enrolled, and institutional policies on enrolment targets, geographical focus, fields of study, scholarships, distribution of fee income, modes of delivery, including off-shore and twinning arrangements, the use of multimedia and distance-education methods, and the provision of promotional information.

Perhaps the most significant component of the internationalisation of teaching is the internationalisation of the curriculum which, if implemented effectively, ensures that the academic benefits flow not only to the international students but also to the institution itself and to its domestic students. An internationalised curriculum is particularly relevant to international students studying off-shore. Alongside curriculum issues, internationalisation of teaching includes staff exchanges, study abroad and student exchange programmes, joint degrees, credit-transfer arrangements, the development of specialist centres that focus on relevant foreign language and cultural studies and the institutional links which facilitate these initiatives.

Internationalisation in research involves a wide range of collaborative projects, institutional links and exchange programmes. These activities make extensive use of the Internet and other applications of information technology. International technical assistance and training projects, often funded by aid agencies and multilateral organisations, apply the expertise of institutions to multidisciplinary problem-solving in an international setting. Student support services are also a crucial element of an institution's internationalisation strategy. Institutional responsibilities for the support of international students are usually described in formal codes of ethical practice designed to ensure that adequate provision is made for a full range of support services to international students.

Internationalisation strategies make up a dynamic and integrated set. Developments in one internationalisation activity can lead to opportunities in another. Back, *et al.* (1996: 17) suggest links between an international student programme, the international research interests of academic staff and the internationalisation of teaching. A new course offered internationally through the Internet may result in links with institutions and staff in countries other than those that have been the traditional partners. Student and staff exchange programmes may lead to international research collaboration.

Internationalisation of distance education and open learning

Off-shore and distance education make up one of the internationalisation programme strategies of a higher education institution. Distance education and open learning have been subject to four internationalisation influences. First, approaches and methods, developed in one national system, have been adapted and adopted by other national systems. Second, as a matter of strategy, the European Union is supporting projects in open and distance learning. Third, the catchments of distance education institutions have been steadily expanded from local and national to regional and international locations. Fourth, distance education materials and approaches have been utilised in twinning programmes and at off-shore campuses.

Adaptation and adoption of distance education across national borders

Distance education and open-learning approaches developed in one national system have been adapted and adopted in other national systems at an increasing pace over the last thirty years.

> The provision of distance education had largely been confined to a few developed economies and to China, until the open learning movement was stimulated by the foundation of the UK Open University in 1969, and its then innovative use of broadcast public television as a core element of its teaching practice. . . .
>
> Developing countries were also encouraged by the immediate popular success of the UK Open University, and its demonstration of the efficacy of broadcast television-radio-print, at least in a small geographic area serviced by a national broadcaster and a dense population with appropriate reception equipment. China TV University demonstrated that broadcast media could also be effective over a large geographic area.
>
> It is crucial to acknowledge the core role of government in establishing distance education institutions. As Daniel (1995: 17) points out, the 'mega universities' (over 100,000 students) were created 'with clear

policy goals in mind, above all to increase access to higher education at low cost'.

(Cunningham *et al*. 1998: 30–2)

European Union strategy

The European Union has been promoting the internationalisation of education. The Treaty of Rome provided for mobility of labour within member countries. This led in turn to a concern for the recognition of qualifications across frontiers and to support for student mobility: the aim of the ERASMUS student mobility programme was for 10 per cent of university students to have the opportunity of studying abroad. The European Commission then moved on from actual mobility to consider virtual mobility. The Commission had already been supporting experimental work in telematics, seen as being of potential economic benefit to Europe. As a result of these twin interests, in education across frontiers and in the application of telematics to education, the Commission made a formal decision to support projects in open and distance learning. Since 1995 the European Commission has been funding cooperative projects that involve partners in three or more European countries through open and distance learning. This work is now beginning to extend into eastern Europe and will continue into the next century.

The widening catchment of distance education institutions

The catchment of individual distance education institutions has steadily widened in the last decade. This widening has been driven by the same factors that had led to the internationalisation of universities. An additional and important factor has been the availability in recent years of new information and communication technologies.

The British Open University has sought international markets, and 'had 13,000 students outside the UK in 1994, mostly in the European Union, Hong Kong, Singapore and the former Soviet bloc' (Cunningham *et al*. 1998: 30). Today the number has increased to 25,000 in ninety-four countries and using four hundred examination centres (Daniel 1998).

The specific mandate of the Commonwealth of Learning, established in 1988 with its headquarters in Canada, is to encourage the development and sharing of distance education materials, expertise and technologies for students throughout the Commonwealth and other countries. The Expert Group, whose report led to its establishment, saw as a long-term aim of the Commonwealth of Learning that any learner, anywhere in the Commonwealth, should be able to study any distance-teaching programme available from any *bona fide* college or university in the Commonwealth (Briggs *et al*. 1987).

Off-shore campuses

Distance education is one part of a spectrum of flexible delivery. The traditional distance education model in Australia is predicated on isolated students. It is resource based with little, if any, regular face-to-face teaching, although students may be brought together once or twice per year for 'residentials' – short periods of intensive teaching on-campus. In Europe and North America some distance education is resource based, while some universities have adopted a different model in which students are collected as a class in dedicated facilities at a satellite campus and are taught by videoconferencing (Cunningham *et al*. 1998: 24).

British and Australian universities have developed off-shore campus models extensively, in countries such as Singapore and Malaysia, to offer twinning programmes. As described by Lewis and Pratt (1996: 211), the general characteristics of a twinning programme in Malaysia tend to be:

- a local private college provides the equity for campus and buildings, the administrative infrastructure, employs local academic staff and is responsible for obtaining approvals from the Ministry of Education;
- a foreign sponsoring university provides intellectual property in curricula and academic staff expertise;
- students spend one or two years studying at the local private college in Malaysia, while concluding their degree study in the final year(s) at the foreign university;
- the degree is granted by the foreign university.

In Australian universities in 1997, 20 per cent of international students were at off-shore campuses (IDP Education Australia 1998: 2). Lewis and Pratt (1996: 211) describe the popularity of these programmes, where, along with other international links, 'around twenty Australian universities [there are thirty-eight in total] currently have some form of twinning arrangement with a private college in Malaysia, either on a one-to-one joint venture, or via a consortium'.

Back, *et al*. (1996: 55) used the Royal Melbourne Institute of Technology (RMIT University) as a case study and identified five types of cooperation in a study of twinning. Asia's economic and financial crises of 1997–8 have added to demands for programmes enabling students to study in their own countries for at least part of their courses which leads to a sixth type. They are:

- programmes carried out off-shore with local partners to upgrade local diplomas to RMIT degrees;
- programmes carried out off-shore with local partners to offer RMIT undergraduate or graduate programmes;

- programmes involving one or two years at an off-shore twinning partner followed by one or two years onshore at RMIT;
- distance education programmes offered in conjunction with local partners;
- the provision of course materials for programmes to be offered off-shore by other education institutions or organisations;
- programmes offered totally at off-shore campuses.

The spectrum of flexible delivery is complete when on-campus students use resource materials developed for distance education. Deakin University in Australia provides an example. Since its foundation it has been university strategy to provide distance education with flexible delivery. Students did not need to attend a study centre, and there was no requirement for residentials. Deakin University describes its flexible course delivery:

> All Deakin students have choices about the way they study. The traditional distinction between on-campus and off-campus has been superseded at Deakin by flexible course delivery. A flexible approach to course delivery means choosing the best teaching methods and the best technologies to provide real choices for students in the mode, place, time and duration of their study.

Technology in international education

IDP Education Australia in 1996 commissioned research on Technology in International Education which described the merging of information technology and telecommunications.

> The combination of information technologies and telecommunications has meant that world events are no longer localised, but spread around the world within a split second via technologies ranging from Email to satellite video links. For those with access to these technologies, the global village has arrived.
>
> This global transmission of information is not restricted to current events, but extended to learners from kindergarten to senior citizens who, although they may live in the United Kingdom, participate in learning experiences delivered from other countries in Europe, the United States or Australia, for example.
>
> Information technologies and telecommunications build on existing distance education courses by adding value to the design of internationalised learning experiences.
>
> (Alexander and Blight 1996: 20)

Approaches to international study

The report described case studies that exemplified the state of the art in the use of technology to internationalise teaching, through the content or form of the curriculum, for language learning, for virtual international mobility and for international delivery of distance education and lifelong learning. It identified five case studies in the delivery of distance education and lifelong learning, which actually or potentially allowed for international study.

* 'Deakin Interchange', from Deakin University in Australia, was a suite of software for accessing a variety of networked services at the university with an easy to use graphical interface. It allowed access to these networked services either by direct network connection on campus or via modem from off campus locations (Alexander and Blight 1996: 40). In 1997, Deakin Interchange was replaced with a web-based platform of delivery using local Internet service providers.

* The Graduate Certificate in Open and Distance Learning from the University of Southern Queensland in Australia is a course which is offered solely via electronic media. It was developed for academics and trainers needing professional graduate education in the use of open and distance learning techniques. It incorporates flexible-learning techniques and explores real learning systems. The learners participating are staff working in organisations involved in open and distance education in Australia, Brazil, Canada, Hong Kong, Malaysia, Mexico, Solomon Islands, South Africa and USA (ibid.: 44).

* 'On Line and Distance Learning' is an elective subject for students studying educational technology at the Faculty of Educational Science and Technology at the University of Twente in The Netherlands, most of whom are studying at Master's level. The students, from eight countries, are engaged in exploring the design and creation of materials for the support of tele-learning, and in particular materials for access via the worldwide web (ibid.: 47).

* 'Teleteaching 96' was a virtual conference held in conjunction with an on-site conference of the International Federation for Information Processing, the theme of which was 'Practising what we preach'. Several months ahead of the on-site conference, delegates were directed to a specially developed website where a number of international experts in aspects of virtual universities posted papers for discussion, as well as links to selected locations which illustrated the practices and theories under discussion. For two months, virtual participants discussed issues,

ahead of the on-site conference, where small groups of participants discussed the issues raised in the virtual conference (ibid.: 57–8).

- The 'Knowledge Media Stadium' is a desktop platform, developed by the Knowledge Media Institute at the UK Open University for the purpose of hosting electronic events around the globe. The Institute has the aim of defining the future of lifelong learning by harnessing and shaping the technologies which underpin it. The Stadium is used as a hardware and software platform for professional update master classes, international symposia, syndicates, town meetings, specialist and celebrity netcasts and hindsight analysis of an event in detail after it has taken place (ibid.: 60–2).

Distance education and lifelong learning

In Deakin Interchange and Knowledge Media Stadium, Alexander and Blight (1996: 9) describe two common desktop software platforms from which a number of different courses or learning experiences are delivered. The Graduate Certificate in Open and Distance Learning, On Line and Distance Learning and Teleteaching 96 exemplified the design, development and delivery of international education at the level of a whole course, a subject and a conference.

In respect of distance education, Alexander and Blight conclude from an Australian perspective:

> Developing a capacity to deliver courses internationally is of critical importance to all levels of education in Australia, with benefits which include improved educational outcomes for students, economic sustainability, and humanitarian factors. The possibilities for information technologies to deliver international education are appealing, because of their potential to overcome Australia's geographic isolation.
>
> (ibid.: 9)

Policy issues

A number of policy issues need to be addressed in the context of the internationalisation of higher education. They include questions of quality and student support, of the content and form of curricula, of intellectual imperialism and the globalisation of accreditation, and of access.

Quality and student support

International delivery of distance education and off-shore campuses raise specific issues of quality assurance and student support. Lewis and Pratt

(1996: 215), discussing the need for new 'distribution channels' for international business education, suggest the need for international business schools as separate multinational business corporations: 'The challenge will be to achieve this without eroding academic standards and educational quality'.

The new distribution channels include the international delivery of distance education, off-shore campuses and twinning programmes, often involving the use of new technologies in delivery. In the Australian context, Back, *et al.* (1996: 129–32) surveyed universities on their use of new technologies and on their quality assurance programmes. Most universities used technology such as the Internet, including all seven universities with off-shore campuses, twenty-two of twenty-five universities with twinning programmes and all twenty-two universities involved in international delivery of distance education. Few universities had specific quality assurance programmes. Of seven universities with off-shore campuses, five used the same quality assurance programmes for teaching and learning at off-shore campuses as at Australian campuses while two had specific programmes. For twinning programmes, seven of twenty-five universities used specific programmes. For international delivery of distance education, twenty of twenty-three universities used the same quality assurance programmes as those for Australian distance education and three had specific programmes.

Australia's Review of Higher Education Financing and Policy (1998: 59–61) discussed the absence of face-to-face teaching under the heading 'Technology will revolutionise higher education teaching' and noted that 'many of the academics and students the Committee met stressed the educational importance of placing learning within the academic community, and of the dialogue between teacher and student, and between student and student'. It acknowledged 'the fears felt by some in the academic community that the new technologies may reduce opportunities for human interaction and in this way reduce the quality of teaching'. It also noted that face-to-face teaching does not always live up to its ideal image and was convinced that 'technologies offer significant opportunities to higher education institutions to enhance the quality, accessibility and cost-effectiveness of higher education teaching and research' (ibid.).

The Higher Education Quality Council in the United Kingdom dealt with the issue of quality in off-shore programmes in its *Code of Practice for Overseas Collaborative Provision in Higher Education* in 1996. The Code required that 'Arrangements for the quality control of approved collaborative links should be explicit, comprehensive and documented in detail. They should be no less rigorous than the arrangements operating internally in the UK institution'. Its detailed provisions included:

- adequate monitoring, including regular visits by staff from the awarding institution;

- clear and properly supported administrative systems to provide reliable information to the awarding institution on the operation and management of collaborative programmes;
- external examining procedures in accordance with the requirements of the awarding institution;
- sufficient visits, in both directions, between the home and overseas institutions, by academic and administrative staff;
- use of reliable local representatives to oversee the arrangements on the ground;
- knowledge of, or involvement in, appointments procedures for local staff by the British institution;
- the availability of British staff for consultation between the partner institutions;
- complaints procedures and provision for student appeals to the awarding institution;
- proper student records;
- student assessment procedures comparable with those used internally.

The Quality Assurance Agency, successor to the Higher Education Quality Council, has issued a *Consultation Draft* on developing a quality assurance and standards framework for UK higher education. It proposes a single, comprehensive and generally applicable code of practice on all matters relating to the assurance of quality and standards including aspects such as distance learning, programme monitoring and review, student guidance, welfare and counselling and student appeals, complaints and grievance procedures.

Hong Kong has also introduced quality assurance mechanisms. Its Non-local Higher and Professional Education Ordinance has been framed to protect Hong Kong 'consumers' of non-local higher educational services against the marketing of substandard courses in Hong Kong. Courses, which involve the physical presence of the non-local institution or its agent in Hong Kong for lectures, tutorials or examinations, must go through a registration process. It is designed to ensure that courses offered in Hong Kong are offered by accredited institutions, that the courses offered are accredited in home countries and that they are the same as those offered in home countries, with the same range of elective subjects. Consistent with 'one country, two systems', courses from institutions in the People's Republic of China are covered by the Ordinance.

Content and form of curricula

There is a link between international student programmes and internationalisation of the content and form of the curriculum.

Internationalisation of the student population leads to internationalisation of research interests, which in turn leads to internationalisation of teaching. There is demand for international student exchanges on the part of Australian students. Where there is a large international student population, the professional responsibility of academic staff leads to internationalisation of the curriculum. Universities seeking a competitive export product ensure that the curriculum is international.

(Back, *et al.* 1997: 47)

Curricula may incorporate international content, through case studies drawing on international examples, through assignments involving research from the Web and other international resources, through interviewing of international students or others from different ethnic backgrounds or through the development of course material in collaboration with international partners. Universities with off-shore partners may undertake international staff exchange and may share ideas and curriculum developments with partner institutions. Curricula may be further internationalised by including options for language studies as part of a degree programme, encouraging and supporting international fieldwork and study tours; and promoting study abroad programmes. New technologies may allow a virtual internationalisation of the form of the curriculum.

Intellectual imperialism and globalisation of accreditation

A number of authors on higher education see internationalisation and globalisation as different but dynamically linked concepts. Knight, for example, suggests:

Globalisation can be thought of as the catalyst while internationalisation is the response, albeit a response in a proactive way. The key element in the term internationalisation is the notion of between or among nations and cultural identities. A country's unique history, indigenous culture(s), resources, priorities, etc., shape its response to and relationship with other countries. Thus national identity and culture is key to internationalisation. The homogenisation of culture is often cited as a critical concern or effect of globalisation; internationalisation, by respecting and perhaps even strengthening local, regional and national priorities and culture is therefore seen as a very different concept.

(Knight 1997: 6)

The concept of globalisation of education can be explored through an analogy with the cinema. The British film producer Lord Puttnam was a partner with the Open University, the BBC and the British Council, in a proposed, though abortive, World Learning Network. This venture led to widespread speculation about the potential for convergence of global media networks and higher education (Cunningham *et al.* 1998: 62). Puttnam told the *Los Angeles Times* in August 1997 that he was keen to 'thwart any attempt by American entertainment conglomerates to establish the same sort of stranglehold over education and information that their movie divisions exert over worldwide distribution channels'. He argued that:

> We're now moving toward an information and education age in which the values and skills of entertainment are destined to affect and infect other areas of the economy. If we end up going down the same road in those two critical sectors that we've gone in movies, the implications for the world's economy, and even elements of the world's stability, are serious.
>
> (*Los Angeles Times*, 10 August 1997)

Globalisation of higher education involves a supranationalism that straddles national boundaries, ignoring cultural identity. Technology often goes hand in hand with globalisation, magnifying the threat. A concern emerging from globalisation is the potential for international accreditation systems. Increasing mobility of human capital, demands for mutual recognition and globalisation of higher education could pose threats to the accreditation of higher education by national systems. International accreditation systems themselves straddle national boundaries and may involve cultural imperialism.

In contrast with globalisation, internationalisation of higher education recognises nations and describes a process of interchange of higher education between nations. It involves partnerships, between nations, between national systems, between accreditation systems, between institutions. Without partnerships, there is no international education.

Access to borderless education

There is at least the potential for excess capacity in many universities in the USA, Canada, Britain, Australia and New Zealand. At the same time there is substantial unmet demand for higher education from countries in Asia and Africa. Open and distance education and off-shore strategies are elements in the process of supplying higher education to satisfy demand and may help match supply and demand here. New technologies have the potential to reduce the costs of delivery.

This is not to say that the economics are easy. The World Bank's Etienne Baranshamaje explained the costing structure of the African Virtual University project to Cunningham *et al.* (1998: 87):

> Our mission is that it has to be affordable to the African income. We're counting on economies of scale to make that possible. . . . But it's a lot

cheaper being done by the World Bank for the whole of Africa, but it wouldn't make sense for an individual in one country to undertake such a project. . . . The most costly aspects are not the equipment on the ground, but the content and the development. Being multinational, multidisciplinary, multi-language and multi-country has a cost, but it's a worthwhile one from my perspective.

We have the possibility of a new learning architecture. Do new technologies, with their potential to reduce the costs of delivery, allow widespread border-less access, through partnerships, to an internationalised, quality higher education system such as Australia's, with its long tradition of education across vast distances? The Commonwealth of Learning (http://www.col.org) has a vision of this:

> Distance education is now a part of the mainstream of education and training. It enables students to learn at the location, time and pace of their choice, for far less money and with far greater results. COL's goals include maximising the transfer of information, ideas, innovations and resources to support this rapid evolution of distance educational training.

Dhanarajan's (1998a: 11–12) views of the future are pertinent:

> Partnerships, especially with institutions located in those parts of the world where the demand for learning will far exceed the ability to supply, will be particularly helpful as nations begin to accelerate the agenda for greater equality of opportunity.
>
> The 21st century will witness, I am certain, the emergence of a number of pan-global open learning systems. They do not necessarily have to be funded by the public purse, but by entrepreneurs who will work in partnerships with either like-minded individuals or public-funded institutions which will not impede the movement of students, courses, learning materials, credits and staff. . . .
>
> Partnerships of the 21st century cannot be about territorial preservation (cyberspace does not recognise this), it will be about student volume and economics, learner choice and autonomies, mobility of jobs and people, explosion of knowledge and technology and interdependency and universalisation.

References

Alexander, S. and Blight, D. (1996) *Technology in International Education*, research paper presented to the 1996 Australian International Education Conference on Technologies for the New Millennium, October.

Australian Vice-Chancellors' Committee (AVCC) (1995) *Code of Ethical Practice in the Offshore Provision of Education and Educational Services by Australian Higher Education Institutions*, Canberra.

Back, K., Davis, D. and Olsen, A. (1996) *Internationalisation and Higher Education: Goals and Strategies*, Higher Education Division, DEETYA, Evaluations and Investigations Program, Canberra, 96/15.

Back, K., Davis, D. and Olsen, A. (1997) 'Strategies for internationalisation of higher education in Australia', in J. Knight and H. de Wit (eds), *Internationalisation of Higher Education in Asia Pacific Countries*, European Association for International Education (EAIE)/IDP Education Australia (IDP), Amsterdam.

Blight, D. (1995) *International Education: Australia's Potential Demand and Supply*, research paper presented to the 1995 International Education Conference, Brisbane, October.

Briggs, A. *et al.* (1987) *Towards a Commonwealth of Learning*, London: Commonwealth Secretariat.

Cunningham, S., Tapsall, S., Ryan, Y., Stedman, L., Bagdon, K. and Flew, T. (1998) *New Media and Borderless Education: A Review of the Convergence between Global Media Networks and Higher Education Provision*, Higher Education Division, DEETYA, Evaluations and Investigations Program, Canberra, 97/22, January.

Daniel, J. (1995) 'The mega universities and the knowledge media: implications of the new technologies for large distance teaching universities', MEd. thesis, Montreal: Concordia University.

Daniel, J. (1996) *Mega-Universities and Knowledge Media: Technology Strategies for Higher Education*, London: Kogan Page.

Daniel, J. (1998) *Distance Learning. The Vision and Distance Learning. The Reality: What Works, What Travels?*, address to a conference on Technology Standards for Global Learning in Salt Lake City, 26–8 April.

De Ridder-Symoens, H. (1992) 'Mobility', in H. de Ridder-Symoens (ed.), *A History of the University in Europe*, vol. 1, Cambridge: Cambridge University Press.

De Wit, H. (ed.) (1995) *Strategies for Internationalisation of Higher Education: A Comparative Study of Australia, Canada, Europe and the United States of America*, EAIE, Amsterdam.

Dhanarajan, G. (1998a) 'International and inter-institutional collaboration in distance learning', paper presented at a conference on Learning Together – Collaboration in Open Learning, John Curtin International Institute, April.

Dhanarajan, G. (1998b) 'Delivery of training programmes: changing design', delivered to the UNESCO/UNEVOC International Conference on Vocational Education in the Asia/Pacific Region, Adelaide Institute of TAFE, Adelaide, 25–7 March.

IDP Education Australia (1998) 'International students in Australian universities: first semester 1998', May, unpublished paper.

Knight, J. (1997) 'Internationalisation of higher education: a conceptual framework', in Knight, J. and de Wit, H. (eds), *Internationalisation of Higher Education in Asia Pacific Countries*, Amsterdam: EAIE/IDP.

Knight, J. and de Wit, H. (1995) 'Strategies for internationalisation of higher education: historical and conceptual perspectives', in H. de Wit (ed.), *Strategies for*

Knight, J and de Wit, H. (eds) (1997) *Internationalisation of Higher Education in Asia Pacific Countries*, Amsterdam: EAIE/IDP.

Internationalisation of Higher Education: A Comparative Study of Australia, Canada, Europe and the United States of America, EAIE, Amsterdam.

Lewis, P.E.T. and Pratt, G.R. (1996) 'Growth in Malaysian demand for business education – the Australian response', *Journal of Higher Education Policy and Management*, 18, 2.

Review of Higher Education Financing and Policy (1998) *Learning for Life – Final Report* (*West Report*), Canberra: Australian Government Publishing Service.

UNESCO (1997) *Statistics Yearbook 1997*, Paris: UNESCO.

Web sites

Commonwealth of Learning: http://www.col.org
Deakin University: http://www.deakin.edu.au

Chapter 3

The impact of telecommunications

Robin Mason

Electronic communication by written message, by audio interaction and by video exchange comprises the field of educational telecommunications. The technologies which correspond to these different means of communication vary considerably, and as they are currently the focus of intense research and development, they are always changing.

There are three broad categories within which current technologies that support distance education can be divided:

1   text-based systems, including electronic mail, computer conferencing, real-time chat systems, fax, and many uses of the Web;
2   audio-based systems such as audioconferencing and audiographics, and audio on the Web;
3   video-based systems such as videoconferencing, one way and two way, video on the Internet with products like CUSeeMe, Web-casting and other visual media such as video clips on the Web.

The implication of this list is that text, audio and video are discrete media. While this is partially true today, the evolution of all these systems is towards integration – of real-time and asynchronous access, of resource material and communication, of text and video: in short, of writing, speaking and seeing. The fourth category and the best illustration of this convergence is:

4   the Web, which integrates text, audio and video, both as pre-prepared clips and as live interactive systems, both real time and stored to be accessed later, and furthermore which provides text-based interaction as well as access to educational resources of unprecedented magnitude.

Pedagogical advantages of telecommunications

It is no coincidence that the use of telecommunications media in education is growing at the same time as education budgets are decreasing. Nevertheless, the use of telecommunications media in distance education is not driven solely or even primarily by cost incentives. Each of the media described below allows institutions to provide more flexible and wide-ranging access to their courses, and possibly to increase student numbers without the usual increase in costs. Educational reasons are more significant than costs, and image is often most important. In many areas of the curriculum, practical knowledge and experience with on-line communication is becoming *de rigueur*.

Text-based systems

Without doubt the most commonly used telecommunications technology for communicating with students at a distance is electronic mail and various forms of written group communication. Text-based interaction, whether many-to-many in conferences, or one-to-one in electronic mail, is practised at most institutions of higher education in developed countries, whether students are geographically remote, or actually on-campus.

Some institutions use standard electronic mail systems (which include the facility for sending messages to a group) to communicate with students at a distance. Those accessing from abroad usually use the Internet; those living locally may use a modem over telephone lines. The primary use is for students to ask questions of the tutor, but an additional use is the electronic submission of assignments, as an attachment to a mail message. This is the simplest and most accessible of all the telecommunications technologies, with the possible exception of fax.

More commonly in distance education, a proprietary computer conferencing system is used. FirstClass is a very successful product among educators, and Lotus Notes is common particularly in Business Schools and in training organisations. Web bulletin boards are also becoming very popular and most of the proprietary systems have integrated with the Web, so that conferences can be accessed from a Web browser. Computer conferencing systems allow students on one course to share discussion areas, to have subconferences for small groups, and to have easy access to all the course messages throughout the length of the course. Computer conferencing systems are slightly more complex than e-mail, and they may require the student to have client software. A faster modem may be necessary as well, or at least highly desirable.

The fax is most often used in distance education for sending and receiving students' assignments. For example, the Open University in the United Kingdom provides a fax machine to those of its UK-based tutors who have students in continental Europe.

Text-based systems can be divided according to whether they are primarily synchronous or asynchronous in use. More accurately, while the technologies usually support both, in practice one or the other is the primary intended use, and this influences the design of the interaction features. Figure 3.1 shows a screen from the FirstClass conferencing system in which messages are listed as separate items and comments on messages are apparent from the subject descriptors. While FirstClass includes a real-time chat facility and some educational uses are made of it, the most significant applications of the system are asynchronous.

Most text-based communication systems are used primarily to *support* students (with the *contents* of the course delivered through some other medium); however, some educators run 'on-line courses' in which the primary content of the course is the discussions and activities taking place among the students. For example, Applications of Information Technology in Open and Distance Education, part of the Master's degree offered by the Institute of Educational Technology at the Open University, is run almost entirely on the Web through collaborative work, readings, discussions and electronic assignments.

One of the major advantages of text-based media is that they facilitate interaction for those using their second language. Most people are more able to write than to speak in another language. Furthermore, asynchronous systems allow time for reading messages slowly and composing a response with the aid of a dictionary. Not surprisingly, there is a range of very successful asynchronous text-based programmes at an international level for second-language teaching. Usually they provide natural language practice with

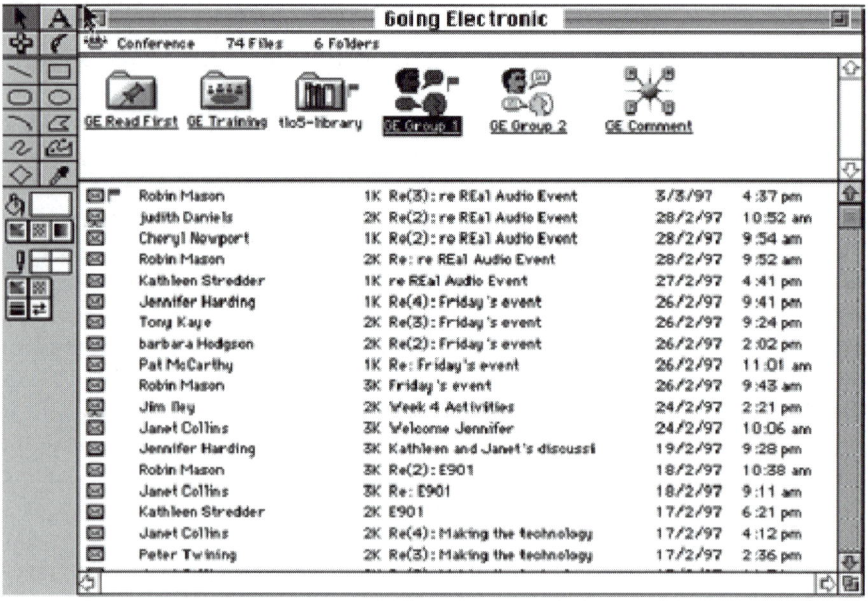

Figure 3.1 FirstClass messaging

mother-tongue speakers, which is much more engaging and profitable educationally than artificial classroom practice.

Another primary advantage of any text-based system for distance education is that many people worldwide can access them using a personal computer and telephone line from their home. In fact, although there are a few uses of real-time chat or even computer conferencing in which students go to a study centre, campus computer room or training centre, most uses of these systems are asynchronous and from the student's own machine (whether at home or in the workplace).

My third advantage of text-based systems is rather more contentious. Much has been made of the equalising effects of textual communication – the concentration on what is said rather than who says it. While it remains the case that the disabled and the disadvantaged can participate without the usual judgemental reactions, text-based systems do not remove bias and advantage; they merely shift it around a bit. Clearly, those who have regular access (for example, from both work and home) or have no concern about the cost of access, are advantaged in terms of being able to participate in discussions more easily than those who have restricted access and cost considerations. Furthermore, those who have good writing skills tend to dominate by the very quality of their messages, in that less literate participants defer to them or are simply deterred from putting in messages themselves. Finally, the openness of these systems to anyone, anytime to make their opinion known, to respond to other viewpoints and to engage in dialogue, is true in theory, but in reality, messages not following the main thrust of the discussion (keeping up with the ongoing conversation) tend to be ignored. Abuses of the openness of the system, such as 'flaming' (a jargon term to describe the all-too-common phenomenon of sudden heated confrontations between on-line participants often over misunderstandings due to textual communication), sexual harassment (also a common occurrence in on-line systems), and unsociable behaviour generally, have driven participants away and somewhat damaged both the image and the value of text-based communication (although this is much less prevalent in educational than social uses). So what was originally hailed as a new democratising medium, inherently more open than other modes of communication, has been shown in practice over time to be as flawed as the human beings who use it. Nevertheless, for some groups of people, text-based interaction allows access to education in a form ideally suited to their situation.

Audio systems

Straight audioconferencing using ordinary telephone lines is a low-tech solution to supporting students in the developed world, owing to the near ubiquity of the telephone in these countries. Many print-based distance education programmes use audioconferencing to help motivate students, and it has also been used for small group collaborative work at postgraduate level (Burge and Roberts 1993). Nevertheless, there are relatively few uses of this technology in group-discussion mode (as opposed to simple student-to-tutor telephone calls) in distance education.

An extension of pure voice interaction is audiographics: voice plus a shared screen for drawing or sharing pre-prepared graphics. This technology has had more extensive use in distance education (Idrus 1992; Nordin 1992), and examples of it being used between sites in different countries also exist (Mason 1994b). As with audioconferencing, audiographics use with more than two sites requires an audio bridge to connect all the lines together. There is no technical barrier to doing this internationally; cost is the primary deterrent. The term 'audiographics' is used less and less now that shared screen and multiway audio are possible on the Internet.

Audio on the Web is a developing technology which many institutions are beginning to take seriously as an educational tool, especially when combined with various forms of real-time, text-based interaction. RealAudio, for example, is a product which allows real-time lectures with 'overheads' on a shared screen (http://www.realaudio.com/). Many distance education systems have involved sending audio cassettes out to students through the post. With audio on Internet products like RealAudio, it is possible for large numbers of students to access these 'broadcasts' in both real and delayed time.

Figure 3.2 is a screen from the Open University's use of RealAudio to

Figure 3.2 An illustrated lecture on KMi Stadium

deliver a global lecture and discussion session with a series of experts. The interface which has been developed on the Web to support the events, called the KMi Stadium, provides facilities for slides associated with the lecture (http://kmi.open.ac.uk/stadium/).

Before leaving audio systems, it is worth highlighting another up-and-coming technology: voicemail. Currently, this technology is being used by both distance teaching and campus-based institutions for mini-lectures, timely comments from the lecturer and for various types of assignments requiring a student response. The student dials into a special number and can listen to the pre-prepared message from the tutor. It is another low-tech solution to adding interactivity and responsiveness to the learning environment.

Video systems

Some educators feel that videoconferencing is not necessary in supporting students at a distance, and that audio, especially audiographics, works better because it concentrates attention on content rather than distracting the learners' attention with the visual image of the speaker. For them, the significantly higher cost of providing video is not justified by the educational benefits. Others feel that we live in a visual age in which it makes no sense to restrict the learner to audio exchange. Video, when well used, contributes to the motivation of the student, makes the learning environment more social, and facilitates the delivery of exceptional learning materials in almost every area of the curriculum (see Mason 1994a).

One-way video (with two-way audio) systems have widespread application in North American distance education and some of these systems use satellite delivery to extend coverage. The National Technological University (NTU) is one of the best known and successful examples of this teaching method. Two-way videoconferencing is taking over from the one-way systems, and a number of multi-site applications are in use, for example, in Australia (Latchem, et al. 1994).

Despite the popularity of videoconferencing, there are many educational technologists who disparage its use. The following is a particularly incisive critique:

> The widely held view that face-to-face teaching is inherently superior to other forms of teaching has spawned a major industry worldwide. It is difficult to believe that videoconferencing would have become such a major influence, especially in North America, without the intellectual complacency associated with the tyranny of proximity. The investment in videoconferencing has been quite staggering despite the widely held view that the lecture is a process whereby the notes of the lecturer are transmitted to the notes of the student, without passing through the minds of either. . . .

The apparently unwavering enthusiasm for the proliferation of video-conferencing systems for the purpose of enhancing teaching and learning represents 'the tyranny of futility'. If most lectures are relatively futile from a pedagogical perspective, why spend vast sums of money promoting expensive futile exercises?

(Taylor and Swannell 1997)

Streaming video on the Internet, however, is a developing technology which may have more lasting potential, precisely because it is more closely tied to the model of personal computing, just-in-time learning and Web-based resources, than it is to the notion of teaching and learning through traditional lectures. While technically feasible today, video on the Web is restricted by the bandwidth available to most distance learners. In theory it allows the image to be downloaded by remote sites in real time. More realistic today is the use of video clips integrated with text-based material, to illustrate and highlight rather than to deliver large amounts of live lecturing.

The Web

There is little doubt that the Web is the most phenomenally successful educational tool to have appeared in a long time. Evidence for such a statement can be found in Collis (1996) and Khan (1997). It combines all the media described above: text, text-based interaction, audio and video as clips and, with somewhat less robustness, multi-way interactive audio and video. Its application in distance education is unquestioned. Although access to the Internet is hardly universal, and large segments of the global population are more remote from access to it than they are to print and post-based systems of distance education, nevertheless, vast numbers of people worldwide do have access, many from their home, and this access is growing exponentially.

The Web is merely a collection of protocols and standards which define access to information on the Internet. The three defining characteristics of the Web are:

- the use of URLs (Universal Resource Locators) which provide the addressing system;
- the HTTP standard (Hypertext Transfer Protocol) by which the delivery of requested information is transacted;
- the development of HTML (Hypertext Markup Language) through which links between documents and parts of documents are made.

Fundamental to the nature of the Web is its client-server architecture, whereby the client (Web software residing on the user's machine) requests a particular document from a Web server (a program running on a computer whose purpose is to serve documents to other computers upon request).

Having transmitted the documents, the server then terminates the connection. This procedure allows servers to handle many thousands of requests per day. One of the mechanisms for implementing audio and video on the Internet is through the programming language called Java and the HotJava browser:

> HotJava interprets embedded application <APP> tags by downloading and executing the specified program within the WWW environment. The specified program can be an interactive game, animation or sound files, or any other interactive program. Also, when a file or application requires particular viewers, such as for video, Java anticipates this and calls these viewers up automatically.
>
> (Collis 1996: Interface 3)

Now that it is possible to download programs from the Web along with data, and to receive the appropriate software to handle the program automatically, the institution wanting to deliver course material can manage the maintenance and updating of any software required for the course. The student no longer needs to struggle with the installation of massive packages, and, furthermore, can use a relatively low cost machine – even a portable.

Synchronous versus asynchronous distance education

As is apparent in this description of different technologies for delivering education at a distance, some of the systems rely on real-time interaction, while others can be accessed asynchronously. This difference has major implications for the design and delivery of distance education, as well as for the study requirements of the learner. There are advantages to both forms and in the end, personal learning styles and the larger educational context determine what is most appropriate. We can examine the major benefits of each mode in an educational context.

Asynchronous delivery

There are four crucial advantages to the asynchronous media and I have arranged them in descending order of significance:

- flexibility – access to the teaching material (e.g. on the Web, or computer conference discussions) can take place at any time (twenty-four hours of the day, seven days a week) and from many locations (e.g. oil rigs);
- time to reflect – rather than having to react on one's feet, asynchronous systems allow the learner time to mull over ideas, check references, refer

back to previous messages and take any amount of time to prepare a comment;

- situated learning – because the technology allows access from home and work, the learner can easily integrate the ideas being discussed on the course with the working environment, or access resources on the Internet as required on the job;
- cost-effective technology – text-based asynchronous systems require little bandwidth and low end computers to operate, thus access, particularly global access, is more equitable.

Synchronous delivery

There are four equally compelling advantages to synchronous systems, although I am less confident of general agreement about the order:

- motivation – synchronous systems focus the energy of the group, providing motivation to distance learners to keep up with their peers and continue with their studies;
- telepresence – real-time interaction, with its opportunity to convey tone and nuance, helps to develop group cohesion and the sense of being part of a learning community;
- good feedback – synchronous systems provide quick feedback on ideas and support consensus and decision-making in group activities, both of which enliven distance education;
- pacing – synchronous events encourage students to keep up-to-date with the course and provide a discipline to learning which helps people to prioritise their studies.

Implications for students, teachers and organisations

> In general, conferencing technologies should be tools to help human activities. But like models of teaching, they are not neutral tools. Their use will reflect whatever values the educator holds – consciously or subconsciously – about her/his relationship with learners, and their use will invariably bring advantages and disadvantages.
>
> (Burge and Roberts 1993: 35)

The context in which any of these technologies is used reflects attitudes to education on the part of the organisation and the particular teacher. This context defines the advantages and disadvantages for all concerned. What telecommunications technologies have in common is that students are not in the same location as the teacher and/or other students, at least not during use of the medium. This fact has a number of implications – for equipment provision, learning styles, preparation of teaching material, and not least, training and support.

Implications for students

Most evaluation studies on educational uses of conferencing include feedback from students regarding their reactions to learning from the medium. Almost invariably reports are enthusiastic. Students are usually positive about the advantages the medium has brought them – a wider curriculum choice, less time and money spent travelling, more interactivity with the teacher and their peers. Where reports are less favourable, these are from quasi-laboratory studies in which students are put into both remote classrooms and face-to-face teaching situations and the results of tests compared. The fact is that with a few exceptions, these systems are used to meet specific needs such as time, distance and interaction. When these systems are used outside of any context of need, the results not surprisingly show less user acceptance.

How well do these systems meet students' needs? The travel time and distance needs are best met by home-based technologies, or workplace settings. In some distance education systems, the study centre provides access to equipment and to a very convivial setting with a long cultural tradition. The social and interactive needs of students vary considerably – some students prefer to learn in isolation; others want some contact with their peers. Face-to-face contact is the only satisfactory form of interaction for some students; others find the curiously intimate but anonymous quality of computer conferencing contact very appealing. Undoubtedly videoconferencing is most satisfactory to most students in meeting social and interactive learning needs. Home-based access is likely to increase costs to students for the initial purchase of computer equipment and the ongoing cost of telephone calls. Training, maintenance and upgrading of the equipment are additional problems with costs attached.

Computer conferencing is the medium which most challenges the traditional lecture format. In fact, computer conferencing requires much more self-direction, motivation and initiative on the part of the student than do most other media. Although applications in this area are also growing very fast, the overall student acceptance level is probably lowest. Computer conferencing is hard work for students, much more so than listening to a lecture. There are not many precedents for interactive discussion in education – discussions in which one is expected to formulate a point of view, express it and modify or defend it in the face of comment or criticism. Many teachers cannot or choose not to use interactive teaching methods. Any experience students have had in doing this is almost invariably spoken rather than written. Although many students are very enthusiastic about computer conferencing, there is no doubt that many others are not.

Most tutors report that their main difficulty lies in encouraging students to participate.

Some students are very nervous about making presentations via video-conferencing. Having to manage equipment and being seen on monitors simply add to the general level of stress in presenting their own work. Asynchronous presentations through Web pages and on computer conferences cause less concern, as there is no camera to record embarrassment and nervousness.

The impact of these technologies on students varies with how active and interactive they choose to be. Students who want to take the initiative in the learning process and who enjoy engaging with their peers are empowered by these technologies. Others will use them to learn this independence and interdependence. Nevertheless, there will always remain a minority resistant to these technologies, for whom face-to-face is the only satisfactory learning mode.

Implications for teachers

Most reports about technology-mediated teaching indicate that preparation time is much greater than for equivalent face-to-face teaching. This preparation is of two sorts: producing material (for the Web or to illustrate a lecture) and planning the format of the course. The more interaction desired, the more planning is necessary.

The quality of the visuals used is a significant element in the success of videoconferencing. The size and legibility of the lettering and drawings, the production of graphics or other images require that the teacher be competent in the use of graphics software or have access to a support team. Sequencing the images to be used requires planning at the story-board level of detail – what course concepts will be conveyed with each image and how to make one flow into the next to create a meaningful narrative. One set of guidelines suggests:

> Questions to learners participating at distant sites should be preplanned and range from low-order (recall of knowledge) to higher-order (syntheses, analysis, problem solving etc.) on Bloom's taxonomy of cognitive questions. The teleteacher needs to ask a lot of questions in order to 'force' interaction with the learners. After posing a question, the teacher should allow sufficient 'wait' time for students to process information before they answer.
>
> (Barker and Goodwin 1992: 15)

With videoconferencing, teachers need to project themselves, rather like actors, and create a dynamic presence to convey their subject over a monitor.

The role of the computer conferencing teacher is the farthest removed from that of the traditional lecturer. Course design is equally as important as with the other technologies and preparation entails the structuring of conferences and topics, and the design of activities and small group work. During the course, however, the teacher's role is definitely one of facilitator and host, rather than one of content provider and star of the show.

> The facilitator needs to pay careful attention to welcoming each student to the electronic course, and reinforcing early attempts to communicate. In the first few weeks, I make sure that my notes in the conference specifically reference prior student notes. I send many individual messages to students commenting on their contribution, suggesting links to other students, suggesting resources, and generally reaching out to students. The coaching function is key to easing the students' transition to computer-mediated communication.
>
> (Davie 1989: 82)

While the teacher's role is particularly time consuming in the initial phase of a computer conferencing course, it usually reduces as students take over the discussions. Nevertheless, some reports indicate that teachers spend up to twice as long, overall, to give a course via computer conferencing as they do to give a course by traditional means.

Most teachers who take on the challenge of teleconferencing, particularly those who develop collaborative learning strategies for their courses, report tremendous satisfaction, despite the greater effort required. The reward lies in their sense of working towards the goal of developing independent, questioning learners. Almost all find that using these technologies is a tremendous learning experience for themselves:

> These experiences also taught me how to teach differently than in a traditional classroom. They have led me to reflect on my role as a teacher, and have enabled me to change my teaching style to facilitate learner-centred instructional systems that promote knowledge generation through collaborative learning. The quality of student interactions and performance has shown that students were able to generate knowledge, to innovate, to collaborate, and to analyze their own learning. The teacher's role in interactive telecommunication teaching is best portrayed as that of a facilitator guiding and supporting the learning process. This is no easy task, and consumes much more time and energy than does teaching a traditional class. The role changes I have experienced as a result of distance teaching have been transferred to my traditional teaching in that my teaching style has become learner centered and interactive.
>
> (Gunawardena 1992: 70)

Implications for organisations

A number of case studies and evaluations of telecommunications applications underline the importance of top-level administrative support to the
success of any programme. Although many small-scale uses of these technologies begin at grassroots level, with a few enthusiastic teachers, their
growth within an organisation must have backing at the highest levels,
because so many major policy issues are at stake involving, among others,
questions about student support and about costs.

Support

The provision of support for students is a major issue an organisation must
address. The quality of support services is equally as important to student
motivation and performance as are the teleconferences. The organisation
must consider the preparation and delivery of training materials to students.
Many institutions offer their distance students telephone office hours for
direct queries with their teacher. Individualised feedback from faculty
on assessments and access to library resources (increasingly via electronic
communications) are other forms of support. Operating a help desk for
queries about equipment and communications systems is another institutional consideration for those involved in computer conferencing. Given
the technical complications of the current telecommunications scene, many
organisations adopt the policy of expecting students to turn to their local
dealer for this support. Managing and supporting the equipment through
its lifetime is another issue which some institutions face for the first time
with telecommunications. For some organisations, a whole new unit and
type of staff are necessary. Many underestimate the extent of this element
of telecommunications.

> To understate the dollars required to operate, maintain, upgrade, and
> train to the system is to undercut its assimilation into the instructional
> process. When this happens, technology remains supplemental, making
> it even more vulnerable to cost reductions.
>
> (Maloy and Perry 1991: 45)

Cost savings

Cost studies of actual uses of these technologies are very rare (Bates 1995).
Generalisations from the few which exist are notoriously difficult to apply to
other contexts. Examples of the introduction of technology reducing unit
costs are most easily found in industry, where training by videoconference in
the workplace replaces expensive face-to-face residential sessions (see for
example, Lange 1994). Examples of unit cost reductions within education are

much harder to find. This is partly because the introduction of technology slowly changes the whole cost structure of course preparation, presentation and support. It then becomes difficult to compare before and after costs as they are literally no longer comparable: different staff are required and different kinds of students take the courses. However, more often the technology is an added cost, either because old systems exist in parallel, or because technology enriches but does not actually replace old systems.

Many practitioners have concluded that telecommunications systems do not save money in the long run. What they do is extend access to courses, improve the quality of current provision and meet needs which cannot otherwise be accommodated. Even this statement needs qualification, however, because in some respects the introduction of technology limits access and disempowers the technologically illiterate, the impoverished and those remote from networks. The most comprehensive study of this very complex issue is Rumble (1997).

One of the pitfalls of many attempts to reduce costs in education is to turn to information and communications technology as the cost saviour, and to assume that what is delivered in one medium (e.g. face-to-face lectures) can be transferred to another medium (e.g. videoconferencing, the Web) with minimal cost. However, the effectiveness of any medium is invariably dependent on exploiting the unique characteristics of that medium. Web courses need to be tailor-made for the hypertext structure; videoconferencing should exploit the two-way interactive facilities and the visual potential of the medium; computer conferencing courses need to build on the possibilities of collaborative group work, and so on. Consequently, technology-mediated courses are often cost-effective, but at the expense of educational quality. An alternative pitfall is to use the technology as an add-on to the course, thereby improving the quality, but increasing the cost.

> New technology is usually employed to add richness or accessibility to otherwise unaltered programs; thus it tends to increase costs rather than lower them. If staff are able to save money in one area, they generally do not reduce prices and may not even be able to do so; instead the money is reallocated to other pressing needs within the same program.
>
> (Ehrmann 1996: 126)

Ehrmann concludes from his study that it is easier to achieve lower costs while maintaining quality and openness if the programme is created from the start to address this triple challenge. He describes these three interdependent elements as the quality of the learning process, the accessibility of the course, and the costs, both to the providing institution and to the student (Ehrmann 1996: 11). Costs of open and distance learning cannot be assessed without also considering the quality and accessibility of any programme.

Consortia are a growing solution to sharing the high costs of videoconferencing, or the teaching and expert resources of a range of educational institutions. An emerging example of a consortium is the Western Governors University in the United States which has formed from existing institutions in order to address the need for accessible, relevant lifelong learning. It acts both as broker and as course provider. The University of the Highlands and Islands is a United Kingdom version springing from a similar vision.

Another resource-sharing solution to high costs is the joint use of study centres. In some places these are called tele-cottages, in which various kinds of teaching media are at the disposal of the local community. As competition among educational providers increases, these tele-cottages will allow students to access courses from a variety of sources and will offer a wider market for niche courses.

Conclusion

Has technology-mediated distance education been oversold? Undoubtedly yes. Will technology-mediated distance education increase? Undoubtedly yes. This is the paradox of technology and of humanity's perpetual attraction to the new and exciting. However, there are educational benefits to be gained from telecommunications technologies: wider access, greater flexibility, more engaging learning environments and better communication with other learners and teachers.

References

Barker, B. and Goodwin, R. (1992) 'Audiographics: linking remote classrooms', *The Computing Teacher*, April 1992, 11–15.

Bates, A. (1995) *Technology, Open Learning and Distance Education*, London: Routledge.

Burge, E. and Roberts, J. (1993) *Classrooms with a Difference. A Practical Guide to the Use of Conferencing Technologies*, Toronto: Ontario Institute for Studies in Education.

Collis, B. (1996) *Tele-Learning in a Digital World*, London: International Thompson Computer Press.

Davie, L. (1989) 'Facilitation techniques for the on-line tutor', in R. Mason and A.R. Kaye (eds), *Mindweave: Communication, Computers and Distance Education*, Oxford: Pergamon.

Ehrmann, S. (1996) *Adult Learning in a New Technological Era*, Paris: OECD.

Gunawardena, C. (1992) 'Faculty roles for audiographics and on-line teaching', *American Journal of Distance Education*, 6, 3, 58–71.

Idrus, R.M. (1992) 'Technological innovation towards adult self-directed learning in the Off-Campus Academic Programme at the Universiti Sains Malaysia', *ICDE Bulletin*, 28, 48–54.

Khan, B. (ed.) (1997) *Web-Based Instruction*, Englewood Cliffs, NJ: Educational Technology Publications.

Lange, J. (1994) 'ISDN videoconferencing for education and training', in R. Mason and P. Bacsich (eds), *ISDN Application in Education and Training*, London: The Institution of Electrical Engineers.

Latchem, C., Mitchell, J. and Atkinson, R. (1994) 'ISDN-based videoconferencing in Australian tertiary education', in R. Mason and P. Bacsich (eds), *ISDN Application in Education and Training*, London: The Institution of Electrical Engineers.

Maloy, W. and Perry, N. (1991) 'A navy video teletraining project: lessons learned', *American Journal of Distance Education*, 5, 3, 40–50.

Mason, R. (1994a) *Using Communications Media in Open and Flexible Learning*, London: Kogan Page.

Mason, R. (1994b) *Evaluation Report on Courses over JANUS*, Vol. 1: *Delta Deliverable*, Brussels: European Commission.

Nordin, M.R. (1992) 'Workshop on audiographic teleconferencing at Universiti Sains Malaysia, 20–1 May 1991', *Open Learning*, 7, 2, 60–1.

Rumble, G. (1997) *The Costs and Economics of Open and Distance Learning*, London: Kogan Page.

Taylor, J. and Swannell, P. (1997) 'From outback to Internet: crackling radio to virtual campus', in *Proceedings of InterAct97, International Telecommunications Union, Geneva, September, 1997*, Geneva: ITU (CD-ROM).

Chapter 4

Professional reflective practice and lifelong learning

Patrick Guiton

While professional continuing education may have been comparatively slow to recognise the significance of open and distance learning, the number of distance and off-shore MBAs and similar credential courses now offered by universities, colleges and commercial training bodies indicates that professional workplace learning is changing rapidly. The context in which many professionals work is being transformed as information technologies and more particularly the PC and access to the Internet are giving more working professionals direct access to career upgrading and problem-solving information on a day-to-day or even an hour-to-hour basis. Reflective practice (Schön 1987) can now involve the keyboard in addition to and perhaps increasingly in place of the seminar. This chapter looks at some of the possibilities which are now emerging for professionals to guide and direct their own career-long learning.

The changing world of professional continuing education

When Schön (1987) wrote about 'reflective practice' he was concerned primarily with the need to establish the practicum as a basic element in the initial training of undergraduates in university professional schools. He quotes the dean of a maritime engineering school who recognised that he was teaching students how to build good ships but not which ships to build: there was a clear need for training to be placed in a context which would better enable graduate professionals to apply their specialist knowledge effectively.

Universities have tended to recognise two categories of graduate. Postgraduate describes those who remain in the system in order to proceed to higher degrees. A broader term for those moving on into careers, jobs and other post-university lifespans is alumni, which carries connotations of completion, celebration and in most cases a more or less tacit expectation of future financial contribution. But most of the contexts into which alumni, and indeed many postgraduates, pass after graduation have become increasingly fluid. Job security, even for the highly skilled, is less certain and professionals must adapt to that workspan reality. While some relish the flexibility which peddling their specialist and highly portable skills offers in select competitive markets, most must work strategically and continuously to upgrade or redirect hard-earned entry skills in anticipation of several, quite possibly involuntary, career changes. In these circumstances, reflective practice attains a new measure of urgency.

Many universities have moved quite rapidly to acknowledge this change even though in the nature of universities they have tended to do so by offering new credentials such as graduate certificates and diplomas often drawn from the existing curriculum rather than starting by exploring the range of needs of the reflective practitioners themselves. In this they have often been guided appropriately enough by professional associations, employers of graduates and groups of employers. They have also been motivated by two other significant factors. In almost every university mission statement we now find specific commitment to develop lifelong learners: opinion may vary as to whether this means the development in undergraduates of skill to continue learning independently throughout their working lives without further assistance or whether it acknowledges that apprenticeship training of initial graduates from whatever faculty is no longer sufficient and must be supplemented. The other major motivator has been the capacity, long denied, for universities to charge students for postgraduate award study. An MBA, endorsed by employers, perhaps by an entire industry, becomes a worthwhile investment for a professional employee and also a worthwhile and profitable enterprise for a providing university. That is a win, win, win situation which of course explains both the prevalence of MBAs and their cost.

There is one other factor of particular relevance to the Commonwealth of Learning. At the time of COL's foundation there was a rationale, more or less overt, which argued that if it had become too expensive for students from developing countries to go to study in developed countries then it was necessary to take the courses to the students at home. The very significant growth in undergraduate places in many Commonwealth member nations has now made this challenge somewhat less relevant at the first degree level. However, the widespread imposition of full fee charges for overseas graduates pursuing post-initial qualifications and updating courses has now made the original COL rationale one of particular significance for postgraduate and professional students for whom provision at home may well be sparse or non-existent.

The university and recurrent education

Many universities have longstanding and highly regarded extension programmes through which academics have been able to contribute to the community by offering courses of interest from their particular expertise on a not-for-credit basis, and increasing recognition of the significance of lifelong learning means that this will remain a most important activity across a wide range of subject areas. However, more specialised contributions to continuing professional learning, often guided by the influence of that profession's association or crediting body, have served three major categories of professional need:

1   further credentials: for graduates with a background in the subject area but requiring greater depth and sophistication;
2   updating: again for graduates with a background but whose major concern is to guard against the outdating of their original training;
3   changing direction: designed for graduates who want to add a new, possibly complementary, skill to their original training but who do not have that discipline background.

Strategies for meeting these needs have almost invariably focused on structured coursework, a medium with which most academics are familiar and which lends itself readily to organisational arrangements favouring economies of scale. However, the increasing availability of on-line resources makes it more possible, and perhaps more likely, that professionals will seek to direct their own upgrading and change of direction.

University structure and lifelong learning

The adoption by universities of a flagstaff commitment to the development of lifelong learners is raising consciousness that graduation is both more and less than completion of an apprenticeship. Professional schools will always have the spur (or in some cases perhaps the drag anchor) of a gatekeeping professional association, but there can be few faculties left in which either students or staff still see the initial BA/BSc as a 'meal ticket'.

Universities have grown increasingly aware of the competitive nature of continuing professional education. In many countries it is no longer practicable for them to expect the community, its stakeholders and members, to come cap in hand to a seat of learning. There are other universities, some close at hand, some perhaps on the other side of the world, with ready marketing and organisational access to any supposedly local catchment area. There is ever-increasing readiness of graduates to look at other educational sectors for the technical and vocational knowledge and not to be hung up by artificial status considerations. In addition, there are now a significant number of providers of continuing professional education from the commercial sector, while several professional associations and many individual employers provide specialist in-house training for their professional staff geared to their own specifications.

Linked to, or underpinning, this competitive situation have been the radical changes offered for teaching and learning practices through the new computer-based interactive and asynchronous technologies. Because practising professionals are almost by definition computer-literate and desktop-active in their daily working lives, the potential for applications in continuing professional education is boundless. The capacity of providers to exploit this potential will rest on a range of factors, including technical infrastructure capacity, the skills to use it effectively and the motivation of, and incentives provided for, those with control of the knowledge base.

Flexible teaching and learning and professional development

All stakeholders in higher and continuing education now accept the value of, or at least the necessity for, increasing flexibility in the provision of teaching and learning. But, as with most aspects of openness in education, interpretations of flexibility are as elastic as the term itself. Academic course structures are generally carefully constructed around the long-term aim of graduation as the outcome of years of cumulative study, and this mind-set does not adjust easily to the notions of customisation and fee for service which are of prime importance in professional development education. Knight (1997) uses somewhat cumbersome terminology in developing an important perspective on this issue when he distinguishes between short half-life knowledge (SHK) and long half-life knowledge (LHK). LHK is acquired over months or years in formal academic programmes: it is generally seen to deliver positive economic and social, as well as purely individual, benefits and is therefore a good candidate for public-sector finance and delivery and for presentation to cohorts of students across a standard academic year. SHK by contrast, can be acquired relatively quickly and often has a short useful life: it is likely to be practical vocational knowledge such as a new surgical technique or new computer software which, unless practised immediately after acquisition, is easily forgotten. By definition this learning on demand is ill-suited to the student-cohort structure and in contrast to long half-life knowledge, SHK is therefore 'an excellent candidate for private sector provision and finance by individual members of the labour force or by companies' (Knight 1997). At one time it might have been argued that universities had little if any place in the provision of SHK, but increased market awareness and the need to broaden funding sources has changed that perspective. At the same time, it is of course no accident that faculty groups most responsive to SHK learning needs are likely to come either from professional schools or those with well-established consultancy programmes in industry or government: these links provide both the opportunity and the legitimacy for adopting customisation as a core component of educational provision.

Most customised professional training programmes are offered as courses with varying degrees of flexibility for participants to determine their own pace of study or to select from component parts of the material. By arrangement with employers, courses may be offered to groups at their workplaces or increasingly on-line.[1] But while public-funded universities are now comfortable in sharing curriculum design for an individual module or a non-credit course with an employer partner, most would baulk at the notion of a privately designed award curriculum to be delivered and accredited by the partner university. A current example of such a structure is one recently formalised between an Australian university (University of Technology, Sydney) and the country's largest insurance company (AMP): it was significant that the commercial partner reported its difficulty in finding such a collaborating university because 'most universities couldn't even have the conversation'. Many universities have wrestled with this issue of private-sector patronage in relation to research funding with varying outcomes and some professional associations have long exercised influence in the universities' development of curricula for training their prospective members: it is therefore interesting to consider how far they may go in extending this influence to the point of contracting out to a university the teaching of a specific set of professionally determined objectives. At what point is academic integrity compromised and is that point necessarily more elastic in professional faculties than in others?

The development of increasing numbers of on-line courses, modules and updating packages is opening up much broader access for individual professionals who may be self-employed or working in small partnerships without ready access to workplace group training programmes.[2] Courses and modules of courses meet a large proportion of the demand for professional development education, particularly where this is geared towards the earning of credentials or meeting employers' expectations of recurrent updating of professional skills. This is the dominant sector of the fee-for-service market for professional education; it is relatively straightforward to organise, cost and implement and, even where customised, it lends itself readily to the development of profitable economies of scale. But it does not provide for the full range of need for professional development.

Reflective practice and personal professional development

Many professionals will continue to be involved in some formal credentialled learning at various stages or even throughout their careers. But all reflective practitioners will be more or less actively involved in self-directed informal learning on a day-by-day basis as they cope with the challenges of their job, and there is no particular reason to distinguish here between those in formal professions and any other workers who take an active reflective interest in their jobs. In times of rapid technological change, reflective practice is virtually an occupational necessity for everyone. Informal learning is widespread and significant (Candy 1991; Gear, *et al.* 1994; Becher 1996) but has generally been regarded as irrelevant in higher education, because it is not readily translated into credentials: at best something for extension activity. It tends also to be submerged by employers as 'not measurable for promotion or work release' and even by the practitioners themselves who often see it as 'just broadening my perspective'. But recent studies have demonstrated the significance of such activity. In a study conducted from the University of Hull, Gear *et al.* report examples of architects teaching themselves about computer graphics, stonework restoration and church-bell technology in order to enhance their capacity to cope with emergent job demands, engineers pursuing capital investment strategies and railway signalling, and lawyers studying alternative dispute resolution, book editing and library cataloguing. The list of learning needs is broad and diverse but not random: we find reflective practitioners seeking quite systematically to improve their professional skills in relevant ways, but also in diverse subject areas which formal postgraduate coursework awards could never hope to anticipate. Becher emphasises the importance to professionals of informal, often casual, interactions and consultations extending throughout their careers – common-room discussion addressing specific task-related factors at the workplace. Reporting on a British study, Becher notes the marginal role of higher education institutions in meeting the continuing education needs of his professional subjects which 'stems from their (universities') tendency to regard formal courses as the most appropriate mode of teaching provision, while practitioners in general take a different view' (Becher 1996: 54). More optimistically, however, Becher reports that 'universities were seen as valuable sources of specialised knowledge and as helpful in resolving technical problems'. This comment is highly significant when considering the changing role of universities because it focuses attention on the opportunity for academics to be consultants to individual professional learners in addition to, or in place of, their more familiar role as curriculum specialists in developing courses to accommodate established professional needs.

Is there a way in which higher education can exploit the rapidly increasing use of asynchronous computer-based teaching and learning interaction to benefit its advantageous position in the provision of specialist knowledge to reflective practitioners? In a report for the Association of European Universities, Edwards (1996) anticipates such a development when he speculates that 'the university may well find itself becoming a sort of "learning broker", in a situation where learning demands and learning resources must be matched'.

Learning brokerage and reflective practice

Because they have made a heavy investment in the development of course-ware, universities are happy when they can enrol postgraduation learners in courses or in sets of units drawn from courses or in modules or sets of modules drawn from units. This modular structure is cost-effective, and where it also includes scope for customisation to accommodate the needs of corporate clients it will remain the staple of continuing professional education delivery. There is also a range of modules in print, on CD-ROM, and increasingly on-line, available for a fee and offering updating in dentistry, medicine, engineering and other professional areas for clients who are clear about their specific updating targets.

But there is another market. Because this market deals with the less well-defined but no less important learning needs of individuals, or of potential groups with similar interests, rather than with cohorts and classes, it is more difficult to operationalise and to cost. However, the rapid development of flexible-learning techniques and a focus on guided independent study both on- and off-campus offers increasing legitimacy to the role of learning broker. Most universities have a *Guide to Academic Expertise*, the major purpose of which has often been to provide the media with spokespersons on issues of the day. But what if this *Guide* became recognised as a systematic standard for reflective professional practitioners to the 'specialised knowledge and assistance in resolving technical problems' already identified by Becher as one of the university's major strengths? (Becher 1996). A number of current projects developed at the University of Sheffield are exploiting the flexibility of asynchronous (and therefore reflective) computer conferencing to foster interprofessional interaction as 'just in time open learning' (McConnell and Hammond 1997). Meanwhile, at Stanford University a well-recognised capacity for using communications technologies for outreach into industrial worksites is being expanded by the introduction of 'asynchronous access to the desktop' (Harris and DiPaola 1996). Significantly, these authors report that:

> the essential power of the emerging technology may be to provide sufficient flexibility so that ... greater numbers of students can be approached as specific cases in a cost effective manner. Ultimately this customisation might reach the level of the individual student.
>
> (Harris and DiPaola 1996)

Of course any such schemes which seek to involve academic staff as sources of specialist information for individual practitioners or as facilitators of computer-based discussion of professional issues will need to address at the outset vexed issues of recognition and reward for such inputs if they are to succeed.

One regularly expanding source for professional development education of all types is a university's alumni. While most professional schools and teacher-training establishments have long recognised that their alumni are not just past graduates but ongoing professional colleagues this is not necessarily a dominant perspective in other areas where conferral of a degree can all too easily be seen by both parties as a termination. There are, however, commentators now arguing that the concept of graduation is outdated and becoming increasingly irrelevant and that degrees should indeed carry with them a type of maintenance contract of the sort familiar to purchasers of household appliances to provide a systematic and recognised basis for ongoing professional development.[3]

Professional development education and the developing Commonwealth

In all discussions of educational development, the question of disparity of access for people in countries at different stages of technological infrastructure development is pertinent. The widespread imposition of full-cost fees by the traditional provider nations has challenged COL and other facilitators to seek ways of taking professional education to students in their home countries rather than taking students to overseas-based courses. A significant example of how this challenge is being met is provided by the current development of a Commonwealth MBA and MPA using collaboration between existing distance education university providers to construct a high status programme which students in developing countries, or their sponsors, can afford.

It will be interesting to see whether this principle can be extended to meet the needs of a broader range of Commonwealth professionals. It can be assumed that ever-increasing numbers of such professional people will gain access to and competence in using computer-based educational resources in their workplaces. They are, however, all too likely to lack the financial resources to access on-line courseware, computer conferencing and asynchronous interaction with academic specialists, technical experts and fellow practitioners on any sort of regular basis. Perhaps it is time for a new Colombo Plan, one which this time provides a number of selected practising professionals in developing countries with a financial subsidy enabling them to participate in the rapidly growing networks of on-line reflective practitioners. In due course, these initial participants in Commonwealth-wide networks would be in a good position to act as catalysts for the development of local networks both on- and off-line, designed to give meaning to that critical and ever more challenging requirement so often used as a throwaway line at graduation ceremonies – 'make sure you keep in touch'.

Notes

1 Examples are customised training programmes offered in industrial contexts by the Open Learning Agency of British Columbia; and more specifically by Washington State University Engineering Faculty on the Boeing aircraft site. 'On demand' on-line courses and modules are available in corporate sites from the Stanford University Centre for Professional Development through ADEPT (Asynchronous DE Project).
2 For example, the University of Pennsylvania School of Veterinary Medicine CAL Updates programme.
3 See, for instance, the Open Learning Katholicke Universiteit Leuven, Belgium, Homepage: http://www.kuleuven.ac.be

References

Becher, A. (1996) 'The learning professions', *Studies in Higher Education*, 21, 1, 43–55.

Candy, P. (1991) *Self Direction for Lifelong Learning*, San Francisco: Jossey-Bass.

Edwards, K. (1996) *Restructuring the University: Universities and the Challenge of New Technologies*, Brussels: Association of European Universities.

Gear, P., McIntosh, A. and Squires, G. (1994) *Informal Learning in the Professions*, Hull: University of Hull.

Harris, D. and DiPaolo, A. (1996) 'Advancing asynchronous distance education using high-speed networks'. Available HTTP: http://stanford-online.stanford.edu

Knight, P. (1997) 'The half-life of knowledge and structural reform of the education sector for the global knowledge-based economy'. Available HTTP: *http://www.knight-moore.com/html/halflife.html*

McConnell, D. and Hammond, M. (1997) 'Just in time open learning: issues and possibilities'. Available HTTP: *http://www.shef.ac.uk/uni/projects/jitol*

Schön, D. (1987) *Educating the Reflective Practitioner*, San Francisco: Jossey-Bass.

Chapter 5

Flexible learning and university change

Louise Moran and Brittmarie Myringer

In the last thirty years, distance education has moved from the margins to the mainstream of higher education policy and practice in many countries, accompanied by a spectacular growth in programmes, institutions and enrolments. Governments, in particular, increasingly see distance education as a valuable economic and social tool in meeting the demands of an information society. The methods and technologies surrounding distance teaching and learning have been systematised, so that those involved now take for granted the way things are done, just as educators in more conventional environments take for granted the way face-to-face, classroom teaching should occur. However, such is the speed of change nowadays that this status quo cannot last.

Throughout this expansion phase there has been an assumption that distance education and face-to-face teaching are different forms of education, each with its own value systems, organisational arrangements and teaching/learning systems. Although hard to sustain in practice, this has been largely due to distance educators' search for legitimacy and status. The separateness has been reinforced by the organisational structures of distance education: on the one hand, open universities entirely dedicated to distance teaching; on the other, distinctive distance education department/centres within dual-mode universities. The quest for legitimacy also sprang from the desire to distinguish distance education from its predecessor, correspondence study. We argue here that what is now occurring is far more than simply evolution of distance education into a third stage, as Nipper argued in 1989.

We suspect that the days of distance education, as such, are numbered. An unsteady, problematic, profound process of change is under way. Distance education methods and systems are converging with those of face-to-face teaching, strongly influenced by new electronic technologies. This process, we believe, will transform university teaching and learning as a whole, not merely add some distance teaching here, and some on-line technologies there. The watchwords today are flexibility, student-centredness (or client-centredness), networked learning, quality and efficiency. What might such a transformed learning environment look like? We outline a concept of flexible learning based on our experiences in Australia and Sweden, and use examples from these countries to illustrate some of the major issues with which universities are now engaging. They represent versions of the dual-mode model which is by far the most common environment within which distance teaching presently occurs.

Triggers for a paradigm shift

Broadly speaking, for advanced and developing nations alike, the triggers for change in university teaching are declining funds, advancing technology and the demography of students.

In most industrialised nations, the advent of the information society and demand for educated professionals is, paradoxically, being accompanied by a decline in public investment in education and greater emphasis on the individual's responsibility to pay for education. In countries like Australia and Britain, a typical first response to financial crisis was to increase class sizes and academic workloads. When this overloaded the system unbearably, the search intensified to find alternative ways of teaching which reduce unit costs, satisfy academic criteria of quality and meet customer needs. In Sweden, the government now requires universities to meet their obligations to serve labour-market needs especially through distance education and professional continuing education (Government of Sweden 1997). Students' costs have traditionally been met by the state, but government is now also encouraging universities to pursue education contracts with employers, again through distance education in particular.

Electronic technologies are triggering change in every area of work and social life in the developed world. Universities are responding to an imperative to adopt on-line technologies that will enable them to provide up-to-date education and training, support larger enrolments, and remain competitive in a global educational economy. In Sweden, for example, the elaborate national communications technology infrastructure appears to offer a robust solution to a decline in public investment in higher education while serving a sophisticated technologically oriented economy and society.[1]

The third trigger – the changing demography of students – is partly a function of the shift from elite to mass higher education, and partly a consequence of a growing demand for recurrent, lifelong education. Broadly speaking, universities are educating far greater numbers of students, drawn from more heterogeneous socio-economic, age and gender backgrounds, with diverse prior educational experiences and levels of knowledge and skills, and varied learning styles. Rigid times and places of formal teaching do not suit the requirements of many potential learners who must juggle study with work and family commitments and may be some distance from a campus.

These factors are triggering turbulence in universities. The physical, intellectual and social boundaries around universities are loosening as they explore notions of real and virtual campuses, and seek greater flexibility in who, where, when, what and how they teach. A three-way convergence of distance and face-to-face education and electronic technologies may seem inevitable in these circumstances, but the reality is far from straightforward. A recent International Council for Distance Education (ICDE) taskforce identifies a formidable range of barriers to change: resistance to new learning theory and practice, rigidity of organisational structures, the tyranny of time, persistence of traditional faculty roles and rewards, assumptions about learning content, constraints of regulatory and accrediting practices, and traditional funding formulas (Hall *et al.* 1996). Australia's National Council for Open and Distance Education, in producing quality guidelines for universities contemplating such moves, points to a similar set of inhibiting factors – ingrained conservatism among many staff and students who continue to favour traditional modes of instruction; academics' insecurities about the nature and continued tenure of their positions; a distaste for standardised learning packages and/or a fear of technology; students' difficulties in learning how to take responsibility for their own learning; and fears that flexible learning will be imposed on universities in the simplistic belief that it is a cheap solution to large-scale delivery (NCODE 1996).

An emerging concept of flexible learning

There may be widespread agreement that the paradigm shift is occurring, but the pace and characteristics of change vary considerably, and paradoxes abound. Even the terms employed exemplify the confusion. In North America, terms such as 'distributed learning', 'technology mediated learning' and 'telematics' are common. In Britain and Australia, the term 'resource-based learning' emphasises the resources and media for student-centred learning in a mass education context (NCODE 1996). It represents a partial response to political pressures to increase enrolments at lower cost. Another term – 'flexible delivery' – dominates Australian vocational education (TAFE 1993; OTFE 1996). It implies a narrow emphasis on one-way delivery of education and reflects also a political assumption that education is merely an industry delivering educational product.

In Sweden, continued use of the term 'distance education' when the actual environment is increasingly blended, is causing some confusion in public debate and resource allocation, but the term 'flexible learning' is rapidly penetrating public discourse. This term is gaining popularity elsewhere, too, especially in Australia where several universities have created flexible learning centres (at least one incorporating a former distance education centre).

Some consistency in trends is apparent across national borders, but has yet to be consolidated into a rigorous theoretical construct and coherent practical framework for university teaching and learning. Our own experiences lead us to believe that piecemeal approaches to change are counter-productive, and that what is needed is comprehensive university-wide strategies, based on explicit integration of a well-articulated set of institutional values about learning, with a range of teaching strategies and technologies, plus a set of organisational systems and networks to support them. Distance education and face-to-face teaching disappear as separate constructs, to be replaced by flexible, networked learning. We define the ideal of flexible learning as approaches to teaching and learning which are learner-centred, free up the time, place and methods of learning and teaching, and use appropriate technologies in a networked environment.

As concept and practice, flexible learning draws qualities or experiences from its three parents. For example, it takes from distance education the idea that education should go to people and not the other way around, and harnesses extended experience in fostering student-centred learning. It builds on distance educators' expertise in designing and producing learning materials, and choosing and using technologies appropriate to the learning purpose. And it also draws on experience in interinstitutional collaboration and networking to support learning. From campus-based education flexible learning draws a recognition of the importance of interaction and personal contact between teacher and learner (although distance education has shown that personal contact need not be face to face for effective, stimulating learning). Moreover, since learning is a social activity, greater flexibility and use of technologies have implications for campus learning spaces and facilities, and for the roles of networked study centres or virtual learning environments. The third element in the fusion is information technologies which can change dramatically the variety, amount, sources and media of information required in learning. Moreover, the communications capabilities of the new technologies have the potential to reduce significantly the old bogey of distance education – students' isolation from each other and their teachers.

What, then, might a comprehensive approach to flexible learning mean for a dual-mode university? One example is that of Mid Sweden University, a young, multicampus, dual-mode institution of 14,000 students and 500 staff, located about 400 kilometres north of Stockholm. Its mission statement places the student at the centre of its activities and emphasises networking within the University and with its various regional and national communities and budding international connections. In 1998, Mid Sweden has accepted a definition of flexible learning as one which (MSU 1998):

- applies to teaching and learning wherever they occur – on-campus, off-campus and cross-campus;
- frees up the place, time, methods and pace of learning and teaching;
- is learner-centred rather than teacher-centred;
- seeks to help students become independent, lifelong learners;

- changes the role of the teacher who becomes a mentor and facilitator of learning.

Implementation requires the integration of:

- teachers who have the skills in course design and teaching necessary to support student-centred, lifelong learning;
- students from diverse backgrounds, learning styles and motivations to study

to assist them to achieve their personal goals and the University's goals for qualities of its graduates, through strategies such as:

Courses

- Entry arrangements which ensure greater access and equity for students from various backgrounds;
- degree and course plans which set out specific learning outcomes and generic graduate qualities, and the ways in which each will be achieved;
- course content which takes account of students' backgrounds and recognises that we live in a global community.

Teaching and learning

- Use of learning materials and technologies which are appropriate to the subjects and needs of the students;
- teaching methods which free up the time, place, mode and pace of learning;
- information literacy and support programmes which assist students to become independent lifelong learners.

Organisational arrangements

- Teachers working in networked partnership with academic support specialists;
- organisational structures, planning and resource mechanisms which enable rapid, networked support to flexible learning;
- collaborative networks across the campuses and with outside bodies in order to free up modes of teaching and the range of courses available anywhere, any time.

Based on

- Evaluations of experience and practice in flexible learning;

• research into the educational, social, technological and policy issues underpinning university teaching and learning in a rapidly changing environment.

Change of the magnitude planned by Mid Sweden University will not be easy or fast. We are sceptical of quick-fix technology based solutions. For Mid Sweden, this long-term transformation requires simultaneous attention to the University's culture, the knowledge and skills of academics as teachers, the organisational and resource arrangements supporting learning and teaching, and its networks of relationships within the University and with Swedish and international communities. In 1998 it is a unique approach for a Swedish university, but several Australian universities are pursuing similar lines (for example, see Moran 1997). From our experiences in both countries, we have identified four of the major issues confronting dual-mode universities moving into flexible learning: the changing role of the teacher; learning materials production systems and infrastructure; mixing real and virtual campuses; and collaboration and networking.

Role of the academic teacher

As the learning paradigm changes, so do the teacher's role and relationships with students, exchanging transmission models of teaching for constructivist, collaborative models of learning. Constructivism is not new, and good teaching has always emphasised deep learning through dialogue. However, the transmission model is easier when teaching large numbers or when academics have a limited repertoire of teaching skills. It is also an easier response to students who are reluctant to abandon their initial dependence on the teacher and seek autonomy as deep learners. It is now increasingly difficult to sustain this as a prime model of university teaching. In the teaching task, the role of information provider declines; that of mentor and collaborator in learning grows.

Commitment to student-centred learning has been common in distance and open learning for years, but there remains a tension between the desire for individualised learning, and the standardisation inherent in self-instructional learning packages delivered to large numbers. For the teacher also, there is a risk of alienation within a quasi-industrial educational system (Peters 1989), and a fear of losing authority in the learning environment; perhaps also of losing one's job to encroaching technology. A gulf is opening between academics' present levels of knowledge and skills as teachers, and those they increasingly require – not only in choosing and using technologies for course development, teaching and assessment, but also in curriculum development more broadly.

In response to these changes, staff development and training is beginning to assume a central place in university approaches to flexible learning and technology adoption. In the United Kingdom, the Dearing Committee has recommended major investment in staff training and development by all universities, and a national (but voluntary) system of teacher accreditation under the aegis of a national Institute for Learning and Teaching in Higher Education (NCIHE 1997: 8.56 ff.). In Australia there have been calls for staff development to be placed at the core of university activity in recognition of the vital link between institutional strategic development and individual professional development (AVCC 1995; Moran 1995; Stanley 1996).

Latchem, Lockwood and their collaborators (1998) outline the multiplicity of ways in which distance teaching universities, in particular, are addressing staff development needs. In distance education, broadly speaking, staff development has been a by-product of the emphasis on quality in course materials. In dual-mode systems, where the same staff teach courses on- and off-campus, these skills may well spill over from distance teaching into the classroom, but the strength of staff development support has resided in a pragmatic, technology focused orientation to course design and delivery. This is unlikely to be sufficient as the teacher's role changes, and a more systematic, deeper and broader understanding of the nature of learning and teaching is required.

One major difficulty in responding to the need for staff development is the shortage of well-qualified, multi-skilled staff developers or instructional designers with backgrounds in both distance and classroom teaching and advanced understanding of a technologically mediated learning environment. The role and skills base of this position do not easily fit traditional characteristics of academic work and are often misunderstood when it comes to salary levels and tenure. Status and career paths are often unclear and may not encourage people into the area. One solution is to maximise the ability of centralised expertise to support academics by creating networks of departmental academics who become the local flexible learning guide and mentor to their colleagues. This solution has the added advantage of helping academics to construct their own knowledge and skills as teachers.

There are signs that this and other factors are influencing new models of staff development and instructional design support are emerging to support flexible learning. At Mid Sweden University, for example, a project was begun in 1996 (and is now being mainstreamed) called the Växthus, or Greenhouse, whose goal is to nurture the flowering of interest and expertise in flexible learning within each department (Myringer 1996). This small central group provides just-in-time specialist services to a Flexible Learning Network comprising a member of each academic department. At least 10 per cent of the academic's teaching load may be assigned to their participation in the Network and support to their departmental colleagues. The Network is intended to stimulate interdepartmental and cross-campus communication and sharing of expertise and experience.

In Australia, there is a trend towards integration or transformation of the former roles of distance education centres and academic development units, the goal being 'one-stop academic and technology support services for all modes of teaching and learning' (Latchem and Moran 1998). Their work is driven by priorities set by the increasingly explicit strategic plans of universities for teaching and learning, technology implementation and internationalisation.

Learning materials production

The single-mode open universities pioneered elaborate in-house centres and processes for production of learning packages, predominantly print materials. In Australia's dual-mode system, cadres of instructional designers and specialist production staff, working on course materials, took priority over the student support functions which many distance education centres also carried. While the model may continue to be valid and cost-effective for the mega open universities, it is losing strength in dual-mode universities, especially where financial constraints are biting. The model has rarely applied in the erstwhile conventional universities. We predict that flexible learning/ distance education units in future will be concerned primarily with educational design support, project management, quality control and student support, but not with materials production as such.

There are three reasons. One is a renewed battle for centralised versus decentralised control. Most of us are familiar with complaints that the distance education centre receives resources which should go to the real educators who should control what is done with them; and the impatience of the 'gung-ho' enthusiast who is way ahead of the more cumbersome and bureaucratically inclined central department. The second reason is closely related – the intimate relationship between the technologies being employed and the kind of production systems and expertise needed to make and deliver learning materials. Production of electronic materials does not involve the same kind of linear production processes which print materials have required. The availability of educational software packages and in-house templates arguably reduces the number and type of specialist production personnel one needs to support the academic author.

Third, there is a trend – borrowed from industry – to emphasise core business and to outsource other tasks in the interests of cost-efficiency and rapid response to changing demands. Publishing and multimedia production require heavy investments in facilities, equipment and specialist staff which do not sit well with universities honing their core business to teaching, research and community service. In contrast, the rapidly burgeoning multimedia industry offers sources of expertise and facilities which can be accessed on demand, at competitive prices, to nominated quality. In these circumstances, core business for a flexible learning centre is helping academics to become more expert, innovative and flexible in curriculum design and delivery; supporting students in various ways, especially in networked and virtual environments; and pulling together the special management and quality control facets of flexible learning.

It may well be easier for universities without an established in-house production infrastructure to implement more streamlined systems to cater for flexible learning on- and off-campus. Swedish university distance education, for example, has typically taken a do-it-yourself approach to distance education rather than the industrial model typical of open universities and many of the larger dual-mode systems. That is, the individual academic has been responsible for development and production of learning materials and Swedish universities have not built up either instructional design or materials production specialist centres (Brändström 1992).

This craft approach has had disadvantages of cost inefficiencies, inconsistent quality in learning materials and teaching processes, and lack of access to specialist support services. However, the craft tradition leaves two important advantages. First, many staff have experimented with various aspects of flexible learning and using learning technologies, and so already have expertise to offer the in-house Flexible Learning Network (see above). Second, the university is not constrained by pre-existing costly infrastructures of materials production, nor by heavy reliance on one technology (notably print), so is able to choose rapid response strategies based on on-line technologies which suit the external environment. It can hire in production expertise just in time – with an added benefit of helping to support a small, but growing, local multimedia industry.

In Australia, two trends are becoming evident. One, exemplified by conventional universities embarking on flexible learning, is to re-form academic development units into flexible learning centres and provide advisory services for learning materials production. Progress may be hampered by the shortage of well-qualified staff and the need for existing developers to expand their knowledge and skills to accommodate to the new learning paradigm. Most of the major distance teaching universities, on the other hand, are embarking on major changes to their distance education centres ranging from disbandment and dispersal into faculties, to down-sizing of technical production facilities and personnel, to redefinition of the roles of instructional designer and editor. They may encounter problems of lack of staff developers with expertise in individual performance of teachers. Instead of viewing a distance education programme holistically in terms of scheduling and costing, there is a trend towards treating courses or groups of courses as projects for which the distance education centre provides an integrated set of services, including management of the relationship with external multimedia services providers.

These trends pose particular problems for the single-mode open university, at least in advanced countries, where the entire systems and rhythms of academic and organisational life are geared to materials production on an industrial scale. From positions of near-national monopoly over distance education, they now face vigorous competition from institutions unencumbered by their complex, Fordist assembly-line systems and lengthy timeframes. Developing more flexible, just-in-time responses to demands for particular courses will require fundamental changes to the value systems as well as complex internal relationships and roles of academics and other staff.

Real and virtual campuses

Distance education, by definition, takes education beyond the physical borders of a campus even when, as has been common in Sweden and Canada, much distance education has relied heavily on distributed face-to-face teaching. For campus-based universities, moving outside their walls and playing-fields can be a daunting experience. Increasing flexibility in who, where, when, what and how courses are taught and learned means that traditional physical boundaries lose their potency as identifiers of a learning community and its inhabitants. Moreover, as students increasingly mix and match their places of study, and as courses adopt mixed teaching strategies and technologies, the physical facilities requirements of campuses and networked study centres will change – in some cases, radically.

Daniel (1997) distinguishes two types of distance education: a synchronous form in which teacher and students are linked in real time; and an asynchronous form, in which a variety of media helps students study in their own learning environment when it suits them. Universities increasingly have several options with place as well as time – to teach on a campus, or in a physical dimension somewhere other than a campus, or in the virtual dimension of cyberspace – or all three. The concept of a virtual university is presently rather confused. Some emphasise a global market for on-line education, and fear the local consequences of having to compete with alliances of mega corporations and internationally prestigious universities. Others worry about the likelihood of cultural and linguistic imperialism in the ways in which virtual courses are designed and taught. For many universities, though, the immediate issues are how to develop a virtual presence alongside the physical one, so that students and teachers can move easily between the two. For the conventional university, this may well be its point of entry to a more comprehensive approach to flexible learning.

Some on-line technology initiatives are ignoring a sound lesson from distance education – the need to maximise interaction and student support – assuming instead that the technology alone will be sufficient to sustain the teacher–student relationship. The need for student support will be intensified in internationalised university programmes, when learners come from different cultural backgrounds, home languages and styles of learning and expression from those of the teacher, and remain in their own environment throughout their study. The twinning programmes developed in several

South-East Asian countries during the 1980s by local organisations partnering overseas universities have shown the importance of local mentoring and a variety of learning and practical support programmes in assisting student success. They point the way to effective globalisation of education through a combination of local and on-line interaction.

Within national boundaries, study centres have long been an important part of distance education systems and have provided the model for effective international twinning programmes. Evaluations have consistently shown that they are most effective when they are embedded in the social life of the local community, and provide learning support, access to technologies not readily available to students, and a place for informal social interaction. When these roles are emphasised and integrated with communications technologies, they enable creation of virtual learning centre networks linking local communities with not one, but many, educational organisations. The TeleLearning Network of Western Australia is but one example; several Canadian provinces have others.

In some systems – for example, in Sweden, the UK and India – study centres have also offered a significant amount of face-to-face teaching. In Sweden, study centres have been akin to mini-campuses, contracting with various universities to provide nominated courses which the study centre believes are needed in the area. In the 1990s, the study centres have formed networks to negotiate with universities from strength. The largest network – called NITUS – comprises thirty-eight study centres and was initiated by local communities rather than government or the universities. Another (with the acronym KHIS) was established in the sparsely populated northern area of Sweden in the 1980s, initially as a project of Umeå University, and subsequently as a network of community-owned study centres and the three northern universities (Dahllöf, et al. 1993; Gisselberg 1993). Teaching strategies have relied predominantly on synchronous teaching through videoconferencing or face-to-face tuition (and students going to the campus for regular intensive programmes). As more courses are offered on-line and through other flexible learning strategies, this approach will become increasingly expensive for both university and study centre. It will also become unduly restrictive of student choice. On the other hand, the study centres, reinforced by their history of collaboration, are likely to have an even stronger role as virtual learning centres.

Collaboration

Collaboration has become an almost ubiquitous element of distance education over the last decade, but mostly as relatively discrete projects. Where flexible learning becomes the university's *modus operandi*, interuniversity collaboration is likely to be mainstreamed into course development and materials production, credit transfer and articulated pathways for entry, teaching and support arrangements (including local learning centres) and investment in expensive technology infrastructures. University–external client collaboration is likely to become a major part of university programmes as custom-tailored courses are provided on a contractual basis. And university-communications technology company collaboration is likely to become a common feature of global on-line education provision.

Universities need cogent reasons to change as radically as this mainstreaming and flexibility imply. Collaboration is easy to justify on educational and social justice grounds if the outcome is improved access to a wider range of courses, study modes and support arrangements. By far the most pressing reason, however, is the lack of resources to meet demand. For some universities – especially younger, less prestigious ones – collaboration is becoming a basic survival strategy in an increasingly competitive and global environment. Sometimes there is little choice, where government forces universities into consortia or brokerage arrangements; success then hinges on the openmindedness with which the partners approach the project. Paradoxically, as is occurring in Australia, government may also be demanding that universities behave as industrial bodies competing against each other in a deregulated market. One outcome may be that universities cooperate less with each other and more with non-university partners or with universities in other countries.

Even with good will, collaboration is hard to achieve and sustain. Moran and Mugridge (1993) found three prerequisites for success, regardless of the particular features of the venture. First, a willingness on the part of all partners to accommodate different institutional cultures and practices by adapting one's own practice to harmonise with partners. This can be hard enough within one social milieu; in the international arena it requires especial sensitivity to different assumptions about curriculum and pedagogy. The second prerequisite is the building of sustained relationships based on personal trust and shared values, typically through champions in each university in a position to negotiate and coordinate the arrangements. This trust needs also to be embedded in the interinstitutional relationship as well as in the interpersonal ones. Third, a successful collaboration requires that all partners perceive the mutuality of benefits involved. This is a binding force even where the consequences for each partner differ greatly.

Nevertheless, collaboration is burgeoning. Two aspects of particular interest for flexible learning are the expanding number of consortia and the growing number of international collaborative programmes. Canada's Open Learning Agency was an early prototype, developing a credit bank in the 1980s which enabled students to choose from courses across a variety of institutions in British Columbia. The model was adapted in the 1990s by Open Learning Australia. Both have been predicated on marginal additional costs to partner institutions, but have experienced various problems caused by lack of trust and/or unwillingness to accommodate to different institutional cultures. The Australian consortium has recently reformed with largely different partners and an explicit intention to collaborate in order to compete with other Australian universities as single entities.

In Sweden, in contrast, interuniversity competition is not as fierce, and social values of cooperation and compromise are strongly embedded in the culture. Three university consortia have emerged in the 1990s, with an emphasis on joint course development, materials production and credit transfer (for example, see Holmberg *et al.* 1996). In 1997, the three began discussions of ways to collaborate further among themselves with a view to increasing access, expanding the range of courses, and reducing costs. In addition, collaboration is seen as an essential strategy to help Swedish universities preserve and nurture Sweden's unique cultural and linguistic heritage in the face of an increasingly globalised education system.

Conclusions – the future of flexible learning

The university, as an idea and as a social institution, has weathered profound changes since the twelfth century. Its modes of teaching have changed to accommodate new technologies (e.g. the printing press which enlarged access to accurately duplicated material from the 1450s); social movements (e.g. the advent of mass higher education since the 1960s); and changes in paradigms of knowledge (e.g. empirical scientific methods in the nineteenth century and postmodernism in the twentieth). The last forty years have been a period of dramatic growth and change, the pace of which is still accelerating, not least because of technological change. The authority of the nation-state is faltering against the power of multinational corporations, and states' capacities to maintain resources for social welfare and education are threatened even while higher education and training are acknowledged as critical to prosperity and progress. Universities are being described and treated as industries rather than cultural and intellectual repositories and creators. They are also being forced to reassess the place, time and methods of their teaching. Today's polarities of distance and face-to-face teaching cannot withstand the onslaught of declining resources, political pressures and institutional survival instincts.

Distance education, too, has weathered major changes to take advantage of new technologies and communications systems, and rise to the challenge of educating large numbers of people. Correspondence study became feasible as an organised form of university learning when reliable transport and communications systems became available from the late nineteenth century. Distance education flourished once television and print production systems became sophisticated and affordable. In the last twenty-five years, we have worked hard to achieve legitimacy and credibility (inside and outside universities) for distance education's methods and the quality of students' learning outcomes. Therein lies a paradox. At the moment when that hard work is paying off in moving distance education from the margins to the mainstream, it is being transformed into something else. It is likely to be as hard for many distance educators to accommodate to flexible learning as it is for many in more conventional universities.

Nevertheless, flexible learning describes beliefs about teaching and learning which many academics and administrators already hold. It is not a brand-new discovery or something magic, but it does provide a means of bringing together the key facets of the paradigm shift which is now under way. In our experience, it is a way of making sense of an environment which is often confused and stressful, but which also offers exciting prospects for the university as a learning community. While in a sense doing ourselves out of a job, distance educators have valuable insights and experience to bring to the processes of integration and transformation which universities will experience in coming years.

© Louise Moran and Brittmane Myringer 1998.

Note

1   We are indebted to Dr Carl Holmberg of Linköping University and personnel of the Distansutbildningskomitet (DUKOM) for their advice on developments in Sweden.

References

Australian Vice Chancellors' Committee (AVCC) (1995) *Development Bulletin 2/95*, AVCC Staff Development and Training Programme, University of Queensland, Canberra: AVCC.

Brändström, D. (1992) *Distansutbildning – Undervisningsform I Tiden*, Projektrapport 1992: 5, Stockholm: Universitets och Högskoleämbetet.

Dahllöf, U., Grepperud, G. and Palmlund, I. (1993) '*Att vilja, våga, kunna*': en *Utvärdering av Distansprojektet vid Umeå Universitet 1987–93*, Umeå: Umeå Universitet.

Daniel, J. (1997) 'Technology: its role and impact on education delivery – more means better', paper presented to Commonwealth Ministers of Education Conference, Botswana. Available HTTP: *http://www.open.ac.uk/OU/News/VC/botswana.htm*

Gisselberg, M. (1993) *Rapport från Kunskapsresa Norr*, Umeå: Umeå Universitet.

Government of Sweden (1997) *Budget Propositionen för 1998, Utgiftsområde 16*, Regeringens proposition 1997/8: 1.

Hall, J.W., Thor, L.M. and Farrell, G.M. (1996) *The Educational Paradigm Shift: Implications for ICDE and the Distance Learning Community. Report of the Task Force of International Council for Distance Education, Standing Committee of Presidents' Meeting, Lillehammer, Norway*. Oslo: ICDE.

Holmberg, C., Lundberg, M. and Sipos, K. (1996) *Det Första Året: Utvärdering av det Pedagogiska Utvecklingsarbetet inom Konsortiet för Nationell Distansutbildning*, Institutionen för pedagogik och psykologi, Linköping: Linköping University.

Latchem, C. and Lockwood, F. (eds) (1998) *Staff Development Issues in Open and Flexible Education*, London: Routledge.

Latchem, C. and Moran, L. (1998) 'Staff development issues in dual mode institutions: the Australian experience', in C. Latchem and F. Lockwood (eds), *Staff Development Issues in Open and Flexible Education*, London: Routledge.

Mid Sweden University (MSU) (1998) *Mid Sweden – a networked, flexible learning university*, unpublished discussion paper, Sundsvall: Mid Sweden University.

Moran, L. (1995) *National Policy Frameworks to Support the Integration of Information Technologies into University Teaching/Learning*, report of a search conference commissioned by the Department of Employment, Education and Training, Canberra.

Moran, L. (1997) 'Flexible learning as university policy', in S. Brown (ed.), *Open and Distance Learning in Industry and Education*, London: Kogan Page.

Moran, L. and Mugridge, I. (1993) 'Trends in inter-institutional collaboration', in L. Moran and I. Mugridge (eds), *Collaboration in Distance Education*, London: Routledge.

Myringer, B. (1996) *The Development of Distance Education at Mid Sweden University 1996–1997, Decision foundation for the Board of Governors*, Sundsvall: Mid Sweden University.

National Committee of Inquiry into Higher Education (NCIHE; chair R. Dearing) (1997) *Higher Education in the Learning Society*, report to the Secretaries of State for Education and Employment, Wales, Scotland and Northern Ireland, United Kingdom. Available HTTP: *http://www.leeds.ac.uk/educol/ncihe/* (accessed March 1998).

National Council for Open and Distance Education (NCODE) (1996) 'Quality guidelines for resource based learning'. Available HTTP: *http://cedir.uow.edu.au/NCODE/* (accessed March 1998).

Nipper, S. (1989) 'Third generation distance learning and computer conferencing', in R. Mason and A. Kaye (eds), *Mindweave: Communication, Computers and Distance Education*, Oxford: Pergamon. Also available HTTP: *http://www-icdl.open.ac.uk/mindweave/mindweave.html* (accessed March 1998).

Office of Technical and Further Education (OTFE) (1996) 'From chalkface to interface: developing on-line learning'. Available HTTP: *http://www.eduvic.vic.gov.au/c_to_i* (accessed March 1998).

Peters, O. (1989) 'The iceberg has not melted: further reflections on the concept of industrialisation and distance teaching', *Open Learning*, 4, 3, 3–8.

Stanley, G. (1996) 'Rewards will flow from focusing on staff development', *Campus Review*, 6, 8, 7–13 March, p. 8.

TAFE Flexible Delivery Working Party (1993) *Flexible Delivery: A Guide to Implementing Flexible Delivery*, Brisbane: Queensland Distance Education College.

Chapter 6

The costs of distance education

Thomas Hülsmann

Educational decision-makers all over the world are confronted by a rising demand for education, a demand with which the budget allocation generally does not keep pace. The challenge is how to cope with the demand, drive down average costs and keep up or improve standards. At the same time increased flexibility is appreciated since learner constituencies change considerably, part-time and mature students representing an increasing percentage. In this situation educational managers turn towards distance education in the hope that it will offer convenience, cost and quality.

This chapter looks at costs and effects in distance education in order to provide some guidance to managers working in this field. Guidance for managers in distance education can be given in three ways: by drawing attention to structural features of distance education; by drawing attention to case study evidence available; and by putting forward a framework for cost-effective media choice.

Costing issues

In distance education the teacher and the student are separated most of the time. This necessitates the reorganisation of the learning process into two main teaching functions: instruction (content presentation) and dialogue (learner support). Instruction is provided via resource media and learner support via communication media. Resource media make it possible to provide students free-standing, pre-prepared objects such as course material in the form of books, cassettes or CD-ROM. Communication media allow dialogue, contributing to an educational process rather than providing course material; videoconferencing, telephone tutoring or lectures can be used in this way. Resource media allow economies of scale, communication media do not. The more students use a printed book or listen to a broadcast, the lower the unit cost of writing and producing the original text or programme; in contrast, the costs of using communication media to provide dialogue increase with each additional student. To improve the trade-off between economies of scale (a parameter of efficiency) and teacher–student interactivity (a parameter of effectiveness), distance education designs inter-activity into resource media (internal interactivity) while keeping control of the level of teacher–student interactivity (external interactivity). In Table 6.1 we distinguish between technologies in this way.

Cost-effectiveness analysis[1] is a technique designed to help choose between alternatives by examining their costs and effects. It requires us to measure the costs of alternative approaches to achieving the same result: preference is given to the strategy with the minimal ratio of costs over effectiveness scores. We can, therefore, carry out cost-effectiveness analysis at two levels: at the institutional level looking at the comparative costs of dedicated distance-teaching universities and of conventional uni-versities and, at the course level, comparing the costs of different media configurations.

In order to be seen as cost-effective, distance education had to demon-strate that it is possible to teach effectively using media. The media equivalency hypothesis claims that media have little impact on outcome effectiveness, and teaching using media can be as effective as teaching con-ventionally. Understandably many distance educators subscribe to this hypothesis. On the other hand, distance educators are also interested in researching the capabilities of different media in order to make optimal use of them. There is a certain conflict, at least between the radicalised version of the media equivalence hypothesis ('media do not influence learning under any condition'[2]), and the effort to identify media capabilities in order to use them more effectively for teaching.

Once it is accepted that you can teach effectively using media, it is possible to look for economies of scale in distance education and so to establish that it can be cost-effective. Some of the costs of distance education are fixed: capital equipment, or the writing of course material, have costs that are the

Table 6.1 Classification of open and distance learning technologies

	Resource media	Communication media
Examples	print, broadcasting media, audio/video cassettes, CD-ROM, Internet	tutorials, telephone tuition, CMC, videoconferencing, Internet
Type of interactivity	internal interactivity	external interactivity
Cost structure	large proportion of fixed costs (strong potential for economies of scale)	mainly variable cost (weak potential for economies of scale)
Timing	asynchronous	predominantly synchronous
Pedagogy	individual teacher–student contact	allows either group learning or individual dialogue between student and tutor

same irrespective of the number of students enrolled. Other costs are variable: the cost of providing tutoring to students, for example, varies with the number of students. (In practice, fixed costs are often lower in distance than in conventional education because you can teach students at a distance without building classrooms, lecture theatres or student accommodation.) Provided the variable costs per student of distance education are lower than those of conventional education, we can also expect the total cost per student to show economies once we have enrolled enough students. Economies of scale, which seldom arise in conventional education where most costs are variable and are driven by staffing ratios, can be achieved in distance education. There is thus a breakeven point for an institution, or a course, at which the cost per student is the same for the two methodologies that are being compared. Whether student demand allows us to reach this point remains an empirical question. Case study evidence can help to identify the conditions under which cost-effectiveness of distance education can be achieved.

Institutional costs

Historically, distance education has served a niche market, responding to needs for flexibility of specific learners. The foundation of open universities signalled that distance education was ready to compete in the mainstream. As this necessarily entailed competition for funds, the question of the comparative cost-effectiveness of distance teaching institutions became important. The experience of the British Open University demonstrates the significance of fixed and variable costs and of potential economies of scale. In Table 6.2 we can distinguish three types of cost: some are clearly fixed, notably for the development and production of courses. Some are semi-fixed: the cost of the central administration does not need to change if student numbers increase or contract by 10 per cent, but will go up, in lumps, if there is an increase in scale beyond this. Some, for presentation, distribution and student support, are variable and vary with the number of students enrolled. As a result of the significant element of fixed costs, the university would be able to increase its total number of students by 10 per cent with only a 3 per cent increase in its total costs. To meet the increased central cost of servicing an extra 20 per cent of students, however, total costs would have to rise by 7 per cent. Thus the university has the potential to achieve economies of scale but we should not exaggerate their significance.

In comparing the cost-effectiveness of distance teaching and conventional universities we may look at the cost per student or the cost per graduate. There are, then, different methods of calculating the cost per graduate. Rumble (1997: 125) discusses several options. One is based on the assumption that the system has already attained its steady state. In this case Rumble proposes to calculate: (1) cost per graduate = annual budget/annual number

Table 6.2 Summary of the cost structure of the UK Open University

Currency 1996 £ million sterling

Type of cost		Approximate percentage change in cost for x per cent change in student numbers			
		−10	+10	+20	+30
Fixed					
Development of courses	19.93	0	0	0	0
Production of courses	18.86	0	0	0	0
Semi-fixed					
Central costs	29.22	0	0	+5	+10
Variable costs					
Presentation and distribution	28.42	−6	+6	+12	+19
Student support	22.09	−6	+7	+15	+24
Total	118.52	−3	+3	+7	+12

Source: DES 1991: 59; costs have been deflated to 1996 ££.

of graduates. If, however, the institution awards different degrees, or the system is still expanding, it might be more convenient to calculate the cost per graduate by estimating the average time students are likely to need for graduating: (2) cost per graduate = recurrent cost per student × number of years to graduation. If a drop-out rate is available (and little else) it is often convenient to calculate: (3) cost per graduate = (recurrent cost per student × number of years)/graduation rate. The variant used by the British Open University is shown in Table 6.3. It assumes that it takes the average student 4.7 years to reach an ordinary degree and 7.4 years to reach an honours degree (a distinction between types of degree that was part of the university structure at the time of the study).

The German FernUniversität provides data on its costs per student and cost per graduate and demonstrates a different approach to their analysis. The FernUniversität does not consider cost per graduate to be an acceptable measure of cost-effectiveness on the grounds that many students do not enrol for a degree. Indeed 30 per cent of those entering the FernUniversität already have a degree. Therefore the FernUniversität uses cost per full degree equivalence, looking at the costs per credit and then examining the number of credits that need to be obtained to add up to a degree. The UKOU also argues that a performance measure based on CAT (credit accumulation and transfer) points awarded would be more appropriate (Daniel *et al.* 1994).

In Table 6.5, cost per student and cost per graduate are reported for a number of institutions. They show costs per student in five industrialised countries as falling between about £1,200 and £2,200 with only one Canadian institution falling outside this range. These costs are generally between 25 and 50 per cent of the cost per student in a conventional university. These comparisons are, of course, always difficult. One source of difficulty is that

Table 6.3 Calculation method of cost per graduate at the UK Open University

	Currency 1996 £ sterling
Recurrent cost per undergraduate student, excluding research expenditure	1,346
Equipment unit costs	85
Premises unit cost	248
Total annual unit cost per student	1,683
Average number of years taken by undergraduate to gain	
an ordinary degree 4.7 years	
an honours degree 7.4 years	
Average wastage rate, estimated from failures within	
earlier cohorts to reach graduation 2.06 years	
Cost per ordinary BA graduate	
1,683 × (4.7 + 2.06) years =	11,377
Cost per honours graduate	
1,683 × (7.4 + 2.06) years	15,921

Source: DES 1991: 67; figures deflated to 1996 ££.

Table 6.4 Expenditure per student by faculty at the FernUniversität

					Currency 1996 £ sterling
Faculty	Number of students	Cost per student	Number of full degree-equivalents	Number of full degrees	Cost per full degree equivalent
Economics	30,451	613	680	192	27,446
Mathematics	2,232	2,118	69	7	68,498
Liberal Arts	11,656	997	198	45	58,692
Electrical Engineering	3,125	2,006	42	24	149,250
Law	1,660	1,957	101		32,170
Computer Science	6,742	1,151	100	32	77,585
Average	9,311	1,474	198		68,940

Source: Fandel *et al.* 1996: 138; figures deflated to 1996 ££.

they usually omit opportunity costs which are of major importance in, for example, the National Technological University, which feeds teaching to its students' place of work, thus providing major savings in costs of time and travel.

Given the consistency in the cost per students, the much greater difference in cost per graduate is remarkable. If cost per graduate is calculated on the basis of any of the formulae referred to above, the cost depends on the cost per student, the time the student is likely to spend in the system in order to graduate, and the drop-out rate. The number of years required for a degree does vary considerably between countries. The number of years to obtain the standard university degree in Japan is about four to five years in the

Table 6.5 Some performance indicators in tertiary education

Currency 1996 £ sterling

Institution and date	Approx. annual enrolment	Cost per student	Comments on degree types	Cost per graduate	Comparison with conventional education	Notes
Athabasca (Canada) 1996/7	2,000[a]	3,628				b
UKOU (United Kingdom) 1989/90	25,000	1,683	BA ordinary BA honours	11,378 15,923	about 50% of CU[c]	d
FernUniversität (Germany) 1993/4	56,000[e]	1,473	including excluding[f] engineering	68,940 44,065	the cost to the state is $\frac{1}{2}$ to $\frac{1}{4}$ of the regional CUs	g
NTU (United States) 1997/8	3,500	2,212		24,398	50% drop out	h
UAJ (Japan) 1991		1,205	weighted	68,330	30% of cost per student in CU; but up to 4 times the cost per graduate in CU[i]	i
CTU Bourgogne (France) 1994–6	746	1,655	Maitrise	10,925	40% of on-campus alternative	k

Notes
a   FTE.
b   Personal communication.
c   There have been different estimates of the relative cost-effectiveness of the UKOU. We have included the recent one of Daniel (1996: 31).
d   DES 1991.
e   Total number.
f   The average (over 6 faculties) is skewed by the costs of the electrical engineering faculty; hence we add the figure not including electrical engineering.
g   Fandel *et al.* 1996.
h   Personal communication; the 50% completion rate is mostly due to job changes after which students are no longer more eligible for company grants.
i   It is claimed that UAJ will be cost-effective when the steady state is achieved.
j   Muta and Takahiro (1994).
k   Based on Ben Abid 1997.

conventional system and five to six years in Germany, contrasted with three years in Britain, so that our comparators are different. But, in the absence of other data, we must assume, too, that completion rates are notably higher in Britain and France, and for the postgraduate students of the National Technological University, than they are for the German and Japanese institutions.

The negative effect of drop-out rates can also be demonstrated for higher education in developing countries and here the argument that students might come for different reasons than a degree seems to be less convincing. Using early data from Sukhothai Thammathirat Open University we can illustrate the impact high drop-out rates have on cost per graduate. For the two-year programmes 1980/2 and 1982/3 the completion rates were 11.7 per cent and 24.8 per cent respectively (Wichit and Wangsotorn 1985) whereas the completion rate in the conventional sector was given as 85 per cent. The cost per student was between £179 and £261 in 1996 sterling. This gives a cost per graduate between £1,435 and £2,088. Though no figures are provided for cost per student, the graduation rate and the length of the course allow us to estimate that the conventional sector could spend about three to four times as much on their undergraduates and still have the same cost per graduate. As Table 6.6 shows, some remarkably low completion rates have been reported: less than 1 per cent for a two-year degree course at the Indonesian Universitas Terbuka for example. Most institutions report completion rates of about 30 per cent. Where degrees are longer, completion rates seem to drop significantly: a five-year degree at the Korean Air and Correspondence University reported completion rates for two periods of 9.8 and 14.5 per cent.

It seems in view of the recent data that Perraton (1991) may have to adjust downward his estimate that graduation rates for tertiary distance education were likely to range from 40 to 60 per cent with a cost per student between a half and two-thirds of that in conventional education. The data in Table 6.6 suggest a completion rate nearer to 25 per cent rather than 40 per cent. If we assume an 80 per cent graduation rate for conventional education, the figures suggest that a distance-teaching institution could aim at a cost per student of a quarter (0.25) of the cost per student in the conventional institution if it was to produce graduates at a comparable cost. But with a lower graduation rate the cost per student through distance education would have to be reduced to a factor of 0.156 instead of the 0.25 of the cost of conventional education for the cost per graduate to be comparable. Calculations of this simplicity, however, often ignore the dynamics such reductions can trigger: lowering the cost per student by, for instance, reducing learner support might induce a vicious circle in the drop-out rate with negative instead of positive effects on comparative cost-effectiveness. It is in this vein that Kishore (1997) suggests increasing investment in student support, hoping it will have a positive effect on cost per graduate. The only general conclusion which can be drawn is that reduction in per student expenditure must be well targeted as it could otherwise have an effect opposite to the one intended.

It might be conjectured that this has something to do with the better cost recovery rate in distance education. Quite often government funding for distance education institutions is low and contribution from student fees

Table 6.6 Completion and graduation rates at some open universities

Currency 1996 £ sterling

Institution	Type of course	Date	Enrolment	Graduation	Pass/ completion rate %	Conventional university rate	Notes
China TVU	equivalent to junior college degree	1988/9			>80	n/a	a
India IGNOU YCMOU BRAOU	first degree	1991/2			22.5 34 29	55–60	b
Indonesia UT	two-year degree	1984–8	65,000	443	0.7	n/a	c
Korea KACU	two-year degree	1977–85	10,837	3,684	34	n/a	d
		1980–8	17,104	5,150	30.1		
	five-year degree	1981–91	28,266	4,111	14.5	n/a	d
Thailand STOU	two-year degree programme	1983–91	35,698	3,511	9.8		
		1980–2	82,139	9,594	11.7	85	e
		1982/3	69,561	17,236	24.8	85	e

Source: This table is based on Perraton (forthcoming) but the data are from the sources cited in the references.

Notes
a   Ding 1994: 161.
b   Ansari 1994: 83.
c   Wilson 1991: 261.
d   Kim 1992: 61–5.
e   Wichit and Wangsotorn 1985: 11–13.

relatively high: the Indian government meets 71 per cent of costs at IGNOU with students' fees contributing 26 per cent. In Thailand STOU receives 24 per cent from the government and the rest from students. Korea receives 50 per cent and Sri Lanka 56 per cent from government. In this case the degree is especially important in order to allow the student to recover the private investment in education.

Costs of media

Within a project funded by the European Commission SOCRATES programme, we have been collecting data on the costs of media used within open and distance learning. These make it possible to answer some questions about the cost-effectiveness of alternative media. There are, however, conceptual difficulties in doing so. If we assume, as already proposed, that media can be regarded as being equivalent in their effectiveness, we cannot at the same time seek to rank them in terms of student performance. In order to compare them we therefore suggest considering learning time as a proxy for effectiveness and asking about the cost per student learning hour. Once this is established for any particular medium, the manager has a default rule for cost-effective media choice to give preference to the medium with the lowest cost per student learning hour. The manager may then move away from the default rule when course designers can convincingly argue that specific tasks require different media.

Student learning hours

Some types of media, such as broadcasting or the use of cassettes, lend themselves easily to measurement in student learning hours. In these cases we can take exposition time as learning time so that one hour of following a television lesson is equivalent to one student learning hour. In the case of print we need to make an assumption about the length of time the average student will spend on printed text of a given length. Following the practice of a number of distance-teaching institutions, we have taken fifty pages of print as providing ten to fifteen student learning hours (SLH). It is even more difficult to estimate the time a student will spend using interactive media, such as CD-ROM, so that it is necessary to ask the course designer how much time students are supposed to spend with the medium in question.

On these assumptions, we can identify the cost of developing materials per SLH in each medium, which we have done partly on the basis of reports in the literature, partly on case studies carried out at a number of European institutions of higher education. Figures for the costs of resource media are set out in the Appendix, Table 6A.1. For many communication media, it is much more difficult to relate costs to student learning hours, mainly because the amount of time used for interaction is not tightly controlled. Estimates are given in Appendix Table 6A.2.

It was not always possible to attribute costs to the different media; staff often spend time working in more than one medium so that, in the absence of sophisticated activity costing, it is not possible to attribute their time to different media. In some cases, too, there are difficulties in inferring the number of student learning hours for a particular educational package. The increasing adoption of credit accumulation and transfer (CAT) frameworks is making it possible to infer the SLH from the CAT value of the course so that these calculations may become easier in the future. In practice, however, the SLH inferred from the CAT value is

Table 6.7 Development cost per student learning hour by medium

Currency 1996 £ sterling

Medium	Cost per SLH	Ratio to print cost
Print	500	1
Radio	27,000	×50
	15,000	×30
Television	125,000	×250
	90,000	×180
Video	84,000	×170
	18,000	×36
Audio	17,000	×34
CD-ROM	20,000	×40

Source: Perraton and Hülsmann 1998.

often bigger than the SLH calculated on the basis of the provided inputs, reflecting assumptions made by course administrators about the amount of time spent by students studying independently. Table 6.7 gives a synopsis of our findings.

Comparative costs

The evidence we have collected is consistent enough for us to reach several general conclusions. The importance of scale is confirmed: reasonable average costs can be achieved, even with high costs per student learning hour, where there is a high enough enrolment on a particular course. One challenge is therefore to design resource material in a reusable form so that it can be made available to the maximum audience. We draw four other main conclusions.

First, text is all important. Education is heavily reliant on text: no matter what the medium, educators usually start with a text so that its development always forms one core cost. Indeed, it is difficult to separate development cost per medium because the text also provides the script which integrates the non-textual elements. Text is, too, generally the most cost-effective medium with the lowest cost per student learning hour. Video and audio cassettes have considerably higher development costs. They have often been treated by course developers as add-ons, provided to increase the interest and attractiveness of a course, and to distinguish it from a simple correspondence course.

Second, text can be presented either in print or on screen. The development costs are the same as long as the text is not re-edited in hypertext format. Where material is presented on screen, with the intention that the students should download it, the costs of distribution and of printing move from the institution to the learners. If the text is a simple one, with no further facilities, such as search capacities, learners as well as providers tend to prefer the printed format. The effectiveness of providing enhancements to text depends on the learning objectives. Increased interactivity increases demand on student time so that, for example, hypertext formats are not always seen as an advantage to students and may also disorient them.

Third, teaching by means of networked computers has a substantial effect on the cost structure and on development costs. It makes it possible to increase internal interactivity between a student and the text but at an increased development cost per student learning hour. It can provide new opportunities for external interactivity, and so reduce the delay in getting feedback from a tutor. While this may have educational and social benefits, it puts pressure on student support costs and is therefore likely to reduce scale economies. It is unlikely that this increases effectiveness, where this is assessed against print-based curricula, although other educational benefits may be identified.

Fourth, more advanced technology tends to increase reception costs, so that the cost to the learner is increased. There is a danger that the drive for more technology will widen access differentials to distance education, both nationally and internationally and so a threat that the new styles of teaching, that can readily go across barriers of distance, may at the same time widen rather than narrow the differentials between industrialised and developing countries.

Notes

1 For a comprehensive overview see Levin (1995) and Mace (1992). For cost-effectiveness analysis of distance education see Orivel (1987).
2 Russell (1997) and Clark (1983: 445). A criticism of Clark's view is found in Kozma (1991). For a systematic exploration of media capabilities see Laurillard (1993). Carter (1996) summarised the debate in *Open Learning*.

References

Annenberg CPB Project: (1997) 'The Flashlight Phase I Report'. Available HTTP: *http://www.learner.org/edtech/rscheval/flashlight/challenge.html* (8 June 1998).

Ansari, M.M. (1994) 'Economics of distance education in India', in G. Dhanarajan, P.K. Ip, K.S. Yuen and C. Swales (eds), *Economics of Distance Education: Recent Experience*, Hong Kong: Open Learning Institute Press.

Ben Abid, S. (1997) 'Analyse coût efficacité du centre de télé-enseignement de Bourgogne', unpublished DEA thesis, Université de Bourgogne.

Carnoy, M. (ed.) (1995) *International Encyclopedia of Economics of Education*, Oxford: Pergamon, Elsevier Science.

Carter, V. (1996) 'Do media influence learning? Revisiting the debate in the context of distance education', *Open Learning*, 11, 1: 31–40.

Clark, R.E. (1983) 'Reconsidering research on learning from media', *Review of Educational Research* 53, 4: 445–59.

Daniel, J. (1996) *Mega-Universities and Knowledge Media: Technology Strategies for Higher Education*, London: Kogan Page.

Daniel, J., Peters, G. and Watkinson, M. (1994) 'The funding of the United Kingdom Open University', in I. Mugridge (ed.), *The Funding of Open Universities*, Vancouver: Commonwealth of Learning.

DES (1991) *Review of the Open University*, Milton Keynes: Open University.

Dhanarajan, G., Ip, P.K., Yuen, K.S. and Swales, C. (eds) (1994) *Economics of Distance Education: Recent Experience*, Hong Kong: Open Learning Institute Press.

Ding Xingfu (1994) 'Economic analysis of Radio and TV universities education in China', in G. Dhanarajan, P.K. Ip, K.S. Yuen and C. Swales (eds), *Economics of Distance Education: Recent Experience*, Hong Kong: Open Learning Institute Press.

Fandel, G., Bartz, R. and Nickolmann, F. (eds) (1996) *University Level Distance Education in Europe: Assessment and Perspectives*, Weinheim: Deutscher Studien Verlag.

HEQC (1997) 'Regulatory framework for assuring academic standards in credit based modular higher education', London: HEQC.

Kim, S. (1992) *Distance Education in Korea*, Seoul: Korea Air Correspondence University.

Kishore, S. (1997) 'Cost-effectiveness and cost-efficiency of correspondence education', *Indian Journal of Open Learning* 6, 1/2, 55–61.

Kozma, R.B. (1991) 'Learning with media', *Review of Educational Research*, Summer 1991, 61, 2, 179–211.

Laurillard, D. (1993) *Rethinking University Teaching: A Framework for the Effective Use of Educational Technology*, London: Routledge.

Levin, H.M. (1995) 'Cost effectiveness analysis', in M. Carnoy, *International Encyclopedia of Economics of Distance Education*, Oxford: Pergamon.

Mace, J. (1992) *Economics of Education II*, London: University of London External Programme.

Mugridge, I. (ed.) (1994) *The Funding of Open Universities*, Vancouver: Commonwealth of Learning.

Muta, H. and Takahiro S. (1994) 'Economics of the expansion of the University of the Air of Japan', in G. Dhanarajan, P.K. Ip, K.S. Yuen, and C. Swales (eds), *Economics of Distance Education: Recent Experience*, Hong Kong: Open Learning Institute Press.

OECD (1996) *Education at a Glance: OECD Indicators*, Paris: OECD.

Orivel, F. (1987) *Costs and Effectiveness of Distance Teaching Systems*, Dijon: IREDU.

Perraton, H. (1991) *Administrative Structures for Distance Education*, Vancouver: Commonwealth of Learning.

Perraton, H. (forthcoming) *Open and Distance Learning in the South*, London: Routledge.

Perraton, H. and Hülsmann, T. (1998) *Planning and Evaluating Systems of Open and Distance Learning*, London: DfEE.

Rumble, G. (1997) *The Costs and Economics of Open and Distance Learning*, London: Kogan Page.

Russell, T.L. (1997) 'The "No significant difference" phenomenon as reported in 248 research reports, summaries and papers', Raleigh, North Carolina. Available HTTP: *http://www2.ncsu.edu/oit/*

Wichit Srisa-an and Tong-In Wangsotorn (1985) *The Management and Economics of Distance Education: The Case of Sukhothai Thammathirat Open University Thailand*, paper presented at International Council for Distance Education World Conference, Melbourne, 13–20 August 1985.

Wilson D.N. (1991) 'A comparison of open universities in Thailand and Indonesia', in M.E. Lockheed, *et al.* (eds), (1991), *Educational Technology Sustainable and Effective Use*, Washington DC: Population and Human Resources Department, World Bank.

Appendix

Table 6.A1 Resource media

Currency ££ sterling

	Unit	Development cost	Production cost	Distribution cost	Reception cost		Cost per SLH[a] as compared to print cost
		Fixed/capital	Variable/capital	Variable/capital	Variable/capital	Variable/recurrent	
Print	50pp[b]	6,000	1	0.5	nil	nil	×1[c]
Broadcasting							
Radio	60 min.	30,000	nil	120	radio set 100	nil	×50
TV	60 min.	120,000	nil	700	TV set 500	90/year	×200
Cassettes							
Audio	60 min.	16,000	1	near to 1	cassette radio 250	nil	×25[d]
Video	60 min.	60,000	2–3	near to 2	video TV 800	90 p.a.	×100
PC media							
CD-ROM	disc[e]	80,000	2–4	near to 1	PC/CD-ROM drive 1,000	nil	×30
Internet							
	5 MB[f]	6,000[g]	nil	120 p.a.	PC + modem 1,000	110 p.a. + 5 p.h.	×1[h]
	10 MB	12,000[i]	nil	600 p.a. connect charge 300	PC + modem 1,000	110 p.a. + 5 p.h.	×3[j]
	n ×10MB[k]	40,000[l]	nil	1,000 + n ×100[m]	PC + modem 1,000 connect charge 200[n]	500 p.a. + 9 p.h.[o]	×30[p]

Notes

a SLH stands for Student Learning Hour.

b In terms of SLH we generally assume that 50pp print is equivalent to 10 SLH.

c In this column we write down the cost of development per SLH against the standard of the development costs of 50pp print being taken as equivalent to 10 SLH.

d It would not be unreasonable to assume that a cassette of 60 min. might generate more than one SLH since it might be used several times. This would cut the factor down to 12. However, similar assumptions could be made for the broadcasting media since in practice, they are also recorded.

e Obviously 'disc' is an unsatisfactory unit of measurement. This cost estimate is based on a case study. To cost CD-ROM properly it would be necessary to develop a bench-marking system specifying to which use the CD-ROM is put.

f 5MB is the minimum amount of memory space for keeping a Web site.

g This is for 50pp equivalent of printed text. Obviously pages are not appropriate units in a digitised medium (the ASCII code equivalent of 100 KB might be more appropriate). Reference to the unit of printed text is made since the core costs refer to authoring which is independent of the medium. Without further cost text text can be converted from typical DTP formats like Word into the Internet html format.

h The core development costs for printed texts and digitised texts are the same. Unit costs incurred by the provider are higher for print. If, however, the unit costs of reception are included, unit costs are higher.

i The additional cost for re-editing a 50pp text as hypertext is calculated on the basis of 6 hyperlinks per page on the average. To put them in and check if they work costs about an hour. Hence 1 hour per page or in total 50 hours or 6 full working days costing £200 each.

j The development costs are higher for a hypertext. However, it is possible to argue that the increase in internal interactivity (e.g. including multiple choice questions type of self-assessment) will considerably increase the number of student learning hours generated.

k The more you want to put on your Web site the bigger the memory space has to be leased on a server. Additional memory space is to be bought in blocks of 10 MB.

l We treat multimedia as being an on-line equivalent to CD-ROM. As in the case of CD-ROM multimedia resources provided over the Internet may include sound, images and films on top of text.

m The additional cost of each block of 10 MB adds £100 on top of a base charge of £1,000.

n Multimedia requires higher bandwidth which suggests the installation of an ISDN line (or an equivalent bandwidth increasing option).

o The higher recurrent costs reflect the use of higher bandwidth.

p Since we have treated the development cost of multimedia resources as being similar to those provided as CD-ROM, the factor will be the same as for CD-ROM.

Table 6.A2 Communication media

Currency ££ sterling

	Providing institution[a] setting-up costs[c] — Fixed capital and fixed recurrent cost	Equipment costs — Semi/variable capital costs	Personnel costs — Variable recurrent	Line costs — Capital recurrent and capital fixed	Reception[b] equipment costs — Variable[c] capital	On-line costs — Capital recurrent and capital fixed
Face-to-face tutorial	nil	nil	20–80 p.h.[d]	nil	nil	nil
Correspondence/TMA	nil	standard[e]	20–80 p.h.	postage less than 4[f]	nil	postage less than 2
Telephone	nil	standard	20 to 80 p.h.	telephone charges less than 4	telephone	110–150 base charges 4–5 p.h.
Computer mediated communication	Web site 1,200[g]	PC + modem 2,000	20 to 100 p.h.[h]	host charges about 700 per year[j]	PC + modem 1,000	110–150 base charges 4–5 p.h.
Videoconferencing	dedicated classroom may be provided	VCS[i] (room based) 40,000	160 p.h.[k]	9–25 p.h. for 128–384 Kbps ISDN[l] connect charges 200	1,000–20,000[m]	9–25 p.h. for 128–384 Kbps ISDN[l] connect charges 200

Notes

a   Under providing institutions we list the costs to the institution.

b   Reception costs are generally borne by the learner.

c   This column identifies costs to set up the system. It includes elements without specified lifetime which means that costs cannot clearly be apportioned to a single lecture or course. Equipment costs are also costs encountered when setting up the system but they can often be attributed to the level of a lecture or course.

d   The costs relate to tutor costs. No overheads are included.

e   Computer, telephone and standard desktop publishing software are referred to here. It means no additional equipment above that level is required.

f   Estimated on the basis of student-related fees paid in open and distance learning institutions.

g   The £1,200 are based on the cost of a Web site of 10MB designed and hosted by a commercial provider. Design costs are about £900 and connection charges are about £300.

h   Computer mediated communication requires additional training of tutors which is reflected in the wider cost range.

i   Besides the cost of design and connection costs for a Web site recurrent costs for hosting the site are to be paid to the provider.

j   The range of videoconferencing systems (VCS) is very wide. They range from desktop videoconferencing of a low bandwidth (with less image quality) to room-based systems of a high level of sophistication. The costs indicated here are the ones of a room-based system including a teacher station. (Cost p.h. over lifetime of 5 years given high usage rate is still £90 p.h.)

k   In videoconferencing we have two distinct systems: a symmetrical system where all cost sites are equipped equally for sending and receiving, and the more common and lower cost alternative, where the sending site is equipped to a higher level than the receiving sites. This figure assumes the symmetrical case.

l   The line costs vary with the bandwidth requirements. Generally a 384 Kbps is required for good quality (costing about £25 p.h.) especially if rapid movements are involved. For conversation only, a 128 Kbps rate would be sufficient (costing £9 p.h. only).

m   Generally costs listed under reception were costs incurred by the learner. This is not always so in videoconferencing where the reception sites are often campuses or learner centres and the like. The cost range for videoconferencing given here are ranging from upgrading equipment for a standard PC to roll about system likely to be used in a learner centre. Both options correspond to the asymmetrical case (see note i). (Cost p.h. over lifetime of 5 years and high usage rate amounts to about £20 p.h.)

Part 2

Regions

Chapter 7

Africa

The present volume reflects some of the major growth areas in higher distance education in Africa. The Open University of Tanzania (Mmari) is one of the most recently established in a long line of autonomous, degree-granting distance-teaching universities across the world. The next open university is also likely to be African, in Zimbabwe. Arguably the oldest established open university of all is the University of South Africa, which currently finds itself only one of a number of dynamic single- and dual-mode distance teaching institutions in South Africa (Dodds, Nonyongo and Glennie). Africa has not seen the same widespread development of open universities which has characterised other regions of the world; in fact, almost twenty years ago it witnessed a notable failure – the unsuccessful attempts to set up an open university in Nigeria.

The Continent has a long history of distance education at university level, but this has generally been in the nature of dual-mode provision. Current developments in Southern Africa (Dodds, Nonyongo and Glennie) reflect the growing involvement of conventional universities in distance provision. This trend can also be observed in other African countries; the Universities of Nairobi, Kenya, and Lagos, Nigeria, for example, have both operated distance teaching programmes for many years, but they are by no means the sole providers of distance education in their respective countries.

A number of international agencies have been involved in projects and initiatives in Africa, some of which have proposed ambitious applications of new information and communications technologies, and in promoting international cooperation. The Commonwealth of Learning (COL), for instance, has been active in numerous ways over the last ten years, from encouraging the establishment of associations of distance-teaching institutions in East and West Africa to commissioning studies on the work of existing distance-teaching institutions to brokering exchange arrangements such as the use of education teaching materials from the University of Nairobi, Kenya, in Makerere University, Uganda. Latest information on its activities can be found on the COL Web site at http://www.col.org. The International Extension College, based in the United Kingdom, has been involved for almost thirty years in setting up distance-teaching programmes and institutions at and below degree level, in addition to publishing practical guides aimed at African and other less-developed country practitioners.

The francophone organisation CIFFAD (Consortium international francophone de formation à distance) has been active in organising training involving francophone African countries and French and Canadian institutions. Distance education programmes are offered by a number of universities in francophone countries, but detailed information tends to be hard to come by. Information on distance education generally is at a premium in many African countries, one symptom of the shortage of resources which bedevils all aspects of education in Africa. Pioneering work in collecting and disseminating African distance education information has been done by the UK Open University's International Centre for Distance Learning (http://www-icdl.open.ac.uk).

Cooperation competition or dominance: a challenge in Southern Africa

Tony Dodds, Evelyn Nonyongo and Jenny Glennie

Southern Africa, as currently defined by the Distance Education Association of Southern Africa (DEASA) consists of South Africa, Botswana, Lesotho, Namibia and Swaziland. South Africa has a population of around 40 million, a gross domestic product of US $117,479 billion and twenty-one universities and fifteen Technikons. The four small states range in population from 850,000 (Swaziland) to nearly 2 million (Lesotho) and total less than 6 million, have gross domestic products varying from US $3,845 million (Botswana) to US $711 million (Lesotho), and only one university in each country. The first part of this chapter deals with the four small states (or, as Namibia was recently described by its Minister for Higher Education, Nahas Angula, 'big-small' states). As its author is currently working in Namibia, that country is dealt with in greater detail than the others, to exemplify developments and trends which are almost equally applicable in the others. The second part deals with South Africa and its much larger and more complex structures of higher education. The third briefly confronts the development dilemma posed in the title: is cooperation a possibility in distance education between countries and institutions of such disparate sizes, populations, target audiences and resources?

Botswana, Lesotho, Namibia and Swaziland

The combined history of these four countries is one of dependence on South Africa, though since independence in 1966, Botswana, Lesotho and Swaziland (BLS), until change began to occur in South Africa in 1990, shared a history of resistance to apartheid in the midst of geographical and economic co-existence. Namibia's independence in 1990 and the struggle for and movement towards it, marked the first signs of the crumbling of the apartheid regime. Educationally, the BLS countries set out to chart their own course, often in, sometimes uneasy, cooperation with each other. The University of Botswana, Lesotho and Swaziland (UBLS), established in 1964 and disbanded, in line with the history of regional universities in Africa, in 1982, was the first university in the sub-region outside South Africa. The

University of Namibia was initially a component part of the Academy of Namibia, set up in 1980 along with the Technikon and the College of Out-of-School Training (COST). It was modelled on the Afrikaner tradition of higher education in South Africa, with limited external contacts. The new University of Namibia and the Polytechnic of Namibia were established as autonomous institutions in 1992, and COST was replaced by the Windhoek Vocational Training Institute.

Prior to 1990, only Botswana had any real success in establishing economic independence of South Africa, largely because of prudent management of its mineral wealth. Dramatic political change in South Africa since 1990 has brought about equally dramatic change in the economic, and educational prospects, of collaboration: the Southern Africa Development Community (SADC) has replaced the Southern African Development Coordination Conference (SADCC) which was set up to help the front-line states escape from economic and cultural dependence on and military threats from an apartheid South Africa. The full implications of this change, in terms of collaboration, dependence and the urge for independence, educationally at least, are still being worked out by South Africa and by her neighbours.

Distance education, mainly under its former guise of correspondence education, started early in the sub-region. In the earliest years after independence, the BLS countries sought similar methods, at pre-tertiary level, to achieve educational development of a different nature. Partly to seek the solidarity of the small in the face of threats of absorption by the large, the Botswana, Lesotho and Swaziland Correspondence Committee (BLSCC) was set up in 1972. BLSCC (later the Distance Learning Association (DLA) and now DEASA) welcomed from the outset the distance education arms of non-governmental organisation (NGO) oppositional movements from South Africa and Namibia. Only after independence in Namibia and the institution of democratic government in South Africa did tertiary level bodies from those countries join DEASA. For these historical reasons, DEASA is still largely dominated by pre-tertiary rather than university distance-learning members.

The development of tertiary distance education up to the present

Botswana

UBLS's biggest and most ambitious distance education programme in Botswana in its early years was a collaborative non-formal programme, the Tribal Grazing Lands Radio Study-Groups campaign, run in 1976 by the Department of Extra-Mural Studies (DEMS) with the Botswana Extension College, which reached 55,000 adults in organised listening groups. The first distance credit course to be offered by the University of Botswana, while still a constituent college of UBLS, was a Diploma in Theology launched in 1979. In 1982, UBLS introduced a distance-taught Certificate in Adult Education programme, its only formal distance education programme to date, which currently has an enrolment of thirty-seven registered students. The University is also committed to set up distance education versions of its Certificate in Accountancy and Business Studies (CABS) and its Diploma in Accountancy and Business Studies (DABS) and to develop a distance-taught Diploma in Education, BEd. and MEd. degrees to be taught at a distance over the next few years. Already plans are at an advanced stage to launch the Diploma in Primary Education course to upgrade over 9,000 primary teacher certificate holders to the diploma level.

Lesotho

The National University of Lesotho (NUL) set up its first distance education programme in 1993. This was a BEd. degree in adult education run by the Department of Adult Education of the Institute for Extramural Studies. After seeking authorisation for some years to establish a programme of distance education degrees, the Institute of Education of the NUL has now been requested to set up a programme while the Institute of Labour Studies has launched a non-formal distance education programme mainly using the mass media. Thus there are three different centres of the same university offering different distance education programmes, each with comparatively small student populations.

Namibia

As indicated above, Namibia reached independence with one tertiary institution for which there was one distance education department. Three separate public institutions now offer distance education programmes at tertiary level; the University (UNAM), the Polytechnic and the National Institute for Educational Development (NIED), which is currently responsible for in-service teacher education for basic education. Each caters for between 1,000 and 2,000 students.

Until 1997, the Centre for External Studies (CES), which operated for both the Polytechnic and the University, managed a range of tertiary certificates and diploma programmes; for the Polytechnic in public administration and police science, and for the University in teacher education. In 1997, the Polytechnic decided to set up its own Distance Education Centre. The University launched its first external degree, the Bachelor in Nursing Science (Advanced Practice) the same year, has added the BEd. degree in 1998, and will soon launch a BCom./BBA programme. The NIED in-service Basic Education Teachers' Diploma (BETD), first offered in 1994, has to date enrolled three intakes, totalling 2,000. The Polytechnic is discussing the introduction of some distance-taught BTech programmes during the next few years. All three institutions offer predominantly print-based programmes with varying degrees of face-to-face supplements.

In addition to these programmes offered by Namibian public institutions, several programmes are offered by foreign, mainly South African, institutions. Undoubtedly, the South African 'Big Three', UNISA, Technikon SA and Vista University, have many more Namibian distance tertiary students than do all the Namibian public institutions put together. Some of their programmes are recognised by Namibian accrediting agencies, some are not; some fill gaps which the Namibian institutions cannot fill at present, some are in direct competition. And at least two South African private colleges offer quicker and sometimes cheaper qualifications in direct competition with the Namibian bodies, without accreditation, for professions for which they have no clear track record in South Africa. The student support services offered by such bodies are mainly on paper; their materials, as is the case in many public institutions, are still in the making. Their familiarity with and involvement in professional curriculum development for Namibia are distinctly questionable.

Swaziland

In 1994, the University of Swaziland, the last university in the sub-region to set up a tertiary distance education programme, established its Institute of Distance Education (IDE). The IDE launched its first distance education courses in 1996 with a Diploma in Law, a Diploma in Commerce and a BA (Humanities) in African Languages and in English Language and Literature. In 1997, it added a certificate course in French and a BEd. (Adult Education). The current student population is just over 300; a few courses, such as Law and the BA in languages, have nearly a hundred students but others, like French, have very small enrolments. All courses are offered almost exclusively by printed correspondence materials.

As in all mixed-mode universities, the IDE is wholly dependent on internal faculty, with their variable commitment and enthusiasm, to produce its courses. It therefore suffers from the common problem of falling behind development and production schedules but is not able to compensate by buying into existing materials from other institutions in the region because their curricula do not match those set by the University internal departments.

Issues and challenges for the future

One feature common to all four countries is that, though there is growing political and financial pressure on the universities to embark on distance education programmes, there is no clearly defined or coordinated national policy on distance education development, on the division of responsibilities between institutions, or on collaboration and the sharing of resources. Botswana's recently set up National Commission on Education and the resultant revised government policies on education laid down clear guidelines for a new structure for pre-tertiary distance education provision and clearly demarcated the proposed College of Open and Distance Learning's responsibilities from those to be implemented by the University. It also made a clear call for close collaboration between the College and the University's Distance Education Unit and sharing of resources and facilities. It is not so clear about the rationalisation of existing tertiary distance education programmes. Namibia is in the process of preparing a White Paper on the development of higher education. There are also moves to establish a National Council for Distance Education as a statutory body with financial power to encourage if not force the various distance education bodies to share resources, especially at regional level, and to coordinate their programmes. There appears to be no clear national policy on the organisation of tertiary distance education in either Lesotho or Swaziland.

All the universities in the sub-region outside South Africa are running and developing programmes, many of them very similar across the countries, for relatively small student populations both now and in the foreseeable future. All four countries, for example, offer or plan to offer BEd. degrees, three in adult education and three for school teachers. Two universities are offering nursing science programmes. None of them has much prospect of capitalising on the economies of scale of which distance education is capable. There is, however, in Namibia and probably in the other countries also, a strong 'not-made-here' prejudice which makes it difficult to convince conventional academics that it is not always necessary to reinvent every academic wheel. At the same time there is clear evidence, from Lesotho, Namibia and Swaziland, that factors such as pressure on time will force distance education units to buy in courses from outside, creating a clear dilemma about independence and dependency.

This situation presents two major challenges to the university distance education programmes. First is the question of *cost-effectiveness*. None of the programmes to date has more than a few hundred students enrolled in any of its courses. It seems unlikely that, even over a five-year period (the generally accepted lifespan of a distance education course, unrevised), such courses will cater for more than one or two thousand students. Such numbers, moreover, reflect the backlog of un- or underqualified professionals, such as nurses, teachers and public- and private-sector accountants and managers. Once that post-independence backlog has been provided for, steady state enrolments are likely to remain low. Do such programmes and such enrolments cross the threshold of economic viability and will they be sustainable at that size in the long run, or will they turn out to be emergency programmes to meet temporary upgrading needs?

The second challenge, closely related to the issue of costs, is the question of *quality*. All four countries have as yet only one national university, and in spite of ambitious staff development programmes are struggling to recruit enough qualified staff even to cover their internal teaching requirements. Under such circumstances it is extremely hard for academics to devote sufficient time and energy to the development of quality distance and open learning materials and to acquire the skills to do so. It is even harder to persuade them to keep to agreed production deadlines. The result is often at best rushed and makeshift materials. At worst, there are long delays in providing students with the materials on which their successful studies depend. Both factors contribute to high drop-out rates and low success rates and further exacerbate the problems of cost-effectiveness.

Both these challenges point in the direction of sub-regional collaboration, the theme to which we return at the end of the chapter.

South Africa

Policy environment

South Africa's first democratic election in 1994 heralded huge changes in its policies on education and training. Centuries of colonialism, racism and sexism had resulted in South Africa being one of the most unequal societies in the world, with lavish wealth co-existing with abject poverty. Forty long years after the Freedom Charter had demanded 'that the doors of learning and culture shall be open', an Education White Paper was gazetted in 1995 which stated that:

> education and training are basic human rights . . . and the state has an obligation to protect and advance these rights, so that all citizens, irrespective of race, class, gender, creed or age have the opportunity to develop their capacities and potential and make their full contribution to society.
>
> (Department of Education 1995: 25)

The White Paper commits itself to the redress of education inequalities and the deployment of resources according to the principle of equity. It states that:

> the over-arching goal of policy must be to enable all individuals to value, have access to and succeed in lifelong education and training of good quality. Education and management processes must therefore put the learners first, recognising and building on their knowledge and

experience, and responding to their needs. An integrated approach of education and training will increase access, mobility and quality in the national system . . . [That system] must provide an increasing range of learning possibilities, offering greater flexibility in choosing what, where, when, how and at what pace they learn.

(ibid.: 21)

Central to its strategy for achieving the far-reaching goals identified above is the establishment of a national qualifications framework. This framework prioritises the recognition of the outcomes of learning. As it begins to take effect, how and where people learn will become increasingly less important than what they learn.

These general policy developments open up huge opportunities for distance education providers and for the use of distance education methods. Recognising the potential growth in distance education, the national Department of Education initiated in 1996 a project to develop a quality standards framework for distance education provision. The resulting proposal has been widely discussed, and generally supported. These standards are likely to be included in the operation of quality assurance bodies established under the national qualifications framework. The Department has also provided a framework and guidelines for the development of technology-enhanced learning.

In 1997, a White Paper on higher education was gazetted. Here the Education Ministry recognises the crucial role that distance education has to play in increasing access, providing flexibility and 'integrating lifelong learning into the basic shape and structure of higher education and increasing access to quality programmes' (Government Gazette, 15 August 1997). With regard to cooperation, the White Paper on Higher Education states that 'the Ministry seeks to encourage the development of regional consortia and partnerships involving a range of institutions' and it sees the purpose of such collaboration as jointly developing and delivering programmes including producing courseware; reducing overlap and duplication in programme provision; helping to build academic and administrative capacity where needed, and enhancing responsiveness to regional and national needs. It sees the real import of such regional collaboration as transcending the current divides in the system, and as a potential harbinger of new institutional and organisational forms.

The development of tertiary distance education up to the present

As the White Paper in Higher Education acknowledges, distance education is already a major form of educational provision in South Africa. In 1997, over 124,000 distance education students were enrolled at the University of South Africa (UNISA), 81,000 at Technikon Southern Africa (TSA) and 10,153 at the Vista University Distance Education Campus (VUDEC). In 1995, a further 87,000 teachers were registered in teacher education programmes offered at a distance at colleges of education. New distance education initiatives emerge regularly, with traditional contact institutions increasingly adopting distance education methods. Furthermore, a range of international distance education institutions have entered the South African market. Distance education provision is clearly no longer peripheral. It is a mainstream form of provision, accounting for more than 40 per cent head count enrolments in 1997 and expanding rapidly. Preliminary indications are that about 42 per cent of all 1997 African students studying at university are studying through distance education.

Despite these diversifications of the distance education sector, UNISA and TSA remain the dominant institutions. UNISA was established as a federation of colleges in 1916 (although its roots can be traced back to the founding of the University of the Cape of Good Hope in 1873). As each of the colleges became independent, UNISA gradually came to focus more and more on its provision of 'external studies' until, in 1946, it became a fully fledged correspondence university. It is an autonomous institution under its own statute and governed by its own council. It has six faculties with the vast majority of its 1997 students enrolled in arts (50,000) and economic and management science (42,500). Over 85 per cent of students are enrolled for Bachelor's degrees. UNISA has 1,200 academic and 2,000 administrative staff members.

Technikon SA was established an autonomous tertiary education institution in 1980, prior to which it had functioned as the external studies facility of the Technikon Witwatersrand. It operates under its own statute and is governed by its own council, but is currently subjected to the norms and standards of the Certification Council for Technikon Education. It has three academic divisions: public safety and criminal justice, community and applied sciences, and economics and management sciences. In 1997, Technikon SA had 80,896 students of whom 25,163 were enrolled in police practice. It had 263 academic staff and 886 administrative staff.

In 1995, the South African Institute for Distance Education (SAIDE) conducted an audit of teacher education offered at a distance. At that stage, UNISA (with 37,717 teacher education students), Vista (15,586 students), College of Education South Africa (25,857 students), a Rand Afrikaans University/Lyceum College partnership (16,263 students) and a Pretoria University/Success College partnership (7,403) were the main players in numerical terms. Since then, numbers at both UNISA and Vista have dropped drastically, the College of Education South Africa and the College of Continuing Education have amalgamated, and the two university/college partnerships have expanded considerably. Influential factors have been changes in the relationship between teacher salaries and qualification, and cutting back on the number of teachers and redeploying others.

Issues and challenges for the future

The South African context provides extraordinary opportunities for distance education. The commitment to and need for lifelong learning, as well as the huge requirement for redress for hundreds of thousands of adults structurally prevented from reaching their full potential under the apartheid regime, create an environment in which distance education should thrive.

The Higher Education White Paper acknowledges the extent of the distance/correspondence education infrastructure in South Africa in both the private and public sectors but is concerned about its efficiency, appropriateness and effectiveness; in other words, its *quality*. It proposes a comprehensive audit of all existing distance education institutions and programmes. The National Commission on Higher Education, on which the White Paper was largely based, highlighted various ways in which the distance education sector needs to transform. These include drastic improvement in the quality and relevance of course materials, proper learner support systems, more participatory and democratic governance structures, and extended partnerships among all types of institutions in order to maximise the use of resources and eliminate unnecessary duplication.

The distance education sector faces two major challenges as it seeks to transform: the first is that it needs to demonstrate that it can provide programmes of high quality to its students; second, it needs to be able to demonstrate that it can offer these programmes cost-effectively.

Quality

Two questions emerge: do programmes offer students reasonable chances of success and are the resulting qualifications of real value to students and to the country?

Globally, completion rates in distance education are generally poor by comparison with traditional provision. Often 50 per cent of those who register drop out early in the programme, and in many instances only a tiny proportion of continuing students graduate. In South Africa, the pattern is variable. At UNISA and TSA, for example, course pass rates seem reasonable, but the graduation rate is low. Detailed figures extracted in 1994 and again in 1996, demonstrate that only 10 to 17 per cent of those entering an undergraduate programme graduate over the ensuing nine years. In other words, only one or two out of every ten students embarking on a programme of study complete it successfully. In science, the figure is one in twenty.

At most institutions offering teaching diplomas at a distance, however, the picture is the opposite. While a detailed analysis of success rates could not be obtained, indications are that they are extremely high. What needs to be queried here is the quality of the qualification obtained. A review in 1995 by ten independent teacher educators of course material and exit performance standards concluded that success in these programmes was most unlikely to have a beneficial impact on the quality of teaching and learning in the classroom. Commenting on the quality of the course material, they noted that, in the main, courses emphasise the recall of content with little or no demonstrable commitment to improving practice; have content that is often out of date; pay no attention to developing critical and analytical skills; and contain little conceptual coherence, thereby forcing learners into rote learning.

In both typical configurations described above, distance education provision cannot be said to be successful. Either students drop out or fail, or else they obtain a qualification of poor quality. There are, of course, some exceptions. For example, honours programmes at UNISA seem to have higher graduation rates than the ordinary degree. This may also be the case for private distance education colleges, although information for this sector is not available.

Distance education provides flexible opportunities to people who, for a variety of reasons, cannot, or prefer not to, attend classes at contact institutions. For example, at UNISA and TSA, over 75 per cent of students are working and 74 per cent are over 25. Distance education also provides opportunities for those to whom opportunity was systematically denied in the past. In 1995, in teacher education, 70 per cent of enrolments were women. In 1993, nearly 47 per cent of all African students at university were studying through distance education. At technikons, the figure was 38 per cent. A trend at both UNISA and TSA is the growing number (probably around 30,000) of full-time young students who have enrolled because they could not gain access to contact institutions.

Cost-effectiveness

Thus, while a place at a public distance education institution may be cheaper than at a contact institution, unless students are successful, the provision cannot be considered cost-effective. Because distance education achieves low graduation rates, contact institutions need to achieve graduation rates of only 20 to 34 per cent (i.e. twice those of distance education institutions) for distance education institutions' cost advantage to be lost. In fact, contact institutions do much better than that.

The question arises as to whether and how cooperation can contribute to the resolution of the above key challenge. There is in South Africa, in contrast to the other four Southern African nations, a well-developed distance education policy encouraging cooperation across the spectrum of contact and distance education institutions. It is the implementation of this new policy that presents major challenges for South African institutions.

Cooperation

The first example of cooperation is between the three big institutions, UNISA, TSA and Vista, which in 1997 established the Confederation of Open Learning Institutions of South Africa (COLISA) to coordinate and rationalise their resources in order to address the vast educational needs of the country better than the individual institutions could manage.

COLISA has established nine task teams to investigate such aspects as joint course offering, learner support services, technology, quality assurance, student governance and course design and development. One concrete outcome of the COLISA collaboration is the agreement to share examination facilities and learning centres, especially in those provinces where the three have a limited presence. Already joint UNISA/TSA offices have been established in the Mpumalanga and the Northern Cape Provinces. Interest from TSA in using the UNISA postgraduate diploma in distance education for internal staff development rather than reinventing the wheel is another possibility. Promotion of capacity building in the application of technology is another area where moves are afoot to maximise collaborative efforts. Successful collaboration in COLISA should result in more resources being deployed in particular courses, with resulting improvement in quality and cost-effectiveness. Progress in other areas of cooperation has not been as quick as originally envisaged mainly because of entrenched individual institutions' procedures, processes and priorities. COLISA needs to hasten the implementation of its cooperation ventures and to demonstrate clearly how these have begun to shift their provision towards the improvement of quality and cost-effectiveness within the three member institutions.

The second example was originally envisaged as a wider consortium of six distance education organisations: UNISA, TSA, Vista, TECHNISA, SACHED and SAIDE. But mainly due to uneven financial resources and the varying stages of readiness to participate in the materials development process, only UNISA and SACHED were able to develop materials for the postgraduate diploma in distance education, while the other members have kept a watching brief on progress and undertaken limited critical reading of the materials produced. SACHED's role is limited to the development of materials for two modules of the postgraduate diploma; delivery and accreditation are UNISA's sole responsibility. The contrasting models of materials development used by the two organisations provide useful case studies of how cooperation can be implemented. UNISA employs an internal staff team approach, while SACHED has used a broader regional team of practitioners from various institutions in Southern Africa to adapt existing materials (from the University of London/International Extension College course) and originate new course materials. The consortium's focus on professional development courses for distance education practitioners is one way of addressing the issue of *quality*. However, such courses would need to integrate theoretical knowledge with practical on-the-job application of ideas as part of institutional quality assurance mechanisms.

A rather different type of collaboration, focusing on the development of *quality courseware*, is being coordinated by SAIDE. Initiated by a group of teacher-educators concerned about the poor quality and inappropriateness of most teacher education courses offered at a distance, the project attempts to harness pockets of innovative practice from across the country. With support from the Kellogg Foundation, SAIDE has employed a course leader and a project manager. On the basis of a curriculum framework constructed by the project's advisory committee, these staff seek out, contract and support different module teams from different parts of the country to develop different aspects of the course. The course leader's primary task is to ensure the intellectual coherence of the course materials and to maintain their quality. The course materials for each module, comprising a reader, a study guide, an audio cassette and a video cassette, are being published by Oxford University Press for both individual and institutional use. The project attempts to demonstrate how to harness the on-the-ground experience and talents of a diversity of teacher-educators from across the country for the benefit of many students in a wide range of contexts and institutions.

The fourth example is that of the University of Natal and the South African College for Teacher Education (SACTE), which aims to make a high quality course from a traditional contact institution widely available through distance education. In 1998, SACTE was officially inaugurated, the product of the amalgamation of two separate colleges, the College of Education South Africa and the College of Continuing Education, which were previously part of different departments of South Africa's racially differentiated systems. SACTE, with over 20,000 teachers enrolled in its programmes, has recently entered into a partnership with the Department of Education at the University of Natal, Pietermaritzburg, to offer a Bachelor of Education on a national basis. The Natal Department had traditionally offered face-to-face programmes, but had recently begun to develop learning resources for teachers wishing to enrol for the BEd. programme but working too far away from Pietermaritzburg to attend lectures and tutorials. These students interacted with the materials and then attended weekend tutorial sessions at centres close to their homes. In 1998, the University Department has enrolled over 800 students in the programme, all based in KwaZulu Natal. The partnership with SACTE will permit national enrolment. Within the partnership, the University will be responsible for developing the overall programme and many of its different modules. SACTE will develop some of the modules. Students will enrol with the University but through the offices of SACTE. SACTE will organise the different forms of learner support with responsibility for overall staff development, and monitoring resting primarily with the University. The University will award the degree. The University and SACTE will jointly determine the equitable sharing of students' subsidies and fees. However, the aim of facilitating collaboration be-tween distance education and contact institutions, though noble in outlook and strongly encouraged in the White Paper on Higher Education, might be more difficult to implement immediately, mainly because of concerns about the 'efficiency, appropriateness and effectiveness of much current distance education provision' (Government Gazette, 15 August 1997).

The wide variety of courses available in South Africa in different disci-plines for undergraduate, postgraduate and technical education through dis-tance learning, has resulted in the very strong 'not-made-here' prejudice already mentioned. Courses available beyond the region are rejected mainly for reasons related to copyright and costs, especially because of the dwindling power of the South African currency. In the past, in-country interinstitutional jealousy seemed limited because of the clear lines of demarcation of insti-tutional responsibilities. Contact institutions were not involved in distance education, within which UNISA was responsible for undergraduate and post-graduate academic education, TSA for technical education and Vista for upgrading unqualified teachers. With a number of universities implementing the new policy encouraging the use of distance education methods by all institutions, interinstitutional rivalry is likely to intensify if cooperation is not fostered. In areas where there is already some oversupply of human resources, as in teacher education as evidenced by recent staff retrenchments, such rivalry could be counterproductive, though the Study of Education collaboration provides a good example of areas needing attention within this sector.

These examples of cooperation among South African organisations pres-ent some opportunities for countering the above-mentioned types of preju-dices. The collaborations between SACHED and UNISA, SAIDE and teacher-educators in the Study of Education initiative are also introducing NGOs as partners in higher education provision. The challenges faced in such cooperation relate to unevenness in status and capacity, different insti-tutional culture and reputation and financial constraints (Roman 1997). While, as both examples show, the NGOs have been able to raise course development finance from external funders, it is in the delivery of the fin-ished products that major challenges arise. Will NGOs' roles in distance education be limited to course development or can they expect to be included in the delivery of courses? The SACHED/UNISA postgraduate diploma partnership suggests a rather bleak future for NGO involvement in delivery, partly because of financial constraints facing higher education institutions and the limited number of students registered in this course, but also because of the reluctance to experiment with non-conventional ways of sharing government subsidies in respect of collaborative delivery. Partner-ships in the development of quality courseware are important and need to be encouraged. NGOs might not become involved in the delivery of programmes, but, they could, like SAIDE, be involved in quality assurance mechanisms, particularly in those courses developed through partnerships.

Regional activity

Our earlier comments on the four small states' distance-learning and open learning programmes portrayed more than a hint of parochialism and scepticism about shared courses and collaboration. Insularity and an absence of sharing are common characteristics of those programmes at present. Fortunately that is not the whole story: we have seen optimistic collaborative developments in South Africa and there are also excellent examples of close cooperation between institutions in different countries – for instance, between UNISA and the University of Namibia, where, on request and through negotiation, UNAM was granted the licence to reproduce, edit and adapt, electronically, UNISA's recently revised nurse science courses at very reasonable costs.

There is, however, a dilemma facing organisations like UNISA: is UNAM a competitor in the field of nursing science and in the geographical area which UNISA has traditionally seen as its own? If the cooperation had not happened, could UNISA have enrolled all those students on its own programme? There are two schools of thought in UNISA on this issue, each sitting on opposite horns of this dilemma.

Is all this inevitable? Are we forced to accept crude market forces in this arena? Are the small states of Southern Africa doomed to simply buying in the products of the large-scale South African institutions, both public and private, with limited ability to adjust those products to their own needs? Or can the small states get together and coincide their requirements sufficiently to create a large enough cooperative base to produce their own collaborative materials, or be in a position to negotiate from strength with their South African neighbours so as to be able to ensure that their purchases are adaptable to their specific local, small-scale needs? And is there a serious prospect of South African institutions being interested to buy for their own use such joint products of their smaller neighbours? Is there a growing prospect of cooperation between the newer and smaller South African programmes, especially the consortia, which are themselves experimental, and the smaller institutions in neighbouring states? In short, is there an economically viable regional alternative to sub-regional domination by the large-scale public South African distance education institutions and South African commercial distance education colleges?

In attempting to find answers to these questions we must recognise both the history of problems and failed initiatives in regional university cooperation and the real logistical and academic difficulties of co-development and production of curricula and learning materials for distance education across national boundaries. Issues of intellectual property and copyright, moreover, which are being recognised as barriers to materials exchange throughout the world, will continue to complicate collaborative ventures in the sub-region. There are, however, a few forces working in favour of collaboration, not least economic forces. Self-made programmes for small population audiences cost several times more than bought-in courses, and are in no way guaranteed to be either higher quality or even necessarily more locally relevant. They also put immense production strains on the meagre personnel and financial resources of the distance education units of these small, mixed-mode, universities. Regular exposure to each others' programmes brought about through regular DEASA meetings, moreover, is leading distance education practitioners to call for and to explore possibilities of sharing courses.

Finally, the recent SADC protocol on education calls for all member-states to open their educational institutions to student mobility within the community. While it might be unspecific about the application of this principle to distance education, clearly collaborative efforts and course sharing through distance education are in the spirit of that protocol. DEASA has a major role to play in promoting and facilitating such sharing. Without such sharing, or without an unlikely dramatic increase in the resources available to individual countries, and their universities, it is very hard to see how an increasing dependence on and domination by the large South African institutions, both public and private, not always led by an altruistic concern for the needs of students in the smaller states, can be avoided. It is put forward here that domination by and dependence on the large by the small can only turn into genuine sharing and cooperation if the small can negotiate with the large from a position of strength. That position of strength can only be achieved through prior cooperation between the small. If it can be achieved the prospects for major economically and educationally viable distance education developments in the sub-region must be bright indeed.

References

Department of Education (1995) *Education and Training in a Democratic South Africa: First Steps to Develop a New System*, Pretoria: Department of Education.

International Commission into Distance Education in South Africa (1995) *Open Learning and Distance Education*, Manzini: Macmillan Boleswa.

National Commission on Higher Education (1996) *National Commission on Higher Education Report: A Framework for Transformation*, Parow: CTP Book Printers.

Nonyongo, E.P. and Ngengebule, A.T. (eds) (1998) *Learner Support Services: Case-studies of DEASA Member Institutions*, Pretoria: UNISA Press.

Roman, M. (1997) 'Course material development collaboration in South Africa', in Minutes of the DEASA Meeting held at Botswana Grand Palm Hotel, 20–1 September 1997, pp. 5–8 (unpublished).

South African Institute for Distance Education (SAIDE) (1996) *Teacher Education Offered at Distance in South Africa*, Cape Town: Juta.

Southern African Development Community (1995) *Handbook*, Gaborone: SADC.

Young, M., Perraton, H., Jenkins, J. and Dodds, T. (1991) *Distance Teaching for the Third World*, 2nd edn, Cambridge: International Extension College.

The Open University of Tanzania

Geoffrey Mmari

The following pages recount the experience of this new African distance-teaching university, established in one of the poorest countries of the world at a time of global economic difficulty. The Open University of Tanzania is a young institution whose legal existence dates back to December 1992. Following the announcement that the University would commence activities on 1 March 1993, key decision-makers were appointed in April. The first students were admitted in January 1994; it is from this cohort that we expect to see the first graduates in early 1999 after five years of study.

Tanzania: its political history, economic situation and educational framework

A century ago, the present Tanzania came under German administration during a period of European colonisation in Africa. It remained under German colonial administration until the end of the First World War when, through the auspices of the League of Nations, it became a Mandated Territory under the British colonial administration.

The British governed Tanzania throughout the period leading up to and including the Second World War, and after the War as a Trust Territory. The global anti-colonial movement in turn affected Tanzania, which was granted political independence in December 1961, and elected to be a republic within the British Commonwealth in December 1962.

Off-shore Zanzibar followed a different course. The foreign power was from Arabia, and when the British came on the scene in 1890, Zanzibar became a Protectorate. It gained its political independence from Britain in December 1963, and early in 1964 merged with the mainland to form a union which has lasted up to the present.

Tanzania's chequered history is reflected in its culture, language, architecture, system of education, governance, religion and in many other ways. It is also reflected in its foreign policies and relations. The country's tropical location has determined its agricultural products and its means of production, while its political history has dictated its economic dealings. Since the colonial powers were interested in serving the metropolitan economy, plant-ations were established to grow raw materials for the home industries. This explains the cash economy around sisal, cotton, tea, coffee and cloves as well as mining interests in gold, diamonds and tin.

Communication networks were built to facilitate exports to overseas industrial destinations as well as imports to maintain the emerging local industries and economic interests. In addition to the plantation estate and mining economy, the majority of the people were involved in peasant agriculture based on small farms, using traditional agricultural tools and traditional methods. They also engaged in trade, cattle herding, fishing and other activities for subsistence and for the domestic market. They relied heavily on imported goods for their everyday needs, ranging from clothing to building materials, from school equipment to medical supplies. Govern-ment after government has tried to correct and reverse this economic dependence.

Government attempts to change economic trends have relied on models practised elsewhere, earning the country the name of the 'Great Experi-menter'. For government leaders, these were not experiments but genuine attempts to change the situation while at the same time observing the need for equity and broad participation of the people in guiding their destinies.

The educational framework of Tanzania has also been influenced by the country's political history. There have been German models, British models and models from other countries, especially after political independence in the early 1960s. The current system is based on seven years of primary education for the majority of school-age children. This is followed by four years of secondary education for 13.3 per cent of primary school leavers. Another group moves into vocational training for between one and three years, while the remaining majority enter employment, both formal and informal. The economic crisis facing many countries has affected this group, leading to unemployment.

A two-year period of advanced level secondary education follows the first four years; 25 per cent are able to proceed to this level. The remaining group proceeds to various forms of training for between one and three years for diplomas, advanced diplomas and other professional skills awards. Many others enter formal and informal employment, while others remain unemployed. While the state has taken responsibility for public education at all levels for some twenty years, the private sector is involved in secondary education to the extent that 55 per cent of all secondary pupils are in schools run by private providers.

University education in Tanzania has been described as the least extensive in Africa since only 30 per cent of those who complete A level secondary education proceed to this level. Up until 1994, when the Open University of Tanzania came on the scene, the two public universities had a total of 3,670 students. The establishment of private universities was legally permitted from 1995; half a dozen private universities have already been established and are at different stages of development.

Distance education in the last ten years (1988–98)

The year 1988 represents a watershed in the history of distance education in Tanzania. In this year, the government established a Committee on the Establishment of an Open University in Tanzania, an institution to be dedicated to teaching and learning by distance methods at the tertiary level. There is evidence that at this time, some individuals in Tanzania were taking courses from overseas-based institutions in, for example, Britain and India, but such students were few in number.

The President's decision to split the Education Ministry portfolio into (a) Education and Culture and (b) Science, Technology and Higher Education had an impact on the future of distance education in Tanzania; recommendations made by the Committee established under the Ministry Responsible for Education now fell under two different ministries. In June 1990, the Minister Responsible for Education reported to Parliament that the Committee he had established in 1988 to recommend the establishment of an Open University had completed its task and submitted its report. He promised that his Ministry would deliberate on the Committee's recommendations and report to government.

The Minister also pointed out that institutions under his Ministry, particularly the Institute of Adult Education, were conducting twenty-five courses by correspondence, and that two new ones would shortly be launched in the areas of tailoring and motor mechanics. In July 1991, the Minister Responsible for Education reported to Parliament that 5,000 teachers had been upgraded through correspondence courses and 4,523 were taking correspondence courses with the Institute of Adult Education, including those in practical skills such as tailoring and other technical subjects. In the meantime, it was government's aim to upgrade 5,000 primary school teachers by correspondence in the subject areas of mathematics, English, politics, Kiswahili, history and geography.

In successive years from 1992 to 1997, education ministers have reported in their Budget speeches to Parliament on the achievements of previous years as well as on future plans. The range of courses taught by correspondence has included mathematics, English, Kiswahili, politics, history and geography, as well as practical and professional subjects such as vehicle mechanics, electrical skills, carpentry, management, book-keeping, librarianship and law. The principal provider is the Institute of Adult Education, which operates under the Ministry of Education and Culture. The 1994–5 Budget speech reported that 57,088 people had completed correspondence courses.

The Minister Responsible for Higher Education reported in July 1991 that his Ministry was producing implementation strategies based on the recommendations of the 1990 Committee. In July 1992, he reported to Parliament that a planning committee had been established to deal with (a) drafting a bill to establish the University, (b) identification of basic facilities, (c) location of regional centres, (d) contacting cooperating institutions, and (e) forging international links. In July 1993, the Minister announced that a Bill had been passed in the previous December and that applications had been invited for admission to the January 1994 degree programmes in ten disciplinary areas. Four teaching methods would be used: (1) print, (2) audio cassettes, (3) face-to-face and (4) practicals. In addition, key officers had been appointed in April 1993, and international recognition had been sought.

In August 1994, the Minister reported that 766 students had been admitted in January 1994 and that nine regional centres had been established, in Dar es Salaam, Mbeya, Mwanza, Dodoma, Tabora, Arusha, Moshi, Zanzibar and Mtwara. He also described loan arrangements for students not able to meet all the fees. Since they were supposed to be working adults, government was allowing Open University students a loan of 30 per cent of the figure set for students in conventional universities.

The first group of students could register for the BA, BCom. and courses in education. The demand for sciences and law determined that preparations were made for the admission of students to BSc. and LLB degree programmes in January 1995. The University had received some computer equipment primarily for desktop publishing but also for other purposes such as communication. The Minister reported to Parliament in August 1996 and August 1997 that the University had established twenty-one regional centres and had a student population approaching 4,000.

Student profiles

The following tables illustrate the characteristics of students enrolled by the Open University of Tanzania from 1994 to 1998.

Table 7–2.1 demonstrates that one-third of 1994 students were below the

Table 7–2.1 Age distribution of students: 1994 intake

Age range	Percentage of total				
	BCom.	BA	BA(Ed.)	BCom.(Ed.)	Total
20–24	2.5	–	0.8	–	3.3
25–29	3.9	3.0	4.2	0.2	11.3
30–34	5.3	5.0	7.5	–	17.8
35–39	6.1	4.4	14.8	1.1	26.4
40–44	4.7	6.1	9.5	0.8	21.1
45–49	4.4	4.2	7.0	0.8	16.4
50+	0.5	0.5	2.1	0.5	3.6
Total	27.4	23.2	45.9	3.4	99.9

age of 35. The two-thirds over 35 are people born before independence in 1961. They had the ability and ambition to proceed further but restricted opportunities did not allow them to do so. The large number of enrolments in the BA(Ed.) reflects not only the courses available in 1994 but also the fact that there are many teachers wishing to improve their situations.

Table 7–2.2 provides information on the educational qualifications of 1994 students. One-third had the right number of A level passes for entrance to university, but did not gain admission because of the restricted number of places. Most of the remainder have equivalent qualifications (i.e. they have advanced beyond O level and have acquired sufficient professional skills to benefit from university-level education). Those with equivalent qualifications principally opted for or were selected to do the BA(Ed.).

Other statistics relating to the 1994 intake indicate that 75 per cent are married and therefore have family commitments. Many students have complained that they were not only paying fees for themselves but also for their children and their relatives.

Table 7–2.3 shows that although teachers, bank workers and those who have not specified their professional background account for around 12.5 per cent of the total, the range of backgrounds of BA general degree students is very wide. This perhaps reflects both the broad content of the BA and also the nature of the degree programme as a general foundation for many lifetime opportunities.

Table 7–2.2 Admission criteria met by students: 1994 intake

Level	Percentage of total				
	BCom.	BA	BA(Ed.)	BCom(Ed.)	Total
A level	9.2	13.4	9.2	0.2	32.0
Equivalent qualifications	15.9	8.9	36.1	–	60.9
University graduate	0.5	0.5	0.5	0.2	1.7
Bridging course	1.6	0.2	–	–	1.8
Total	27.2	23.0	45.8	0.4	96.4

Table 7–2.3 Background of students: 1995 intake in the BA(General)

Employment status	Per cent of cohorts
Teaching	12.7
Banking	12.7
Not specified	12.7
Administration	10.6
Business	8.5
Agricultural field officer	4.2
Others	38.6

The 'Others' category includes: auditing, forestry, security, games, stores, technician, youth work, self-employment, editing, peasant, publishing, police, naturalist, secretary, artist, clergyman, planner, library – which account for about 2 per cent each.

It is not surprising that 75 per cent of the students enrolled in the 1995 BA(Education) are teachers. The implications for the Ministry of Education and Culture, the private school system and all employers of teachers are far reaching. If students take their studies seriously, and if the University achieves quality in teaching, there should be a noticeable improvement in the quality of education offered in schools.

Teachers also comprise 50 per cent of the 1995 intake for the BCom.(Education). For two decades, Tanzania has opted for practical biases in its secondary education. One of the four biases is commerce, which explains why so many people with a teaching background have opted for the BCom.(Education). The wide range of backgrounds of students other than teachers is accounted for by the expectations individuals have beyond the completion of their studies, by their background in commerce-related school subjects, and by the range of options in the BCom. degree, which include accounting, marketing, finance, production, human resources and international business.

By contrast, only a very small percentage (3.9 per cent) of students enrolled in the BCom.(General) are teachers. The largest identified groups are employed in accounting (14.7 per cent) and administration (9.8 per cent). Unfortunately, more than 25 per cent of students are classified in the 'Not specified' category. Sixty-six per cent of the 1995 intake into the BSc.(Education) are from the teaching profession. It is a challenge to the University to be able to offer relevant content to cover such a diverse background of scientific-related disciplines. The 1995 BSc.(General) students are from a wide range of backgrounds, pointing to the existence of many men and women keen to study higher education beyond the point they reached in school and training college. Technicians (31.25 per cent) are by far the largest specific group.

Table 7–2.4 demonstrates the relatively high intake into the LLB programme. For reasons which cannot easily be explained, the range of employment and background of students is extraordinarily wide. The largest specified groups are administrators (12.2 per cent) and legal workers (11.9 per cent). The 1995 analyses by age and qualifications are not yet complete. It will be particularly interesting to compare the 1994 and 1995 figures in Tables 7–2.1 and 7–2.2.

Table 7–2.4 also shows enrolment over the first five years of admissions. It is very clear that women are underrepresented at around 10 per cent. Equally clearly, the LLB has been very successful in attracting students. The numbers are already comparable with those for students admitted to education or education-related programmes. An important factor which is not revealed in these statistics is the number of students active after admission. Analysis of

Table 7–2.4 Enrolment pattern by gender, annual intake and degree programme 1994–8

Degree	1994			1995			1996			1997			1998			1994–8		
	F	M	Total	F	M	Total	F	M	Total	F	M	Total	F	M	Total	F	M	Total
1 BA	15	173	188	4	47	51	7	54	61	5	45	50	5	50	55	36	369	405
2 BA(Ed.)	40	319	359	23	104	127	25	167	192	18	115	133	24	112	136	130	817	947
3 BCom.	11	185	196	5	90	95	12	149	161	13	92	105	8	79	87	49	595	644
4 BCom.(Ed.)	1	22	23	0	17	17	17	32	49	2	16	18	3	20	23	13	107	120
5 BSc.	0	0	0	2	30	32	7	67	74	7	63	70	10	77	87	26	237	263
6 BSc.(Ed.)	0	0	0	10	51	61	8	85	93	8	38	46	13	50	63	39	224	263
7 LLB	0	0	0	26	329	355	36	445	481	33	300	333	35	260	295	130	1,334	1,464
8 Foundation course	–	–	–	–	–	–	34	194	228	41	182	223	60	189	249	135	565	700
9 Total	67	699	766	70	668	738	146	1,193	1,429	127	851	978	158	837	995	558	4,248	4,806

this factor will become available at a later stage of student studies, especially in relation to annual examinations.

It is anticipated that in 1999, it will be known how many students admitted in January 1994 have continued their studies and graduated. Efforts are being made to encourage those lagging behind to resume their studies or to overcome temporary hurdles on the way. A thorough study of this group is important in order to improve guidance and counselling services in the future.

Administration of higher education programme by distance learning

The University attempts to reach students in the regions where they live and work. Ten of the twenty-one regional centres have full-time directors, currently with few support staff. The remaining eleven regions are served by those with directors in place and also by the Head Office. As from January 1998, a Director of Regional Services has been appointed to maintain closer contact with the regions. Every quarter, the directors of regional centres meet at the Head Office to compare notes and thrash out student problems of a policy or practical nature. Problems confronting them and students include the delivery of study materials, return of marked scripts, receipts of fees paid into bank accounts, and postponement of studies. Every effort has been made to tackle these problems and improve services.

The Act establishing the University provides for student participation in policy-making organs. It also allows for a students' association run by students themselves. These opportunities have been taken up, and students have attended Council and Senate meetings as well as Faculty Boards where they have made their views heard. Through regional and study centres they are able to communicate to the lowest levels and thus provide an opportunity for further contacts that facilitate solutions to their problems.

Figure 7–2.1 shows how the various levels of the University are linked in an effort to facilitate effective administration of general as well as specific needs of students.

The pace of technological change has been so fast that the University has found itself leap-frogging several intermediate steps others have gone through. When the University was established in 1992, the concern of many Members of Parliament was whether postal services would be efficient enough to make the University effective. Within a half decade, the University has found itself using the latest satellite technology side by side with the old postal system. While the majority of students still rely on the post office, for others options include delivery of their assignment by e-mail, review of literature surveys via electronic library, and using laptop computers for assignments.

The old, well-tried carrier system has proved very reliable as staff have

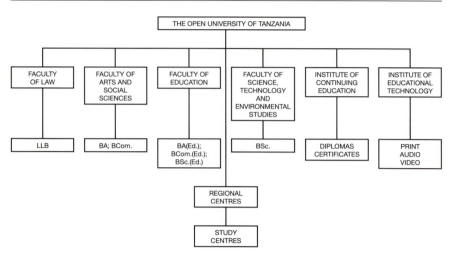

Figure 7–2.1 Organisation of OUT

travelled from Dar es Salaam to Zanzibar with student materials or with parcels and bus drivers have hand-carried envelopes with assignments and tests to directors of regional centres waiting at the other end. Five years' practical experience has shown that nothing is too advanced or too old-fashioned. There is need for imaginative flexibility in trying whatever works at any given moment. Students have appreciated this. This includes delivery in bulk of study materials from Nairobi which would have been very costly by air freight. Stores staff have travelled between Dar es Salaam and Nairobi with import–export papers in their hands, handled customs duties on the spot, and accompanied parcels through border posts. This approach has saved hours, days and even weeks of frustration waiting for study materials.

Experience from other institutions has taught the University to negotiate licence agreements which will permit the reprinting of materials developed elsewhere for a small fee. This approach cuts down on costs involved in transporting these study materials in bulk and on time since the reprinting will be done as and when needed. The acquisition of study materials includes those for special groups such as the blind or those with disabilities preventing them freely using their hands. Arrangements to produce audio tapes are at an advanced stage and hopefully such students will be able to register in January 1999. They will start with the BA(Education) programmes and follow later with the other programmes.

It is with regard to study materials that cooperation with the conventional universities is most evident. To date, the University has published close to sixty titles, the majority of which have been written by academic staff in the conventional universities. Over a hundred titles purchased from Nairobi have been written by academic staff from conventional universities in Kenya.

Arrangements have been made to introduce academic staff in conventional universities to the philosophy and practice of distance teaching and learning. Seminars have been organised using resource persons from well-established programmes as well as from within the University drawing on staff members' previous experience. Academic staff from conventional universities have also been deployed in running face-to-face sessions, and in setting and marking assignments, timed tests and annual examinations. Some have served as external examiners while others sit on Council, Senate, Faculty Boards and other committees. The Open University is also a member of various national and international organisations which facilitate contact with peers in the conventional universities. Experience elsewhere has shown the need for recognition and for quality assurance strategies so that at the end of the day qualifications earned at the Open University will be accepted and respected.

While national manpower needs have commanded top priority in government policy in higher education, social needs have also demanded close attention in recent years. Whereas the capacity of government to employ all graduates of institutions of higher education is now quite limited, the private sector needs these graduates. With liberalisation, far more opportunities are opening up than can be met through existing facilities. The Open University is able to address itself to these issues in a manner complementary to government efforts.

The ability of the Open University to reach students where they are located helps meet the government's equity agenda, which undertakes to make higher education accessible to the broad spectrum of the population irrespective of social origin, gender, geographical location and historical consideration. The very low fees charged by the Open University makes its programmes accessible to practically any serious student. The current fees of about US $730 for the full programme are very low, although students rightly point out that there are also hidden costs: for example, for fares and accommodation as students travel to regional centres for orientation and face-to-face programmes, for tests and examinations. There are more costs borne by those who do science practicals and teaching practice away from their home bases. The solution lies in identifying science laboratories closer to students' homes as well as more centres. But these too mean more investment on the part of the University. With new technologies and based on proper infrastructure, these problems will be contained.

Government policy on lifelong education is well met by the Open University since it makes it possible for a growing body of retired people, including public servants, to pick up new skills. To help them, the newly established Institute of Continuing Education is geared to produce very specific tailormade courses. Some programmes have an appeal beyond the borders of Tanzania, such as the proposed Commonwealth Youth Programme, to be launched soon.

New opportunities

Five years' practical experience at the Open University of Tanzania has shown how new opportunities can and have been exploited in making higher education accessible to far more people than ever envisaged. First and foremost has been the opportunity to cooperate with other institutions in and outside Tanzania. Involving academic staff at existing public institutions has opened a completely new path for cooperation. Writers of study materials, reviewers of manuscripts, publishers' editors and others, setting and assessing work undertaken and involved in face-to-face sessions and general seminars have brought together men and women not previously involved in this way before. This has enriched Open University programmes. Because of their high quality, study materials are now finding their way to students in the conventional institutions, thus indirectly filling a vacuum which has concerned institutional administrators and managers for a long time.

Cooperation has extended to the national library network, science laboratories and information services run by public and private institutions. At the international level, close cooperation has been forged with neighbouring country universities for their study materials, external examiners, resource persons for workshops and now technical expertise in solving problems related to satellite-based delivery systems. Cooperation has extended to Asia and beyond, for example, with Indira Gandhi National Open University (for their study materials and the Masters in Distance Education), the Federal University in Abuja, Nigeria (for their law study materials), the University of South Africa (for their study materials and staff training), the Commonwealth of Learning in Vancouver (for their pan-Commonwealth coordination), the International Centre for Distance Learning at the UK Open University (for their regular supply of CD-ROMs), and many others. The African Virtual University experiment launched by the World Bank in 1997 throws open doors to further cooperation through use of new technologies.

The second new opportunity is in the exploitation of technologies developed on a commercial scale after years of experimentation. The computer, e-mail, the Internet, audio- and videoconferencing and the electronic library are examples of opportunities confined to a minority in the beginning but with potential for wider use. Experimenting with alternative sources of energy is one way of expanding the number of those who can be reached in these ways.

The third opportunity is that lifelong learning becomes a reality to many more people than before. In the past, lifelong learning was associated particularly with literacy and numeracy, functional literacy and such aspects of knowledge sharing. The Open University is providing new opportunities for secondary leavers, PhD holders, the self-employed, cabinet ministers, housewives, diplomats, the retired, soldiers, and the like, to see their future in a new light. Lifelong learning will also help to guarantee lifelong quality assurance in schools, courts of justice and administration, as men and women continually upgrade their knowledge, skills and worldviews.

The fourth category of opportunities is the flexibility in the style of teaching made possible with the Open University but also applicable at conventional universities. The use of new technologies makes it possible to reach greater number of students than was ever possible in the past. At the same time, practitioners of both old and new teaching technologies should be aware of the full range of possibilities so that experience can be made available for the benefit of students.

The fifth category of new opportunities lies in the financing of higher education. With possibilities for greater enrolments, unit costs can drop. With distinguished scholars reaching many more students, the quality of course content will improve considerably. The increasing interest of commercial companies in new applications of new technologies will bring down costs of equipment. And with new technologies which transcend geographical boundaries, it is possible to make access to higher education more equitable at a cheaper cost to national budgets. Tanzania already has concrete examples of students who have transferred from conventional institutions where fees were beyond their reach, and opted for similar courses offered by the Open University.

In conclusion, there is still a great deal to learn from the older distance teaching institutions and from the sometimes expensive technologies which they use. At the same time, it is hoped that the five-year experience of an open university in one of the poorest countries in the world will inspire those in similar circumstances and urge on those who have already started. Events move so quickly that a year from now there could be a new story to tell. For our part, we will carry on and use the best possible alternatives to help all those who have opted for distance learning to realise their goals.

References

Famighetti, R. (1997) *The World Almanac and Book of Facts*, Mahwah, NJ: World Almanac Books.

The following are all publications of the Open University of Tanzania:
   1994–1998 Admission Statistics, 1994–8 (unpublished).
   Open University of Tanzania Newsletter, nos 1–22. Quarterly since December 1992.
   Prospectus. Issued annually since 1994 academic year.
   A Report on the Activities of the Open University of Tanzania. Issued annually since 1993/4.
   Tutors' Handbook, 1993.

The following are all official United Republic of Tanzania publications:
   Act No. 17 An Act to establish the Open University of Tanzania and to provide for matters connected therewith or incidental thereto, 1992.

Budget Speech by the Minister of Education, 1990–91.

Budget Speech by the Minister of Education and Culture, 1991–92 to 1997–98.

Budget Speech by Minister of Science, Technology and Higher Education, 1991–92 to 1997–98.

Government Notice No. 55 The Open University Act (Commencement) Notice Act 1993.

Report of the Committee on the Establishment of an Open University in Tanzania, 1990.

Chapter 8

America

Until relatively recently, distance education in the Caribbean was commonly equated with the University of the West Indies Distance Teaching Experiment (UWIDITE), which has been known for many years for its use of teleconference technology for facilitiating contact between students and university tutors. Brandon's chapter describes recent developments in UWI and in other institutions which are developing their own distance-taught programmes.

Distance education in Latin America has a long history, as Chacón relates in his chapter, and continues to develop apace. Two open universities, Universidad Estatal a Distancia in Costa Rica and Universidad Nacional Abierta in Venezuela, were established twenty years ago at the time when single-mode institutions were mushrooming all over the world. Chacón documents other similar institutions in Latin America established more recently, but the trend towards dual-mode distance education is particularly strong.

Canada, as Shale describes, has a strong tradition of dual-mode distance education in universities as well as possessing the single-mode Athabasca University, the Open Learning Agency, which offers degree programmes in addition to programmes at other levels, and the francophone Télé-université, which is part of the Université du Québec system. The Canadian Association for Distance Education provides a national focus through its *Journal of Distance Education*, its Web site (http://www.cade-aced.ca) and its organisation of face-to-face and teleconferenced meetings and conferences.

Distance education in the United States is much more difficult to encapsulate because of its extensive and disparate nature. There is a parallel with Canadian distance education in that many conventional American universities offer distance-taught courses. In addition, a number of Canadian universities utilise the new information and communications technologies either alone or in partnership with other institutions. The United States experience is characterised by extensive usage of audio- and videoconferencing, cable and satellite television, and computer applications of many different kinds. Distance education is also employed by many different sectors, including public and private education at all levels, business and industry, and the military.

To complicate matters, the term 'distance education' is often employed and interpreted differently in the United States than in almost any other country. One of the major differences is that it is frequently used to describe the linking of several campuses of the same institution through technology in real time. Another term currently encountered in the American literature is 'distributed learning', which refers to learning via computer and telecommunications technologies both on- and off-campus.

The American Center for the Study of Distance Education provides a regular source of up-to-date American developments in its *American Journal of Distance Education*, and in its publications programme, which includes collections of papers presented at ACSDE conferences and workshops. Another extensive source of information on distance education in the United States and further afield is the Web site of the University of Wisconsin Extension, at http://www.uwex.edu/disted.index.html/.

The University of the West Indies

Ed Brandon

The University of the West Indies (UWI) was set up in 1948 to cater to the English-speaking Caribbean, initially as a college in relationship with the University of London, and located at Mona in Jamaica. It received its charter in 1962. In 1960, the Imperial College of Tropical Agriculture at St Augustine in Trinidad and Tobago was incorporated as a second campus, followed in 1963 by the establishment of a campus in Barbados, now at Cave Hill. In 1962, Guyana withdrew from full participation and set up its own university. Enrolment at UWI has risen from the initial thirty-three in 1948, to 1,268 in 1961, 10,026 in 1983, and 18,058 in 1996–7. Besides the three campus territories, the University serves and is funded by another twelve governments, the non-campus countries (NCCs).[1] In 1960–1, the present campus countries provided 66.5 per cent of total enrolment; by the time of the preparation of the University's first development plan in 1988–9 they provided 93.4 per cent. Regular outreach to the NCCs has been offered in various ways, first through extension services now run by its School of Continuing Studies (SCS) which has centres in most of them, then through a system of Challenge examinations in certain faculties which permitted candidates to sit first-year examinations in their home territory, having worked on their own with perhaps some assistance from the local centre, and most recently through teleconference-based distance education programmes. Teleconference sites now exist or are at an advanced planning stage in all the contributing countries and in the Turks and Caicos Islands. In Jamaica and Trinidad there are a number of sites in larger communities, while in Barbados and Trinidad the hospitals associated with the University's Faculty of Medical Sciences are also linked to the network.

The regional context

While exhibiting a variety of socio-cultural forms, the territories served by the UWI are all marked by their history of colonial dependency as slave plantation economies in the British Empire. Their populations are predominantly of African origin, with a group originating in the Indian subcontinent of equal size in Trinidad, and in smaller numbers in several other territories. Belize is exceptional in having a very complex mixture of peoples of different ethnic origins. Politically the territories have exhibited periodic social unrest, that in 1937–8 precipitating the post-Second World War moves towards internal self-government and full independence. Independence came after the failure of the federal attempt (1958–62) when Jamaica and then Trinidad and Tobago became fully autonomous, followed by most of the other territories during the 1970s. At the moment Anguilla, the British Virgin Islands, the Cayman Islands, Montserrat, and the Turks and Caicos Islands remain British dependencies. After Federation, its members set up a loose association (the Caribbean Free Trade Association, CARIFTA, in 1968, becoming the Caribbean Community, CARICOM, in 1973) which permits regionwide consultation and planning, though without any power to enforce its decisions. More recently a wider political grouping, including the Spanish- and French-speaking territories of the Caribbean, has been formed, the Association of Caribbean States (ACS). A political association which includes a shared central bank has been created among the smaller islands of the Eastern Caribbean, the Organisation of Eastern Caribbean States (OECS).

Economically, the countries of the region have been moving away from traditional sugar and banana production to embrace tourism in virtually all cases, financial services (notably Cayman and Anguilla), oil (Trinidad), and bauxite (Jamaica) as sources of revenue. They remain undeveloped in industrial and technological terms, are all very small in international terms (only Jamaica has a population in excess of 2 million; most are below 150 thousand), and most are vulnerable to occasionally devastating hurricanes. Currently, Montserrat is barely surviving a series of volcanic eruptions. Table 8–1.1 gives estimates of some basic statistics for the countries concerned, grouping them as campus countries, OECS, and North-Western Caribbean.

The educational systems of the various territories have been modelled on that of the sometime mother country. They have until recently and in some cases still reflect a duality typical of the nineteenth and early twentieth century: primary education for the masses; secondary for a small elite. All-age schools remain a prominent feature in Jamaica, though much is being done to provide adequate secondary education for a wider proportion of the population. All countries have increased secondary provision, though most of them retain an eleven-plus examination to channel students into secondary schools of varying prestige and capacity. Performance in external examinations is generally disappointing (Cox 1991; Whiteley 1993). Table 8–1.2 reports enrolment rates for the different levels of the system for selected countries, from which one can see the disquieting discrepancy between high rates for primary and secondary schooling coupled with internationally aberrant low rates for tertiary participation.

What is now thought of as post-secondary provision was dominated by

Table 8–1.1 Statistics on UWI's contributing countries

		Area in km²	Population 1995 (1,000s)	GDP per capita 1995	% of population	% of graduates	% of certificate holders
Campus	Barbados	432	264.4	7,015	5.16	11.17	10.64
	Jamaica	11,424	2,486.5	2,092	48.52	47.24	52.05
	Trinidad	5,128	1,261.9	4,101	24.62	32.56	22.43
OECS	Anguilla	91	10.6	5,762	0.21	0.08	0.1
	Antigua	440	64.3	7,690	1.25	0.94	1.48
	BVI	150	18.3	18,497	0.36	0.14	0.18
	Dominica	750	74.2	2,901	1.45	0.82	2.44
	Grenada	345	97.4	2,721	1.90	1.17	1.75
	Montserrat[a]	102	10.4	5,846	0.20	0.38	0.38
	St Kitts	269	42.8	5,331	0.84	0.92	0.72
	St Lucia	616	145.3	3,832	2.84	1.64	2.42
	St Vincent	388	109.9	2,517	2.14	0.98	2.15
N-W	Bahamas	13,942	275.0	12,436	5.37	1.11	1.28
	Belize	22,960	216.5	2,696	4.22	0.73	1.75
	Cayman[a]	264	32.8	27,835	0.64	0.04	0.06
	Turks	417	14.8	6,923	0.29	0.07	0.16
Grand total		57,718	5,125.1				

Source: UWI statistics; Caribbean Development Bank Annual Report 1996.

Note
a   1994 figures.

teachers' colleges, traditionally the poor man's secondary school, but it now includes a burgeoning technical and business-oriented sector, increasingly focused on national community colleges. Some continuing education and professional training has been available through local government training facilities, the faculties of the UWI, the SCS and specific donor-funded projects, some of which were organised for the NCCs by the Office of University Services. For the academic elite there is the UWI, but for the more prosperous or for scholarship holders there are willing takers in North America. Figures for 1995–6 indicate that 3,357 Jamaicans, 2,223 Trinidadians and 2,060 Bahamians were studying in the US alone (though these figures may include the children of first generation immigrants).[2]

The past decade has seen the consolidation of the Caribbean Examinations Council's (CXC) replacement for GCE O level; plans are afoot for a CXC alternative to A level. The period has also seen considerable expansion of post-secondary provision, both public and, particularly in Jamaica and Trinidad, private. There has also been increasing penetration of the region by North American and UK institutions offering forms of distance education or sponsorship.

Table 8–1.2 Enrolment ratios for selected countries

Country	Year	Sex	Primary	Secondary	Tertiary
Bahamas	1994	MF	94	90	n/a
		M	95	88	n/a
		F	94	91	n/a
Barbados[a]	1994	MF	95	85	28.1
		M	95	90	13.6
		F	95	80	33.9
Belize	1994	MF	121	49	n/a
		M	124	47	n/a
		F	118	52	n/a
Jamaica	1995	MF	109	66	6.0
		M	110	62	6.8
		F	109	70	5.2
Trinidad	1995	MF	96	72	7.7
		M	91	66	8.4
		F	102	79	6.8

Source: Data are from UNESCO *Statistical Yearbook* 1997 and *World Education Report* 1998. UNESCO gives data only for countries with more than 150,000 population.

Notes
a   Barbados school figures are for 1989.

The University of the West Indies

For the earlier part of its history, the UWI was almost the only post-secondary institution that concerned the governments of the region. It eclipsed the several teachers' colleges, and the scattered tertiary provision for agriculture, nursing, and the arts that existed. Polytechnic institutions were created in the campus countries, that in Jamaica having recently been given university status (the University of Technology). In several countries, minuscule sixth-forms have been rationalised through a community college. Typically these have expanded to incorporate teacher and other training and are now often offering or planning to offer associate degrees, reflecting the growing tendency for North American models to encroach on traditional British structures.

In this context, CARICOM governments continue to express allegiance to the one regional university, and have made serious efforts to liquidate long-standing indebtedness to it, but there are considerable pressures to pay more attention in practice to their national institutions. These pressures have a large financial component: the UWI is extremely expensive, its costs being equal to or higher than those typical of first-world universities, while the cost of local institutions reflects a generally impoverished public sector. A World Bank study (1993) reported that in the late 1980s each student at Mona cost the Jamaican government US $5,138, while each student in the local tertiary sector cost it $639 (and at a secondary school $257). These discrepancies are not quite so marked for the other governments, but for all of them there is a significant difference between UWI costs and those of local institutions. The University is also popularly seen as exclusive, uncooperative and often too academic. It is widely supposed that local institutions will be more responsive to the demands of those making these criticisms, which have led also to two extensive restructurings of the University itself (1984, 1996), both of which increased national control over each campus.

CARICOM does not yet have a comprehensive plan for tertiary education in the region, though its recent pronouncement on human resource development envisages a significant increase in tertiary enrolments and preserves a key role for the UWI, working particularly through distance education. The OECS is working towards a rationalised system for its constituency within a European Union-funded project; this will attempt to avoid the duplication of capacity in each territory, though the history of the UWI's similar efforts demonstrates how difficult it is to deal even-handedly with students who need to travel and those who can remain in their home country, if not physically at home. Only its law faculty, where enrolment is controlled by a quota system related to the number of places in the professional schools and where demand far outstrips supply, has been able to graduate students from all contributing territories in rough proportion to those territories' populations.

Individual governments have various policies and priorities for higher education. The campus governments sponsor all their nationals who are accepted by the UWI – this means contributing 80 per cent of the economic cost of each student (100 per cent for Barbadians). Most NCCs, on the other hand, severely restrict sponsorship, setting priorities in terms of subject studied as well as numbers of students. Where national colleges have been franchised to teach part of the UWI programme, as in Antigua and St Lucia, there is a commitment to continue sponsorship for all those students moving on to a campus to complete a degree.

Within post-secondary education and training, open access has been very rare, except to some extent in teacher training. Here qualifications have indeed been required for entry, but they have been fairly minimal and attempts to make them more stringent, as in Jamaica in the early 1980s, have often been conjoined with prolonged remediation and compromised standards (Nissen 1996). The UWI has not taken kindly to demands for normal entry requirements to be waived, and does not make special provision to support learners who are without the skills it routinely expects of its normally matriculated intake. Its normal matriculation (two passes at A level plus three O levels or CXCs including English Language) is not high by the standards of its would-be reference group, but with chronically weak secondary school systems few of the contributing countries are producing an abundance of entrants of this type.

Distance education

Distance education has fared better. While people have been taking correspondence courses for decades, the regional use of distance education
methods is due to the UWI. The UWI Distance Teaching Experiment
(UWIDITE) began regular programmes in 1983–4, after some years of feasibility studies. UWIDITE provided a telephone-based system, including tel-
ewriters and slow-scan televisions, which permitted courses and programmes
to be taught by a combination of print material and teleconferences, with
very occasional supplements in the form of video or audio tapes, and some
local support by way of tutorials or practical supervision. Initially the
system linked the three campuses to two NCCs (Dominica, St Lucia), but
other sites were added so that by 1993 eleven NCCs were being served, as
well as several non-campus sites in Jamaica and Trinidad and Tobago (for the
history of UWIDITE, see Lalor and Marrett 1986, 1994). At that point a
loan project, funded by the Caribbean Development Bank (CDB), helped
to sustain efforts to substantially upgrade and reorient the nature of UWI's
distance education. From a budget of US $0.94 million in 1993–4, the
University itself is now allocating US $4 million in 1998/9 explicitly to dis-
tance education. The loan had been triggered by the University's momentous
but ill-publicised decision of 1992 to become a dual-mode institution,
a decision informed by and endorsing the general recommendations of a
report prepared by Renwick *et al.* in 1992. The intended quantum leap for
distance education preserved the teleconferencing skeleton, and indeed is
upgrading it to handle videoconferencing, but saw also the need to shift the
delivery of courses away from the telelecturing typical of UWIDITE
towards self-instructional print materials with occasional local tutorial
support (for more details of the reorientation of distance education at UWI,
see Brandon 1996).

In its first phase, UWIDITE offered certificate programmes in education
and social sciences, as well as a variety of non-credit courses and programmes. The post-CDB loan phase has involved the first undergraduate
degree programme (in management studies, the most highly subscribed
option in the University) and will soon include a BEd. in educational
administration, as well as postgraduate work in engineering management,
continuing medical education and contributions to the 'foundation course'
components of all undergraduate degrees. Independently of the units directly responsible for distance education, but utilising the same teleconferencing facility, and generously funded by the British Development Division,
the then Faculty of Agriculture embarked in 1994 upon a masters programme in agriculture and rural development, using material from Wye
College which it has revised for local conditions. Plans for a set of innovative
bilingual taught masters degrees to be offered in conjunction with institutions in the Dominican Republic and funded by the European Union under

Lomé IV also include a significant Internet element, a portent of things to come in other areas of the UWI's distance education activity. These assorted offerings reflect a compromise between what the University believes to be in demand (it has undertaken a demand survey and many consultations at different times) and what faculties can be persuaded to work on, influenced in several cases by the availability of donor funds.

With UWIDITE as inspiration, governments have seen the potentialities of using distance education in other ways, particularly in the area of teacher training. Distance education for practising teachers has played a large role in the extensive Reform of Secondary Education project (ROSE) in Jamaica; it was also intended to contribute to efforts to upgrade teachers in the OECS; it is mooted by the Trinidad and Tobago government in its plans for teacher training as well as for skills training for adolescents and continuing medical education. Others too have realised its benefits. After many years running a small regional project to train community and youth workers, the Commonwealth Youth Programme's office in Guyana converted it to a distance modality and saw a dramatic increase in trainees.

Management and structure

UWIDITE began at Mona, the brainchild of Professor Lalor, then the Pro-Vice Chancellor for Science and Technology. It was initially funded by USAID, later becoming a charge to what is known as the University Centre, that part of the University directly responsible to the Vice Chancellor, rather than to one of the three campus principals. UWIDITE's activity required assistance from the faculties, but it was not integrated into their regular concerns (for instance, teaching time was not allowed to count in establishing work loads, students were not counted in calculating staff : student ratios; participating staff received a small honorarium). With the CDB Loan Project and the formal adoption of dual mode, a Board for Distance Education was created; it oversaw the development of a Distance Education Centre (DEC), with a presence on all three campuses, but it was not able, despite the dual-mode decision, to have distance education planning properly incorporated into normal campus considerations. An ostensibly faculty-driven model finds the faculties being cajoled into action by the DEC and the top management of the University. There remains great reluctance to see work in distance education as simply part of one's normal duties; little budgetary provision is made for it outside the University Centre, and where it has been made it is conveniently forgotten when pleading lack of resources to undertake any off-campus activity. The campus administrations show little interest in processing distance education students, although the dual-mode decision clearly made these campus responsibilities instead of creating a fourth campus structure to administer distance education programmes.

The UWI was restructured once again in 1996, central academic control being devolved in part to the campuses and in part to three functionally differentiated Boards, one of which is specifically concerned with the promotion of outreach and distance education, and advertises the University's commitment to the NCCs in its very title, the Board for Non-Campus Countries and Distance Education. This Board directs the work of three units devoted to outreach: the Distance Education Centre, the School of Continuing Studies and the Tertiary Level Institutions' Unit (TLIU). It provides a forum where coordination of the other outreach undertaken directly by the faculties can be sought, and it also gives a prominent place to agencies external to the University, in particular NCC governments and representatives of the Association of Caribbean Tertiary Institutions, an organisation established to give coherence and a voice to the growing population of local tertiary institutions. While on the one hand giving outreach and distance education their most prominent formal position to date in the University's structure, this Board lacks anything beyond moral suasion to carry through its recommendations, so that implementation of present programmes and planned expansion has to struggle with the pressing demands of campus-oriented faculties and administrations.

Funding for distance education in the UWI has remained largely a centre matter. Unlike on-campus students, who are charged to their respective sponsoring governments and pay a tuition fee as well, distance education students simply pay a fee per course (1997–8 US $176), calculated on the same basis as the on-campus students' fee. The remaining costs of distance education (the approximately 80 per cent not covered by the fee) are allocated to the Centre, whose total costs are apportioned to on-campus students.

The certificate programmes which have so far been the only regular offering have been predominantly a female affair. The Caribbean has for long been in the lead as far as the feminisation of education goes, with Jamaica one of the regional leaders (Standing 1981, ch. 4; Mohammed 1982; Jules 1991; Jules and Kutnick 1991; Miller 1996); the UWI's enrolment has shown a female majority since 1982–3 (Hamilton and Leo-Rhynie 1996). While there are no official statistics, these programmes recruit teachers some way into their career and lower to middle ranking personnel in the public and private sectors. As usual in distance education, drop-out rates are higher than on-campus, though again there are no recent statistics to be found. Pass rates and throughput for completing students in the education certificates are comparable to on-campus rates and are high; in the social science programmes they are considerably lower, an effect in large part of the required courses in mathematics and elementary statistics when entry to the programme itself does not require any pass in mathematics.

The non-campus countries

Despite long periods of deficit financing because of arrears in subventions, the three campuses of UWI are well entrenched in their respective nations. Enrolments have risen almost every year. There has been little money for capital development from the governments and there have been periods of decline relative to the international market-place, but planned growth seems assured, with the partial exception of the Cave Hill campus in Barbados which is approaching saturation of its presently defined clientele – a situation which does not incline its top officials to view the increasing activity of NCC colleges or the expansion of distance education in a very positive light.

From Table 8–1.1 it can also be seen that two of the campuses have provided their home country with a disproportionate benefit in terms of numbers of graduates. A comparison of the proportion of the population of the UWI's constituency residing in each country with the proportion of undergraduate degree and certificate holders (of whom there are many more degree holders) gives a rough indication of the extent to which Barbados and Trinidad and Tobago have in a way got more than their fair share out of the University's presence. In this they are joined by two NCCs, Montserrat and St Kitts and Nevis. Jamaica, despite having had a campus from the very beginning, has derived what in these terms is simply its fair share of undergraduates. But the other contributing countries have not seen comparable benefits.

The lack of representation of the NCCs in the life of the University has long been a concern and a source of contention. As the table indicates, it has as at least two features: a comparatively mild underrepresentation in the case of the Eastern Caribbean, and a very serious one in the case of the North-Western Caribbean. During the restructuring of the mid-1980s, which revised the formula for the payment of costs by the governments, the NCCs demanded a mark of their importance in the creation of a pro-Vice Chancellor with special responsibilities for their territories. The new post (in an Office of University Services) was given responsibility for the OECS.

The latest 1996 restructuring has attempted to deal more even-handedly with all the NCCs. The unit that in effect succeeded to the Office of University Services, the Tertiary Level Institutions Unit (TLIU) has both a more precisely defined mandate (to promote articulation with and the development of the national tertiary colleges) and staff to cater for all the NCCs. In its first year, it in fact worked as much on articulation arrangements in the Cayman Islands and the Bahamas as in the OECS. The north-western countries have also benefited from the CDB Loan Project, so that they will soon have teleconferencing resources on par with the rest, although the SCS remains without a formal presence in the Cayman Islands and Turks and Caicos. To date, the lack of telecommunication facilities or the inadequate quality of what there was has meant that the north-western countries have not participated as fully as the rest in distance education programmes.

These programmes have always been promoted as an effective means of providing services to the NCCs. Jennings (forthcoming) has noted that, in its first two cycles, the UWIDITE Certificate in Education trained as many teachers from Dominica as had been trained in the entire history of the on-campus programme to that point. The figures in Table 8–1.1 indicate more generally the impact that the various certificate programmes have had upon the NCCs; it can be seen that the proportions of certificates (mostly obtained through distance programmes) markedly exceeds that of degrees in most NCCs.

In addition to much expanded distance education provision, the University's present Strategic Plan envisages a complementary approach to greater NCC participation: the development of the types of franchising and articulation arrangements with the national colleges that have been alluded to above. Although the Distance Education Centre and the Tertiary Level Institutions Unit come under the same Board, the question of how to make their activities complementary rather than competitive has to be addressed as one aspect of a general dialectic between centralised University control and dispersed local empowerment. This was played out in the Challenge scheme, where some had hoped to catalyse the development of local resources, either through the School of Continuing Studies or through the local colleges, but where the opportunity provided by the expanding tele-conferencing technology permitted campus lecturers to take over a considerable amount of the teaching that was being provided *ad hoc* in each country. It must be added, in all fairness, that this campus intrusion was generally welcomed by the students, for whom it represented a seal of approval sometimes thought lacking in the local providers.

While there is a genuine issue of relative autonomy here, there is also an important resource question. The building up of local capacity, in the UWI as well as in the national colleges, has generally tended to involve very considerable reduplication (not to mention a lack of critical mass in many areas at the University). The miniscule size and extensive dispersion of the islands entail that costs of study away from one's home country are particularly high, so that there is strong pressure towards such a multiplication of capacities beyond pedagogical necessity. There is also the real danger of permanent or at least extended brain drain once a student goes abroad. In this context, it is noteworthy that planning for distance education work has so far not been coordinated with long-term planning for the development of the national colleges. The region's lack of comprehensive planning capacity, typical of small states' (cf. Bray 1991), and the University's unwillingness to take a lead, for fear, among other things, of being seen to dictate, has resulted so far in University commitments to work in distance education in areas where the colleges might be considered fairly strong, and could certainly be easily strengthened, but with no formal collaboration even in those areas. Plans are now being made to try to use distance education, including the newly emerging Internet and the expected videoconferencing capacity, to permit intercampus sharing of special expertise.

While it shares with the West Indies cricket team the aura of Federation's attempt to set regional commitment above local identification, the University itself finds it difficult to sustain the broader vision when so much of its life is firmly campus-centred. Most members of staff at one campus see no more of the other campuses than they do of any other campus in the world. The vast majority of students at each campus are nationals of the campus country – even at Cave Hill, specifically designed with the OECS in mind, NCC students represent only about 11 per cent of the undergraduate student body in 1997–8. The latest restructuring has given formal endorsement to what was an ever-increasing campus autonomy with respect to courses and programmes.

It is in general easier to separate and find reasons to separate than to join together. It is certainly difficult to envisage what a united Jamaica and Cayman would have been like, knowing their present situations thirty-nine years since their formal divorce. With Nevis seemingly on the verge of independence, with Cayman and Anguilla deliberately pursuing over-employment in order to discourage immigration, it is difficult to believe we will soon have a regionwide majority favouring greater integration in any enforceable sense. Yet the cosmopolitan vision is shared by many – at the moment one UWI graduate prime minister is inviting another to take Barbados into the OECS – and who knows what *la longue durée* will bring? It is unlikely to give the NCCs a significantly larger or smaller proportion of the constituency (assuming the present contributors remain unchanged), but there is scope for it to bring their distinctiveness more clearly into the general consciousness, to give them a larger proportion of alumni, and to provide their professionals with access to continuing education and networking within the wider region. At this juncture, distance education seems as potent as any other factor to move us in these directions.

Notes

1 They are: Anguilla, Antigua and Barbuda, the Bahamas, Belize, the British Virgin Islands, the Cayman Islands, Dominica, Grenada, Montserrat, St Kitts and Nevis, St Lucia, and St Vincent and the Grenadines. The Turks and Caicos Islands are not technically a contributing country but they are usually included among the NCCs. The School of Continuing Studies does not yet have a centre in the Turks and Caicos Islands; a teleconferencing facility for distance education is being constructed there.

2 The figures were given in the Chronicle of Higher Education, 17 December 1997. Emigration has resulted in a Caribbean diaspora in the US, Canada, and the UK roughly equal in size to the population in the Caribbean; it is highly significant as a source of remittances and as a reference group for those in the Caribbean.

References

Brandon, E.P. (1996) 'Distance education in the restructured UWI: policy and problems', *Caribbean Curriculum*, 6, 2, 35–53.

Bray, M. (1991) *Making Small Practical: The Organisation and Management of Ministries of Education in Small States*, London: Commonwealth Secretariat.

Cox, D. (1991) 'Patterns and trends in the 16+ year English Language examination results in seven CARICOM territories, 1960–1989', in E.P. Brandon and P.N. Nissen (comps.), *Proceedings of the 1990 Cross-Campus Conference on Education*, Mona, Jamaica: Faculty of Education, UWI.

Hamilton, M. and Leo-Rhynie, E. (1996) 'Women in higher education: a Caribbean perspective', in D. Craig (ed.), *Education in the West Indies: Developments and Perspectives, 1948–1988*, Mona, Jamaica: ISER.

Jennings, Z. (forthcoming) 'Distance education at universities in the Commonwealth Caribbean', draft chapter of a forthcoming book.

Jules, V. (1991) 'Continuity and discontinuity of secondary schooling and equality of opportunity to survive to the fifth form in Trinidad and Tobago', in E.P. Brandon and P.N. Nissen (comps.), *Proceedings of the 1990 Cross-Campus Conference on Education*, Mona, Jamaica: Faculty of Education, UWI.

Jules, V. and Kutnick, P. (1991) 'Determinants of academic success within classrooms in Trinidad and Tobago: some personal and systemic variables', in E.P. Brandon and P.N. Nissen (comps.), *Proceedings of the 1990 Cross-Campus Conference on Education*, Mona, Jamaica: Faculty of Education, UWI.

Lalor, G.C. and Marrett, C. (1986) *Report on the University of the West Indies Distance Teaching Experiment*, Mona, Jamaica: UWI.

Lalor, G. and Marrett, C. (1994), *UWIDITE Report 1986–1993*, Mona, Jamaica: UWI.

Miller, E. (1996) 'Illiteracy, gender and high schooling in Jamaica', in D. Craig (ed.), *Education in the West Indies: Developments and Perspectives, 1948–1988*, Mona, Jamaica: ISER.

Mohammed, P. (1982) 'Educational attainment of women in Trinidad and Tobago, 1946–1980', in J. Massiah (ed.), *Women and Education* (Women in the Caribbean Project Volume 5), Cave Hill, Barbados: ISER.

Nissen, P. (1996) 'Mathematics education in teacher training colleges of Jamaica: the emergence of a new philosophy', in D. Craig (ed.), *Education in the West Indies: Developments and Perspectives, 1948–1988*, Mona, Jamaica: ISER.

Renwick, W., Shale, D. and Rao, C. (1992) *Distance Education at the University of the West Indies*, Vancouver: Commonwealth of Learning.

Standing, G. (1981) *Unemployment and Female Labour: A Study of Labour Supply in Kingston, Jamaica*, London: Macmillan.

Whiteley, P. (1993) 'Science examinations' results in Barbados, Jamaica and Trinidad and Tobago, 1982–1991', *Caribbean Curriculum*, 3, 2, 13–33.

World Bank (1993) *Caribbean Region: Access, Quality, and Efficiency in Education*. Washington, DC: World Bank.

Distance education in Latin America: growth and maturity

Fabio Chacón

The aim of this chapter is to show how the Latin American countries have addressed their educational needs through the delivery of distance education programmes, using a variety of approaches and technologies. It also presents a current view of this discipline in the region, addressing the question of whether or not the institutions and practitioners are ready for the adoption of new information and communication technologies, as the twenty-first century approaches.

Distance education has been assimilated in to the contemporary life of Latin American countries as a major innovation expected to contribute to filling the gap between the increasing learning needs of the adult population, and the inadequate provision from the traditional education systems. Increasing educational coverage and educational equity are primary and permanent goals of distance education programmes in the region. Another important goal is to improve quality of education through innovative technologies and methods. The chapter discusses here the extent to which it can be claimed that these goals are fulfilled.

As any social process exists within a context, this particular chapter deals also with the related theme of the professional associations dedicated to distance education in Latin America, the staff development programmes for this sector, and the organisations dedicated to promoting international cooperation in the field. All these aspects form part of an interesting scenario characterised by growth and maturity.

Historic view

Looking back over sixty years, it is clear that distance education in Latin America has evolved in relation to technology shifts; programmes have changed in accordance with developments in communication technology. To some degree, changes have also been influenced by variations in clientele of programmes. However, these changes are not clear-cut, because the old technologies do not completely disappear when a new technology becomes dominant; in fact, some of the less technically advanced programmes continue to benefit their audiences. Chacón and Gonzalez (1997) have identified four main stages in the evolution of distance education provision in Latin America, following criteria of type of technology and of clientele. These stages are briefly described below, using some arbitrary milestones to divide the periods.

Early stage: adult basic education (1946–66)

The initial Latin American movements which constituted early forms of distance education were based on correspondence and radio education. In 1946, the Sutatenza Radio Schools were created in Colombia by Acción Comunitaria Popular, an extension of the Catholic Church. Similar programmes emerged in a short span of time which were aimed principally at improving schooling and life adaptation skills of underprivileged populations, both in the rural areas and in the poor sections of large cities. The main content areas were literacy, numeracy, hygiene, citizenship, agriculture and crafts. Such programmes existed in almost all countries of the region, although they were particularly prominent in Colombia, Mexico, Argentina, Brazil, Guatemala and Costa Rica. The main supporting agencies were governments and the Catholic Church. In the late 1950s, several American and Canadian correspondence schools, including Hemphill Schools and Continental Schools, established branches in Latin America offering courses in Spanish.

The tele-education era (1967–76)

This period is characterised by the pre-eminence of television as a mass education medium; film and radio also occupied important roles. By 1967, the Organisation of American States (OAS) had funded a number of courses designed to disseminate information on educational technology in the region. During this time, there were major exchanges between universities and production centres in Latin America and in North America and Europe with scores of professionals and technicians being trained in skills associated with the design, production and delivery of instruction through audio-visual media. Many television facilities were created in universities, ministries of education and religious organisations. There were serious attempts to establish continental tele-education programmes such as Proyecto Satélite Andrés Bello, by UNESCO, and Proyecto SERLA, by the Organisation of American States, which did not reach the implementation stage because of political differences among the countries. At the end of the 1970s, the initial impetus of the tele-education movement was past but residual benefits included a number of well-trained staff in different areas of educational technology who transferred their knowledge to new generations. In addition, a significant volume of infrastructure was built which is still being used for educational purposes. Finally, several mass education programmes have survived and improved through the years. These include Telesecundaria in Mexico, a television-based schooling programme through which adults may gain a High School certificate, and which supplements the formal education system. These developments were all instrumental in the initiation of the third stage described below.

Modular distance education (1977–89)

The leading event during this period was the creation and further consolidation of open universities and open external programmes attached to traditional universities. Two of the largest Latin American distance universities were created in 1977: the Universidad Nacional Abierta (UNA) in Venezuela and the Universidad Estatal de Educación a Distancia (UNED) in Costa Rica. Similar institutions appeared in many other countries during the 1980s. These programmes were modelled after the successful United Kingdom Open University and other European initiatives which had the main purpose of delivering college-level courses at a distance and later continuing education and postgraduate education. Chacón (1990) has identified several common characteristics.

First, open universities were created to respond to strong demands for higher education which in Latin America were centred on the extraordinary growth of the younger population relating to economics and migration. Second, they responded to the re-entry of many adults into the formal education system for the purpose of improving their skills and qualifications in a more competitive society. Third, these programmes share a model of distance education based on multimedia packages or modules, combining print, tutorials, audio and video recordings, experimental activities, and other media towards the achievement of predetermined learning purposes. Universities dedicated solely to distance education exist in Costa Rica, Colombia, Mexico, Venezuela and Chile;[1] on the other hand, mixed mode instruction, which combines traditional and distance courses, is commonplace in most countries of the region. Many other programmes in vocational and continuing education were created under the influence of this model. Some of the largest distance education programmes are dedicated to training teachers, since many teachers in Latin America lack adequate preparation and formal credentials. Distance education is therefore one major strategy used by governments for improving the quality of the general education system. The multimedia model, however, has not been completely successful partly due to the high incidence of student drop-out and partly due to the difficulty of continuously updating courses to maintain high standards of quality.

The emerging open interactive learning systems (1990–future)

Currently, digital information and communication technologies are being slowly introduced and tried out in distance education programmes. It could be argued that this does not represent a stage at all because only a few institutions have tested the new technologies so far. However, this is the way in which previous stages began; some advanced programmes adopted a technology, demonstrated it to others, and triggered emulations both nationally and internationally. The starting point of this new period is symbolically placed in 1990, the year in which the fifteenth World Conference of the International Council for Distance Education was held in Caracas (Villarroel 1991), attracting over 1,200 delegates. This major event enabled demonstration and discussion of the applications of the new information and communication technologies before many educational leaders and practitioners of the region. For many people, this was their first experience of the new technologies because there had been no previous conferences of ICDE in Latin America.

The current scene

Distance education has been adopted in almost all Latin American countries. Those in which it has achieved the largest coverage in terms of students and programmes areas are Argentina, Brazil, Colombia, Costa Rica, Mexico and Venezuela. Table 8–2.1 presents raw data about distance education programmes in these countries drawn from direct observations and interviews with distance educators of these countries.[2] They have a more indicative than statistical value. It must be mentioned that Bolivia, Chile, Cuba, Ecuador, Peru and Guatemala have also important distance education programmes whose population ranges from a few hundred to two or three thousand.

Two important factors may produce rapid changes in the next few years. First, there are some new programmes for the systematic development of distance education staff, which employ new technologies. Universities in the region run these programmes, which began in 1994 and continue to appear each year. At the time of writing, around ten specialised Diploma or Master's programmes aim to develop distance educators who are familiar with informatics and telematics. Sometimes they are delivered within a single country, but increasingly they are looking for an international audience. Such kinds of programmes exist in Argentina, Brazil, Costa Rica, Chile, Colombia, Mexico and Venezuela.[3] The second factor is significant investment in technological change by public and private education institutions, due to policies of innovation triggered by external changes. The awareness of globalisation, entry into the information society, and the demonstration effect of educational systems in the developed countries play an important part.

Table 8–2.1 Descriptive data of distance education programmes in Latin America

Country	Number of DE institutions	Number of DE associations	Estimated DE/student population	Programmes using ICT	Stated educational mission of programmes
Mexico	51	1	500.000 90 million	15	Undergraduate, graduate, vocational, continuing, secondary, basic
Costa Rica	2	–	15.000 4 million	1	Undergraduate, graduate, continuing, secondary
Colombia	37	1	150.000 34 million	4	Undergraduate, graduate, vocational, military, secondary, basic
Venezuela	5	1	100.000 20 million	4	Undergraduate, graduate, vocational, continuing, basic
Brazil	85	3	350.000 160 million	12	Undergraduate, graduate, vocational, continuing secondary
Argentina	23	2	200.000 33 million	6	Undergraduate, graduate, continuing, secondary

Following these policies, the national governments of Brazil, Chile, Colombia, Costa Rica and Mexico, for instance, have made large investments in computers and networks for schools, and it is expected that other countries will follow. Intensive training programmes accompany the deployment of these new systems for teachers, which in turn creates more demand for graduate-level education. Some private institutions also use information and communication technologies. The Instituto Tecnológico de Educación Superior de Monterrey (ITESM), Mexico, for example, has enabled its twenty-six campuses to interact via top-of-the-range satellite and audio tele-conferencing facilities, computer communications and distributed facsimile. The ITESM has fully developed the virtual university concept (Instituto Tecnológico de Educación Superior de Monterrey, 1996), and is currently offering graduate, undergraduate and continuing education to several countries in the region. The main curriculum areas are education, administration and systems engineering. The influence of this institution has extended even to the Spanish-speaking population of the United States and Canada.

All these are clear signs that a new trend is being established in Latin American distance education. Chacón (1997) calls it the informatic-telematic paradigm while Silvio Pomenta (1998) speaks of the virtualisation of education, giving the following definition: 'virtualisation comprises the representation of processes and objects associated to teaching and learning, research and management; it also involves manipulation of these objects by users, and performing some activities on the Internet, such as registering for electronic courses, learning by interaction with them, browsing documents in an electronic library, communicating with students and professors, and some others'. It is anticipated that, in the course of a decade, most distance education institutions in the region will accommodate to this new paradigm.

Cooperative distance learning in schools

Programmes describing themselves as offering 'distance' or 'open' education operate alongside others in institutions which do not employ those terms, but use distributed environments or virtual spaces for the purpose of collaborative learning. In this way, they also participate in the newest forms of distance education; learning may take place within the premises of an institution or in an informal setting such as a home or a café. An example of this type of semi-formalised collaborative learning, designed and carried out in Latin America, is the Quorum Project, which originated in the pioneering work of researchers in the Public School System of Costa Rica (Centra Latinoamericano de Investigación en Educación, 1996). Their experience was transformed into a large international project, with support of IBM, West Florida University and a number of public and private schools in ten Latin American countries.

Defining the new educational paradigm

The introduction of new information and communication technologies into both distance education and traditional education has generated a wave of change that transcends the mere fact of possessing new machines; it has been termed a new educational paradigm. This means that the basic relationships among the actors in the teaching and learning process are changed. Some of the most distinctive features of this new paradigm are discussed below in order to analyse how they affect distance education in Latin America.

New methods

The new information and communication technologies have impacted particularly significantly in enabling the development of new means of teaching at a distance. The most frequently used means are: enriched modular packages, teleconferencing, individual multimedia and on-line education.

Enriched modular packages

The enriched modular package comprises a combination of the old approach of text-based distance education with access to remote databases, advisory services through e-mail or electronic lists, Web pages with recent information and other resources which complement the modular packages and enable students to communicate more intensively. This approach is used by UNED in Costa Rica and by SUA of the Autonomous University of Mexico. Each course in the curriculum has a computer databank of readings, supporting materials for assignments, and administrative information. Both systems include also access to an electronic library system.

Teleconferencing

Teleconferencing involves the delivery of expert lectures through audio or video communication devices, with the possibility of interaction for students. Many teleconferences are carried out using multimedia computers, to reduce costs by digitising audio and video, and then using the Internet as carrier. The teleconferencing approach is used as a leading medium in the Virtual University of ITESM and in Universidad del Valle in Cali, Colombia; each course has a professor in charge for the whole university and a site coordinator for each campus. The professor in charge interacts with all the student groups via teleconferencing; meanwhile, the site coordinators provide direct support to students, organise practical activities and coordinate discussions at the site level.

Individual multimedia

Individual multimedia refers to the already commonly used educational CD-ROM, loaded with information in the form of text, image, sound, video and programs which can be manipulated in many ways by the user. Educators can design many approaches and techniques to facilitate learning by means of CD-ROM resources: for example, tutorial, simulation, gaming, research, a dialogue. No distance education programme in the region yet delivers instruction entirely on the basis of CD-ROMs, although the University of Colima in Mexico has produced educational and research databanks on CD-ROM which are used in a variety of courses, both traditional and distance. Some of the discs are simply collections of text materials; others are complex databases which are used for research and problem-solving. The Master's Programme in Educational Technology of the Instituto Latino-americano para las Comunicaciones Educativas (ILCE), also in Mexico, has transferred all its textbook materials and course guidelines to a CD-ROM, in a joint project with the University of Colima.

On-line education

On-line education is teaching entirely delivered by means of computer net-working in Local Area Networks or Wide Area Networks, such as the Inter-net. The techniques of on-line education in many ways resemble those of group teaching, for example, employing briefings, discussions, forums, inter-views with experts, project teams and debates (Paulsen 1995). Web-based instruction is also a core component of the Virtual University of ITESM. In addition, on-line education supported by e-mail has been used in the Uni-versity Network Reacciun, in Venezuela for delivering courses on artificial intelligence, virtual reality and other current themes in the area of infor-matics. The approach has been to use a flexible discussion schema or sylla-bus, previously distributed by e-mail, through a number of weeks; each theme is presented in a motivating 'lesson' of a 'speaker' and the interaction is coordinated by course leaders. One interesting aspect of this experience is that each course involves participation of a learning community, including faculty, students, researchers, industry developers and final users.

New principles

The introduction of new technologies has brought about change not only in methods but also in a number of educational principles:

Interactivity

This characteristic relates to person–computer and person–person inter-action, both of which may be enhanced by information and communication technologies. Interaction occurs in tutorial programmes recorded on CD-ROM, simulations, computer-assisted collaborative learning, e-mail exchanges, teleconferencing and many other techniques made available through the new breed of media. Many studies demonstrate that interactive learning is more effective than rote or absorption learning.

Process-centred learning

The new information and communication technologies enable users to explore knowledge in any subject area through devices such as hypertext links or keyword searches. The process of learning at a distance or in the classroom can then focus more on the processes for obtaining relevant information than on the bulk of information by itself; these processes include observation, analysis, integration, comparison and evaluation. Courses incorporating new technologies tend to emphasise these activities more than traditional ones such as memorisation and examinations.

Globalisation

This principle is based on the fact that information from any part of the world can be available at the student's fingertips at any time. Consequently, universities are compelled to provide access to all available sources, which are growing exponentially in number. This has also had an impact on changing traditional notions of authority in relation to teachers and experts. Since the teacher and the expert can be challenged through the production of contrasting points of view, new types of group relations must be established in the educational setting. Concepts such as horizontal organisation, cooperative learning, virtual groups and conceptual networks are in the core of emerging distance education programmes; examples can be found in Latin American distance education.

Knowledge webs

One of the most interesting innovations arising from the extended use of the Internet for dissemination of information is the creation of living knowledge networks, in which each aspect of a discipline is studied by a number of research teams, which prepare summaries and deliver them to a team network. These networks have existed for a long time in universities and research institutes, using slow strategies of communication such as conferences and journals; the new information and communication technologies enable networks to become more complex, faster and more intensive. The benefits are being seen in distance education; for example the server of the Universidad Nacional Autónoma de México runs an embryo of a knowledge web, collecting all papers and contributions written about distance education in Mexico for the use of students and researchers.

Shared virtual environments

The development of simulation techniques, artificial intelligence and robotics has enabled the design of learning devices in which many operations which are costly, dangerous or difficult to undertake in the real world can be carried out in the security of a virtual world. So the student can 'learn by doing' many things that could previously only be learned, less adequately, through reading. This has tremendous implications for distance education programmes. The 'print factory' model which characterises Third Generation distance education programmes may be coming to an end. These programmes place great reliance on printed paper because their key activities for learning and assessment are undertaken by means of books, brochures, readings and examinations. They have therefore been obliged to create elephantine facilities for printing, storing, disseminating and ultimately destroying paper. Fourth Generation programmes will be able, largely but not completely, to put paper aside, by engaging students in direct observation, discussion, manipulation, product elaboration and other real-life activities, with the aid of computer communications and computer multimedia. This is not yet happening in Latin American distance education programmes.

It might be expected that through employing new methods and principles, Latin American distance education programmes can overcome some of their long-standing problems including high drop-out rates, low level of interaction between students and advisors, obsolescence of learning materials, scarce resources for staff development, and diminished public image (Chacón 1990). All these problems result from using a kind of industrialised approach in which the instructional message, entirely planned in advance, is developed by means of several media, and delivered to students, who are in turn assessed on the basis of criteria decided at the planning stage. New technologies may break down the loop that tends to flow in a single direction, substituting multiple loops involving planning, selection of materials, production, delivery, student support and assessment about which decisions are made day by day throughout the duration of a course.

Cooperation agencies

This movement towards renewal in Latin American distance education could decline in a few years in the absence of mechanisms encouraging sharing and seeking of inspiration from external sources. Fortunately, these mechanisms exist and it is likely that they will grow and flourish in the future. The most important agencies of international cooperation dealing with distance education and with new technologies in the region are:

* AIESAD (Asociación Iberoamericana de Educación Superior a Distancia). Formed by the rectors of distance education universities and programmes, its functions include: maintaining a journal on distance education, organising an annual meeting and delivering a Specialisation Program in Distance Education for all the member universities. The

coordinating office is in Universidad Nacional de Educación a Distancia, Spain;

- ATEI (Asociación de Televisión Educativa Iberoamericana). A consortium of institutions, mostly universities and government departments, for planning, producing and disseminating instructional television materials in Spanish throughout the Americas. It uses the HISPASAT satellite as a vehicle for instructional television and also provides facilities for teleconferencing and computer-mediated communication;
- CREAD (Consorcio-Red de Educación a Distancia). An association of professionals and institutions which coordinates exchanges between North and South in the Americas. CREAD headquarters are at the Pennsylvania State University in the United States. This organisation has been involved principally in organising training programmes and professional meetings among distance education specialists of the Americas;
- RIBIE (Red Iberoamericana de Educación a Distancia). Dealing mostly with informatics and telematics applications in education, RIBIE serves twenty-one countries where Spanish and Portuguese are spoken. It promotes meetings for exchange of experiences, training programmes, and a large conference every two years. Coordination rotates among member countries; in 1998, it rests with Universidade Nova de Lisboa, Portugal;
- IESAD (Proyecto Innovación en Educación a Distancia). Sponsored by UNESCO, IESAD provides staff development programmes to all countries in Latin America. Coordination is undertaken by Universidad Nacional Abierta, Venezuela. Its main activity is to disseminate international courses on new technologies and models for distance education in collaboration with ATEI;
- GENESIS. This is the network that supports the Quorum programme; it can be accessed through any IBM branch in the Americas.

Conclusions

The following conclusions can be drawn from the account of distance education in Latin America that has been presented in this chapter.

- Distance education has a rich and productive tradition in the region, extending over a period of almost sixty years, during which several models have been adopted, each influenced by the currently available technology. A constant factor among these changes has been the service provided to underprivileged populations, but methods and contents of the programmes have varied considerably.
- Some distance education programmes in Latin America have already taken advantage of the new information and communication technologies. The main facilitating forces behind these innovations have been

government policies, knowhow accumulated from working with previous models, new staff development programmes, and the existence of a relatively good electronic communications system, including access to Internet across the whole continent.

- Despite inconsistencies in policy in some countries and the general scarcity of financial resources, the introduction of new technologies has already produced important results in the modernisation of instruction. It is to be expected that in the next few years many other Latin American distance education programmes will adopt applications such as enriched modular packages, teleconferencing, on-line education, and multimedia.
- The move of distance education programmes towards the new paradigm is desirable because it will reduce and in some cases eliminate a number of specific problems, including lack of interaction, obsolescence of materials and very high drop-out rates.
- An early beneficiary of the enhancement of distance education through the use of new technologies will be the public education system, a major user of distance education for on-the-job training of teachers. Teachers will be able to take advantage of their experience in working with information and communication media own practice in schools.
- An extraordinary effort of international cooperation will be required to promote the change of paradigm of distance education towards the new technologies in Latin America. One main focus of cooperation must be staff development. Existing staff development programmes may be supplemented with courses from the developed countries and new courses created. There is also a need to stimulate development of distance education in those countries of the region which have not had resources to create significant programmes.

Notes

1 Costa Rica: UNED, *Universidad Estatal a Distancia*; Colombia: UNEAD, *Universidad Nacional de Educación a Distancia* (formely UNISUR); Mexico: SUA, *Sistema de Universidad Abierta* of UNAM and UV-ITESM, *Universidad Virtual del Tecnológico de Monterrey*; Venezuela: UNA, *Universidad Nacional Abierta*; and Chile: *Universidad Gran Mariscal Sucre*.

2 The author is in debt to Marta Mena, Silvia Coicaud and Gustavo Rossi (Argentina), Roberto Salvador (Brasil), Luis Fernando Páramo (Colombia), José Joaquín Villegas (Costa Rica), Antonio Miranda (Cuba), Enrique Pontes and María Teresa Miaja (Mexico).

3 The sponsor institutions of these graduate programmes based on distance education and information technologies as a core are as follows: Argentina: CEDIPROE; Brazil: University of Brasilia; Costa Rica: UNED; Chile: University of Frontier; Colombia: University of the Andes; Mexico: SUA and UV-ITESM; Venezuela: UNA and University Simón Rodríguez

References

Chacón, F. (1990) 'Universidades Latinoamericanas a distancia: una comparación de resultado', in A. Villarroel (ed.), *La Educación a Distancia: Desarrollo y Apertura*, Caracas: International Council for Distance Education, Universidad Nacional Abierta.

Chacón, F. (1997) 'Un nuevo paradigma para la educación corporativa', *Asuntos*, 3, 2, 24–46.

Chacón, F. and Gonzalez, I. (1997) *Visión Histórica y Prospectiva de la Educación a Distancia en América Latina*, Caracas: Universidad Nacional Abierta – FUNDAUNA.

CLIE (1996) *Proyecto Quórum*, México: Centro Latinoamericano de Investigación en Educación. Available HTTP: *http://www.mexico.ibm.com/prodser/educacion/clie.html*

ITESM (1996) *Universidad Virtual*, Mexico: Instituto Tecnológico de Educación Superior de Monterrey. Available HTTP: *http://www.ruv.itesm.mx/homedoc.htm*

Miaja de las Peña, M. (1996) *La Educación Abierta y a Distancia en México*, México: SEP.

Paulsen, M.F. (1995) 'The On-line Report on Pedagogical Techniques for Computer-mediated Communication'. Available HTTP: *http://www.hs.nki.no/~morten/cmcped.html*

Salvador, R. (1995) '1965–1995 Thirty years and a destiny', in D. Sewart (ed.), *One World, Many Voices: Quality in Open and Distance Learning, Selected Papers from the 17th World Conference of the International Council for Distance Education, Birmingham, United Kingdom, 26–30 June 1995*, Oslo/Milton Keynes: ICDE/Open University.

Silvio Pomenta, J. (1998) 'La virtualización de la educación superior', paper presented to the Fourth Congress of RIBIE (Red Iberoamericana de Informática Educativa), Brasilia. Available HTTP: *http://www.niee.ufrgs.br/ribie98/*

Villarroel, A. (1991) *Informe del Estudio de Armando Villarroel, sobre la Educación a Distancia en las Américas*, Mimeo, Washington: Organización de los Estados Americanos.

University distance education in Canada

Douglas Shale

There are some ninety universities in Canada (Association of Universities and Colleges of Canada 1997: 10). A number of these are university colleges, designated as undergraduate degree-granting institutions with no explicit mandate for research or graduate studies. Others are semi-autonomous entities existing within a larger university system. This chapter considers only the comprehensive, publicly funded research universities, of which there are some fifty-five to sixty. We will also consider a number of other kinds of agencies, such as telecommunications-based networks because of their impact on the distance education programming offered through universities. Also discussed are the special providers of university distance education: Athabasca University, a distance education analogue of the traditional university model, the British Columbia Open University/Open College as a component of the Open Learning Agency, and the Téléuniversité, a semi-autonomous body with a statutory basis within the Université du Québec system. The general developments and issues raised in this chapter are necessarily selective and to some degree, idiosyncratic. Similarly, the particular universities referred to throughout the chapter should generally be regarded as illustrative only.

The term 'dual-mode university' is used throughout the chapter to describe universities offering both on-campus instruction and distance education. However, universities providing distance education as an add-on (the majority) are qualitatively different from 'mixed-mode' universities in which the two roles are integrated. In the usual form of mixed-mode integration, teaching faculty have responsibilities for teaching in both modes with students taking courses either on-campus or by distance delivery. However, as the technologies used for distance education become more pervasive in universities, a different kind of blending is occurring in which a single course can be offered through a mixture of distance education and face-to-face methods. The newly founded Technical University of British Columbia offers examples of this.

The political framework

The Canadian constitution devolves responsibility for all levels of education to each of the ten provincial governments. As a result there is no national policy body responsible for education and there are no national educational institutions – although there are institutions that regard all of Canada as their constituency. For example, Athabasca University advertises itself as 'Canada's Open University'; the University of Waterloo (among others) offers its distance courses and programmes nationally. However, an organisation called the Council of Ministers of Education, Canada (CMEC) was established in 1967 by the provincial ministers to provide a voluntary mechanism for provinces to consult on matters of mutual interest in education. The Department of the Secretary of State of Canada serves as the point of contact for education matters with an international scope.

The government of Canada provides funding support for education to the provincial governments in the form of grants and tax transfers. However, the provincial governments have the authority to allocate this financial support in whatever way they wish – and not necessarily to education only. This arrangement of turning money over to the provinces with no control over how it will be spent (and what is worse, with no political kudos for doing so) has long been a sore point for the federal government.

Funding flows from provincial governments to the universities through a grant mechanism that can vary from province to province. Generally the allocation of all revenues is completely under the control of the universities with the allocation process established by each university. Distance education activities are normally funded in this way, which means that distance education must compete with all the other academic activities of the university. Distance education does not fare well in this competition since the politics of the decision process favours the conventional university activities of lecturing and research.

Provincial ministries have traditionally regarded the setting of tuition fees as a matter of public policy and consequently have regulated the amounts universities can charge. In the past, this regulation of tuition fees has deterred the development of distance education in some jurisdictions because universities have not had the latitude to charge for the additional substantial costs associated with distance delivery. Fortunately, distance education tuition fees have now generally been deregulated. One noticeable result has been a widespread development of (expensive) distance MBA and other business-related programmes.

Within each province, each university has the freedom to determine what role, if any, it would like to assume in regard to distance education. Special providers are different because their mandates have a statutory basis. However, distance education in most Canadian universities often began not as a result of institutional vision but by entrepreneurial individuals within the university, often using 'soft money' (money available for a limited period of time only). For example, the very substantial University of Waterloo programme began from four courses offered by a physics professor (Leslie 1986). As a result, Haughey (1989: 161) notes, 'many faculty members are unaware of their own university's involvement in distance education and the implications for the university'. Humble and confounded beginnings notwithstanding, all the comprehensive universities are now dual mode to some extent.

Policies on international students also reflect universities' autonomy. Many universities listed in the Canadian University Distance Education Directory indicate that they will admit international students to their distance programmes. Interestingly, tuition fee policies for foreign students generally do not come under the aegis of government policies for students resident within the province. Tuition policies are increasingly germane because distance education is becoming an important element in universities' internationalisation efforts. Since courses and programmes can be 'exported' to wherever students reside, rather than requiring students to physically relocate, the potential market (and the educational 'product') for foreign students becomes very different. In addition, a larger competitive environment is being created because distance education is not constrained by national boundaries. The major impediments are copyright clearances for international use of materials, costs and the academic integrity of student assessment procedures.

Although the federal and provincial governments are obliged to honour the universities' autonomy, there have been significant efforts to inform the educational policy of these institutions through broad public consultation. One high profile approach has been to use task force/commission style studies that culminate in widely distributed reports. In recent times, the Smith *Commission of Inquiry on Canadian University Education* (1991) is perhaps the best known of these. The Maritime Provinces Higher Education Commission *Report to the Senate Subcommittee on Post-Secondary Education*, 1997 is an interesting regional example. Although both these reports deal with university education at large, each also singles out distance education for special consideration. British Columbia created a 'Distributed Learning Task Force', whose report, *Access and Choice: The Future of Distributed Learning in British Columbia*, is a comprehensive, learning-systems view of how to extend access to post-secondary education in BC. In all these documents, a subtheme emerges: not only are distance education methods a way to increase access, they are expected to do so at less cost.

Some background

Distance education in Canada has extended education to a relatively small population (some 29 million) distributed over a very large geographic area

(about 10 million square kilometres). More than 80 per cent of this population lives in a belt some 200 kilometres wide along the Canada/USA border –
about 10 per cent of the total landmass of Canada. Within this belt there are
relatively large concentrations of people in urban centres and vast expanses
of sparsely populated areas.

Given the geography and demographics of Canada it was natural that
developing an extensive and effective telecommunications network would
become an important national undertaking. Comprehensive radio coverage
was a first step. Television made its debut in the mid- to late 1950s, the exact
timing varying from region to region.

In the late 1960s and early 1970s, the technology of television and the
demographics of the Canadian population developed to the point where a
number of provinces considered it worthwhile to develop speciality educational channels. The potential of television to reach large numbers of
people and its appeal as a powerful instructional medium was a beguiling
combination. The province of Quebec established Radio-Québec in 1968.
Ontario set up the Ontario Educational Communications Authority
(OECA), which in turn established a network of transmitters and created an
agency called TV Ontario. Alberta followed suit in 1973 with the Alberta
Educational Communications Corporation (ACCESS). British Columbia
founded the Knowledge Network of the West Communications Authority
in 1980. TV Ontario's mandate was wider ranging than were those of
ACCESS and the Knowledge Network and TV Ontario produced educational programming that it sold to other agencies. ACCESS and the Knowledge Network were viewed more as distributors for programming produced
by various educational institutions in the province. TV Ontario and the
Knowledge Network have also been involved with other regional institutions
in collaborative efforts to establish telecourses. Cable television was also
expanding rapidly at this time. The then Canadian Radio and Television
Commission, the federal body responsible for telecommunications policy
and licensing, required cable companies applying for a licence to provide a
channel for educational programming.

In the early 1970s Canada became actively involved in using satellites for
telecommunications. Satellites have become integral to Canada's telecommunications network generally and in supporting television broadcasting
in particular (Jelly 1993). There are some circumstances in which satellite
telecommunications have been used very effectively for instructional purposes (for example, see Roberts et al. (1993) on TETRA, The Telemedicine
and Educational Technology Resources Agency in Newfoundland).

Another major landmark in distance education in Canada was the creation
of the 'open universities': Quebec's Télé-université (established 1972);
Athabasca University in Alberta (operational in 1972, established in legislation in 1978); and the Open Learning Institute (set up in 1978, now the Open
Learning Agency of British Columbia). These single-mode institutions were

not only concerned with extending access to university education through distance education methods, they also embodied many other innovations intended to open up higher education, including relaxed (or waived) formal admissions standards, easier transfer of credits, and recognition of credit previously earned. Each institution has a fascinating, albeit turbulent history. Collectively, they represent a difference of kind in the provision of university education in Canada, recasting distance education as a network of connections rather than just an extension of place (Farquhar 1998). They raised the profile of university distance education considerably. And because of their 'learning-systems' view of the higher education world, each institution has become a nexus in the development of all sorts of collaborative arrangements, often drawing in the conventional universities. These institutions are documented by Moran (1993) and Mugridge (1986) (Open Learning Institute/Agency); Shale (1982) and Paul (1989) (Athabasca University); and Guillemet *et al.* (1986) (Télé-université).

Until recently, no other institutions as radically different as the open universities had been created anywhere else in Canada. However, three new universities have recently been created in Canada that signal interesting new developments in the provision of university distance education. All three have incorporated formal commitments in their mandates to the use of telecommunications technologies and distance education methods. The most radical is the Technical University of British Columbia, which is unique because it is committed to offering half of its programming over the Internet and appears to intend to design its courses based on a blending of conventional face-to-face and distance delivery. The University of Northern British Columbia (UNBC) is a conventional campus-based institution which indicates in public documents its intent to reach out to citizens in northern BC through distance education methods. The third new university, Royal Roads, is unique because it is to be operated on a cost recovery basis. Its mandate also mentions using new delivery technologies in offering its programmes.

The fact that distance education figures prominently in these institutions' strategic statements is a major development in Canadian university distance education.

An overview of contemporary Canadian university distance education

Despite the difficulty of ascertaining the exact range and depth of Canadian university distance education, the following summary characteristics are particularly noteworthy.

- All the major, comprehensive universities offer some distance education – but 'some' can vary from not much to a substantial amount.

Universities not indicating an involvement in distance education generally are the smaller, undergraduate teaching universities (but there are notable exceptions).

- Very few universities describe their commitment to distance education in strategic terms. By default, the implication is that distance education has generally been regarded as an add-on to the usual academic activities of the university although this clearly does not apply to the specially mandated providers – Athabasca University, the British Columbia Open University/Open College and the Télé-université – and Canada's three newest universities.

- Within the dual-mode universities, the dominant organisational arrangement is for distance education to be part of a faculty or school of Continuing Education/Extension. Where distance education programming is non-credit, this seems logical. However, when programming is credit, the continuing education/extension unit serves as an administrative unit that acts on behalf of the academic units within the university.

- Distance-delivered programmes can originate from other organisational units as well as from a continuing education/extension function. Continuing medical education seems to originate exclusively from faculties of medicine (or their equivalent). Business education usually originates from faculties or schools of business (but not exclusively). General liberal studies courses and programmes typically emanate from the continuing education/extension office. The rules of thumb are: if the subject matter is highly specialised, or if there is money to be made, the distance education programming will be found in the corresponding academic unit.

- A good deal of distance education academic programming available in dual-mode institutions is non-credit instruction that generally comprises certificate or diploma programmes. On the other hand, there are universities that offer predominantly credit instruction. Most likely the state of affairs in any given university is a function of historical circumstance and institutional politics rather than any kind of a statement about the efficacy of distance delivery for credit or non-credit programming.

- Some institutions offer their credit programming simply as an array of courses not formally organised into degree programme structures. However, the major dual-mode universities offer complete degree programmes at a distance as do the mandated distance education providers – Athabasca University, the British Columbia OU/OC and the

Télé-université. Collaborative degrees (with courses provided by two or more universities) are a growing development, systematically implemented in British Columbia through the Open University Consortium, which comprises the major BC universities, a couple of colleges and the Open Learning Agency. A good deal of credit programming is at undergraduate level, particularly in the liberal arts and sciences. The limited amount of distance-delivered graduate-level programming available is at Master's level. MBA programmes have been a rapidly growing programmatic area.

- Although a wide variety of delivery technologies are used, most institutions settle on one dominant delivery mode – the most common being print and mail. This is the open universities' primary delivery mode, although other delivery technologies are also used in supplementary fashion (for example, Athabasca University uses teleconferencing and the telephone to provide tutoring support to students; Athabasca University and the Open Learning Agency broadcast selected course material over television). The University of Waterloo is unique in its use of audiocassettes. Teleconferencing has long been a popular technology in some institutions. Television and radio have been used on a selective basis. Computerconferencing (beyond just being an e-mail system) has been an important primary delivery technology in some instances. Interactive videoconferencing and the Internet/Web are two newer technologies proving increasingly popular, and with substantial implications for university distance education.

- Not surprisingly the majority of universities use English as the sole language of instruction. The Télé-université works solely in French. And a number of institutions use both languages – Laurentian University and the University of Ottawa being two primary examples.

Communications networks

The development of open learning systems during the 1970s was largely influenced by technological innovation. The three open universities were established during this time, educational television was launched in many provinces and the well-known Hermes satellite experiments occurred (Jelly 1993). However, access has been and continues to be the hallmark of distance education in Canada, and technology that enhances access to education has become increasingly important. In addition to telecommunications networks, television, radio and satellite-supported broadcasting were used as additional ways to extend educational opportunities. Costs, infrastructure requirements and unevenness of coverage (as well as limitations in the capabilities of the technologies for educational uses) resulted in a patchwork arrangement where affordability and availability determined where and when technologies were used.

One response to those challenges has been the creation of educational communications networks, of which the best known is probably Contact North /Contact Nord. According to Croft (1993) Contact North/Contact Nord was meant to test a new form of collaborative venture involving government and post-secondary institutions (later extended to include schools). It was established to extend access to education among the population of northern and north-western Ontario. In its current form it is described as providing 'a reliable, cost-effective network of instructional technology and sophisticated telecommunications that allows learners and educators to meet with each other in spite of the barriers of distance, sparse population and climatic extremes' (http://www.cnorth.edu.on.ca). Contact North is a utility analogous to a telecommunications company with basic core funding from the government. The network is managed by a joint body of representatives from the participating educational sectors with educational services provided by the participating educational institutions. Contact North is responsible for daily operations, creating and maintaining the communications network, and providing expertise in its use. Although the politics and specifics are different, the concept of a collaborative communications network is also apparent in such initiatives as the Open Learning and Information Network in Newfoundland and TeleEducation, New Brunswick. To date, these networks have largely been used to support teleconferencing, but videoconferencing is being used increasingly frequently. The advent of digital, computer-based communications will likely lessen the need for this utility style of communications network, but the success of the existing networks will ensure their continuance.

Other collaborative arrangements

Producing a course in distance education format can be laborious, time-consuming and expensive. Not surprisingly, early efforts at collaboration involved looking for ways to reduce the burden of course production through course sharing and course acquisition. Generally these efforts were bilateral – one institution had a course another institution was interested in. Often the arrangement was a straight purchase deal from a domestic or foreign provider.

Various attempts were made to facilitate the exchange of distance education courses among universities. In the early 1980s the governments of the western Canadian provinces signed an agreement of principle to exchange distance-delivered courses freely and at minimal cost. At about the same time, universities in the area banded together to form a consortium to assist with the sharing of course materials (Carefoot 1982; Konrad and Small 1986). A concurrent initiative was the expansion of the National Universities

Consortium (based in Maryland) into Canada to include the Open Learning Institute (as it was known then) and Athabasca University to become International Universities Consortium (IUC). IUC's objective was to create a pool of distance courses with a major television component. Some of the western Canadian universities tried to establish a similar kind of consortium in the mid-1990s, seemingly with limited success. None of these arrangements worked as well as intended. As Moran and Mugridge (1993) observed, what seemed like a good idea in principle often foundered on ugly practicalities. The tight organisational coupling necessary for one university to acquire and deliver another university's course as its own turns out to be quite a stringent condition in practice.

The buy/sell approach to augmenting course offerings is still used to some extent by the other distance education providers. An alternative is for the producing institution to sponsor students and award credit. Other universities could become receiving institutions by recognising the credit awarded and counting it towards a credential conferred by the receiving institution. The Open University Consortium of British Columbia is a good example of this kind of arrangement (Open University Planning Council 1995). Although a student can earn a degree through distance study from any of the participating universities, an open-learning institution like the OLA can be a key element because of its more liberal accommodation of credit transfer and credit recognition of all kinds.

The continuing impact of technology

Technology has been a major preoccupation in Canadian distance education for decades. In the early 1970s we saw the open universities developing material for a range of media. Educational television and radio figured prominently at this time and the provincial broadcasting authorities were set up. Satellites, cable and fibre optic distribution systems were all important aspects of this. In the late 1970s and early 1980s, Telidon, a form of videotext, appeared on the scene briefly. At this time, teleconferencing became more commonplace as more universities moved towards becoming dual mode. In some instances, audiographic enhancements were introduced. About this time there was also considerable interest in Computer-Assisted Instruction (the PLATO system, in particular, attracted a lot of attention) and to a lesser extent Computer-Managed Instruction. In the early 1990s, computer-managed conferencing became more commonplace and continues to be used in various guises.

Two technologies have come into prominence within the last five years which promise to make a qualitative difference not just in distance education but in university education as a whole. These are videoconferencing and the Internet/Web. As with earlier technologies, there is a lot of 'hype' around these, and many arguable claims being made for them. However, these technologies already have had a major impact because of their ready acceptance and use by the teaching faculty in the universities. This is largely because videoconferencing and the Internet/Web are easier to use than the more technologically and pedagogically demanding technologies that up to now have been used to support university distance education.

Interactive videoconferencing has the additional attraction of the kind of glamour associated with television in its heyday, and a sense by faculty that videoconferencing is 'just like being there' (Shale and Kirek 1997). This technology has increasingly attracted teaching faculty to distance education. The faculty thereby becomes more familiar with, and hence more accepting of, non-traditional teaching and learning. The Internet/Web technology also has huge novelty appeal but its additional attraction is ease of use. Professors can work from home or from a terminal in their offices or homes without need for an inordinate amount of infrastructure support. In time, the pedagogical limitations of the Internet/Web are likely to dampen the current enthusiasm. However, as with videoconferencing, it will have drawn a good number of the professoriate into the realm of alternative instruction – hopefully inducing a long-term change in the general attitude to distance education. At the same time, the Internet/Web technology is increasingly being incorporated into regular classroom teaching in seamless fashion.

Videoconferencing and the Internet/Web have stimulated a marked increase in the distance education offerings of the dual-mode universities. This widespread participation of faculty will do much to address the chronic, continuing problems of credibility faced by university distance education. The problem stems from the objections of the professoriate – often the most damaging criticism is of courses and programmes within the faculty's own university. When the faculty are using distance education, the criticism will necessarily disappear because the distinction previously drawn between educational forms will blur.

Many issues arise from the transition brought about by videoconferencing and the Internet/Web. The time-worn issue of copyright and intellectual property will become even more problematic. The academic will believe that he or she owns the course because that is the situation with lecture materials. However, because a course can have an abiding life independent of the creating academic, the university must also have some rights regarding course use and revision.

Workload assignment is another issue. Professors spend a significant amount of time preparing videoconferencing and Web-based courses. Newcomers are invariably surprised at the amount of effort required. In the case of the Internet/Web, the ease of communicating leads to an expectation that communication will increase and that instructors should be available at any time. Professors have yet to fully discover the magnitude of work associated with unrestricted electronic access by students. The workload problem will become more problematic because workload assignments will have to be assigned in terms quite different from the traditional metrics of numbers of courses, credits or contact hours. There are considerable implications here for collective agreements and contracts with teaching staff. We have already seen an agreement struck between York University and its teaching staff not to force the introduction of technology.

Conclusion

University distance education in Canada has followed an evolutionary path characterised by hard-won, incremental progress interspersed with an occasional blossoming of change such as we saw in the 1970s. In the 1990s, we are again seeing new kinds of institutions emerge concerned with distance education in new ways. In addition, collaborative arrangements have become a necessary strategy in institutional positioning, and the distance education providers are figuring prominently in these. One way or another, the dual-mode universities are also being drawn in by the opportunities provided through distance education and open learning systems. The distinction between face-to-face teaching and distance education is more moot than ever before with the blending of teaching methods through digitally based telecommunications technologies. The public profile of distance education is higher than it has ever been. Hopefully, we have come full circle and are well started on a new era of educational innovation that will rival what we have seen in the past.

References

Association of Universities and Colleges of Canada (1997) *The Directory of Canadian Universities, 1997–98*, Ottawa: Association of Universities and Colleges of Canada.

Canadian Association for University Continuing Education (1997) *Canadian University Distance Education Directory, 1997–1998*, Ottawa: Association of Universities and Colleges of Canada.

Carefoot, J. (1982) 'The birth of a western Canadian committee on university education', unpublished report, Regina: University of Regina.

Croft, M. (1993) 'The Contact North project: collaborative project management in Ontario', in L. Moran and I. Mugridge (eds), *Collaboration in Distance Education: International Case Studies*, London: Routledge.

Farquhar, R. (1998) 'Implications of the virtual university for academic leadership', *University Manager*, winter, 42–8.

Guillemet, P., Bedard, R. and Landry, F. (1986) 'Télé-université du Québec', in I. Mugridge and D. Kaufman (eds), *Distance Education in Canada*, London: Croom Helm.

Haughey, M. (1989) 'Involvement with distance education: issues for the university', in R. Sweet (ed.), *Post-Secondary Distance Education in Canada: Policies, Practices and*

Priorities, Athabasca, Alberta: Athabasca University and Canadian Society for Studies in Education.

Hobsons Publishing (1997) *Distance and Supported Open Learning Worldwide*, Cambridge: Hobsons.

Jelly, D.H. (1993) 'Canada in space', *Journal of Distance Education*, 8, 1, 15–26.

Konrad, A. and Small, J.M. (1986) 'Consortia in Canadian distance education', in I. Mugridge and D. Kaufman (eds), *Distance Education in Canada*, London: Croom Helm.

Leslie, J.D. (1986) 'Use of audiocassettes', in I. Mugridge and D. Kaufman (eds), *Distance Education in Canada*, London: Croom Helm.

Moran, L. (1993) 'Genesis of the Open Learning Institute of British Columbia', *Journal of Distance Education*, 8, 1, 43–70.

Moran, L. and Mugridge, I. (1993) 'Policies and trends in inter-institutional collaboration', in L. Moran and I. Mugridge (eds), *Collaboration in Distance Education*, London: Routledge.

Mugridge, I. (1986) 'The Open Learning Institute', in I. Mugridge and D. Kaufman (eds), *Distance Education in Canada*, London: Croom Helm.

Open University Planning Council (1995) *The British Columbia University Learning System, 1994–95*, report prepared by the Open University Planning Council, Vancouver, BC.

Paul, R. (1989) 'Canada's open universities: issues and prospectives', in R. Sweet (ed.), *Post-Secondary Distance Education in Canada; Policies, Practices and Priorities*, Athabasca, Alberta: Athabasca University/Canadian Society for Studies in Education.

Roberts, J.M., House, A.M., McNamara, W.C. and Keough, E.M. (1993) 'Report on Memorial University of Newfoundland's experimental use of the communications satellite Hermes in Telemedicine', *Journal of Distance Education*, 8, 1, 34–42.

Shale, D. (1982) 'Athabasca University, Canada', in G. Rumble and K. Harry (eds), *The Distance Teaching Universities*, London: Croom Helm.

Shale, D. and Kirek, I. (1997) 'Interactive videoconferencing: the next best thing to being there?', paper presented at the 18th ICDE World Conference, University Park, Pennsylvania: 2–6 June.

Chapter 9

Asia

The largest growth area of single-mode open universities during the 1970s and 1980s was Asia. National institutions were established during this period in China, India, Indonesia, Japan, Korea, Pakistan, Sri Lanka and Thailand. Similar institutions have since been established in Bangladesh, Hong Kong and Taiwan, ROC. Several of these institutions are documented in this volume – by Chung (Taiwan, ROC), Ding (China), Murphy and Fung (Hong Kong), Panda (India) and Rumble (Bangladesh). Although belonging to the same genre, these national institutions differ from one another very significantly. The most frequently occurring common characteristics are size of student population (several have over 100,000 enrolled students) and objectives – almost every one sets out to provide degree-level opportunities in far greater numbers than the conventional system could otherwise make available.

Differences between the institutions are inevitable given the nature of the disparity between cultures, resources and topography of the various countries which are served. Some institutions, however, are unique not only in the Asian region but beyond. Allama Iqbal Open University, Pakistan, for example, offers an extraordinarily wide range of courses from adult basic education to postgraduate levels. Indira Gandhi National Open University, India, in addition to offering its own courses nationally, is responsible for coordinating and regulating distance education in India's state open universities and its conventional universities' correspondence education institutes. Universitas Terbuka, Indonesia, has to cope with the problems of delivering courses to the numerous islands of which the country is comprised. The Open University of Hong Kong, until recently the Open Learning Institute of Hong Kong, initially offered many courses which were acquired through agreements with institutions in other countries, including Australia and the United Kingdom. This situation has changed, with the institution adapting to Hong Kong's new political location.

Although single-mode institutions have been established so widely and successfully throughout Asia, the global trend towards the emergence of dual-mode institutions can also be observed in many countries. India, China and Japan, for example, already possessed extensive dual-mode provision even before their national open universities were set up. In Hong Kong and Taiwan, ROC, there is a pattern of conventional institutions initiating distance-teaching programmes, and in Taiwan, even of municipal open universities emerging. The trend is also apparent in other countries, for example in Malaysia. For many years, the Off Campus Studies Programme of Universiti Sains Malaysia was the focus of distance education in the country. Today, the demands on the education system are so great that several conventional institutions are developing major distance-teaching programmes. Among these is the Institut Teknologi Mara, which hosted the 1997 Annual Conference of the Asian Association of Open Universities (the AAOU Web site is at http://www.ouhk.edu.hk/cridal/professional/aaou.htm/). There is also great interest in, and significant practice of, distance education in countries formerly under French influence, such as Cambodia and Vietnam.

The Middle East is included here with Asia because one of the established Middle Eastern distance-teaching institutions, Payame Noor Open University, Iran, has aligned itself with Asia by becoming a member institution of the Asian Association. The other major distance-teaching institution in the region, the Open University, Israel, has operated successfully for around twenty years. Curiously, distance education has had little impact to date in other Middle Eastern countries, although great interest in distance education has been shown for many years in, for example, Egypt, Libya, Saudi Arabia, United Arab Emirates and Yemen.

The Bangladesh Open University: mission and promise

Greville Rumble

The Bangladesh Open University was formally established by Act of Parliament in October 1992 (Bangladesh Gazette 1992) following a series of studies undertaken by the United Kingdom's Overseas Development Agency (ODA) between 1987 and 1989, and by the Asian Development Bank (ADB) between 1989 and 1991.

The rationale for the BOU Project, spelt out in the ADB's Project Appraisal document (ADB 1992a: 1, 7–8, 9), cited the high absolute levels of poverty, the low per capita GNP, the high population growth, the low adult literacy rate and the inability of the conventional education system to meet the country's requirements, including inadequate access in rural areas, inadequate higher and professional education and training opportunities, the poor quality of educational resources and programmes, and the lack of informal and non-formal educational opportunities. The establishment of a distance-teaching university would, it was believed, help support the government of Bangladesh's efforts to strengthen human resource development by increasing access to education and training in rural areas (including basic and secondary education and vocational training), provide higher education and professional training in selected areas, strengthening informal and non-formal educational programmes aimed at the general population, and enhance the general quality and relevance of educational programmes (ADB 1992a: 15).

The conditions that gave rise to the rationale for the Project still prevail. Adult illiteracy was 65 per cent in 1990 (females, 78 per cent) (World Bank 1994: Table 1). The 1991 data show that the primary net enrolment was 65 per cent (this indicator gives a more realistic idea of how many children in the age group are actually enrolled in school since it nets out under- and over-age children from the primary school enrolment figures). Only 19 per cent of the relevant age group was enrolled in secondary education (12 per cent for girls), and only 3 per cent (4 per cent for young women) in tertiary education. At primary school level, the teacher : pupil ratio was 1 : 63. India – to give a comparator – has 44 per cent of the relevant age group enrolled in secondary school (females, 32 per cent), though its teacher : pupil ratio is not much better than Bangladesh's (World Bank 1994: Table 28). With the population of Bangladesh still expanding (though at a slower rate), and estimated to reach 132 million in 2000 (compared with 115 million in 1991) (World Bank 1994: Table 25), it seems likely that many if not most of the educational needs underpinning the education objectives of the Fourth Five-Year Plan (FY 1990–5) will carry over into the Fifth Five-Year Plan.

Bangladesh had already gained some experience of distance education methods through the activities of the Bangladesh Institute of Distance Education (BIDE), set up to offer a Bachelor of Education degree to teachers, but there was little likelihood that the traditional universities would take on the role of teaching external students by distance means. The only realistic option was to set up a new university to exploit distance-teaching methods. Under the Bangladesh Open University Act, BIDE became part of the new university.

BOU's academic programmes

From the beginning, BOU was required to be more than a traditional university providing degree-level opportunities to those unable to secure places in the traditional universities of Bangladesh. The 1991 feasibility report indicated that BOU's main objective should be to provide flexible and needs-based education to those unable or not willing to enter conventional educational institutions. Its planners argued that if it were to play a real role in meeting the needs of the disadvantaged sectors of society, it would have to offer a wide spectrum of non-formal educational opportunities. There was an insistence that BOU should develop both courses leading to tertiary-level qualifications (diplomas, Bachelor's degrees, and Master's degrees), and non-formal courses and school equivalency courses.

BOU's academic plan has gone through several revisions since the first plan was spelt out in the Feasibility Study (1991). Nevertheless, pending a needs assessment survey, the University worked on the development of courses for its planned Certificate in English Language Proficiency, its Secondary School Certificate programme, and its management programmes (both Certificate and Diploma). Also, the fact that the University had taken over BIDE and its existing Bachelor of Education programme meant that from 1992 the University was enrolling students under its own name.

The scope of the survey was constrained by the fact that BOU's planners were seeking confirmation of demand for a list of programmes that had already been written into the early planning documents, together with other programmes that might be developed in the future. The needs assessment survey demonstrated that there was a substantial demand for many of the products BOU proposed to offer, but it also suggested that there were others for which there was little demand. Finally, the survey indicated a demand for a number of specific certificate level courses in the fields of agricultural and rural development, which the University then set about planning to meet; and for a broadening of the range of management education qualifications, to embrace certificate, diploma, first degree and Master's degree levels.

The survey demonstrated that one of the constraints in Bangladesh is the shortage of places in other higher education institutions, leading to considerable levels of frustrated demand, and this explained the expressed demand for university-level studies identified by the survey. It was also clear that there was considerable demand for higher level skills and vocationally oriented courses. Apart from the changes in programmes identified above, the survey also led BOU to decide to bring forward the launch date of some of its programmes, in order to respond more quickly to those areas where demand was highest. (It was recognised that focusing on those programmes where demand was greatest would have the added benefit that income from fees would be maximised, thus helping to meet the objective of financial sustainability.) Having said that, BOU had already begun to develop some of its new programmes, so that it was able to launch the Certificate in English Language Proficiency programme in 1994, and the Secondary School Certificate, Certificate in Management and Diploma in Management in 1995.

By 1995, following discussions at Board of Governors level, the shape of BOU's planned academic programme was clear, with a range of formal and non-formal programmes identified and approved for development by the Board of Governors. A feature of its plans is the development of a 'ladder' of qualifications whereby students can easily progress from lower to higher level qualifications. Further programmes are under consideration.

Programme development

BOU established a number of multi-disciplinary schools which were charged with developing the courses. Academic staff were recruited to develop the materials. Current plans suggest a total academic staff complement of seventy-nine: in April 1996, thirty-one academic staff were in post – a figure that had not changed greatly over an eighteen-month period. The University has experienced some difficulty in recruiting and retaining academic staff, partly because of the location of the campus outside Dhaka; partly because the long-term financial funding (post the ABD-funding period) had yet to be assured by government; and partly because the pattern of work, involving a punishing schedule of course development, is more intensive than in traditional universities (leading some new recruits to decide very quickly that they wished to move on). Additional support is provided by course authors and presenters contracted to produce particular materials.

By 1995, all the materials for the BEd. degree had been developed. The 1994–5 production year saw something like twenty-seven course books, 116 radio programmes (of 30 minutes each), fifty-eight television programmes (of 25 minutes each), and five one-hour audio-cassettes, produced to support the SSC, CELP, and Certificate and Diploma in Management, together with additional programmes developed in support of the Nonformal Programme. The texts are put out to tender, and printed by the commercial publishing sector; the audio and television components are produced in-house in studios taken over when the University absorbed the Bangladesh Institute of Distance Education.

The target population

BOU's establishment was driven by the perceived development needs of the country. The University was set up primarily to serve those sectors of the population who were currently excluded from the traditional education system and those who, for one reason or another, had dropped out of traditional education. Particularly targeted were students in rural areas, and especially women, out-of-school youth, adults who had to work to support their families, and people in work who needed retraining, professional upgrading and personal development. Also specifically mentioned as beneficiaries were untrained teachers at primary and secondary level; extension agents in agriculture, family planning, health and rural development; and professionals wishing to update their skills (ADB 1992a: 14, 33, 37).

To date BOU has launched five formal programmes: Bachelor of Education (BEd.); Certificate in English Language Proficiency (CELP); Certificate in Management (Cert.M); Diploma in Management (Dipl.M); and the Secondary School Certificate (SSC). The University does not have detailed information on the characteristics of all its students, but as one would expect, their characteristics reflect both the nature of Bangladeshi society and the nature of the qualifications they are seeking to obtain:

- the majority of students taking tertiary level qualifications are male: roughly three in four (77 per cent) of the BEd. students are male, as are 70 per cent of CELP students. However, samples suggest that the proportion of female students is much higher (50 per cent or over) in the SSC. For example, in Sylhet 55 per cent of the students are female (Huq 1995: 23);
- between 75 and 78 per cent of each intake into the BEd. have been teachers. All are graduates, with some 32 per cent having a Master's degree (ibid.: 23).
- two out of three (67 per cent) CELP students have a degree as their highest educational qualification; 3 per cent have technical qualifications; 26 per cent have a Higher School Certificate; and 9 per cent a Secondary School Certificate;
- one in two (51 per cent) of CELP students are job seekers; one in three (34 per cent) are in office employment; 7 per cent are housewives; 5 per cent are in business; and 3 per cent are students;

- the majority of Dipl.M students are working. Nearly three in four (74 per cent) live in the Dhaka region;
- the majority of the students taking the BEd. are aged 30 or over. However, the proportion of students aged under 30 is increasing, from 24 per cent in 1992, to 33 per cent in 1993, to 44 per cent in 1994. The majority of CELP students are under 30 (65 per cent of the first intake in 1994, and 78 per cent of the second intake in that year).

On the basis of this evidence, BOU's tertiary level programmes (i.e. its certificates, diplomas and degrees) are not reaching the deprived, rural masses that BOU was set up to reach. On the other hand, one would not expect formal, tertiary-level programmes to be of great interest to the rural masses where illiteracy is high. However, the number of students entering the Open School's Secondary School Certificate is very encouraging, as is the fact that this programme has students throughout Bangladesh, in both urban and rural communities. The high female participation rate is also very encouraging.

The expectation was that BOU would enrol some 140,000 people during the five-year implementation period of the project (ADB 1992a: 37). Although it could not meet the 1992 and 1993 'targets' set it in the original project appraisal document (ADB 1992a), later enrolment figures have been encouraging, suggesting that BOU is expanding at the rate envisaged in its plans (Table 9–1.1).

Delivery

The University is using a variety of technologies: text in the form of print, audio in the form of radio and audio-cassettes, television in the form of broadcasting, and direct human contact through lectures that incorporate a degree of interactive questioning of and by the teacher. It does not currently use computing for teaching purposes. The norm is to provide 75 minutes of broadcast television and 120 minutes of radio broadcasting to every 45 hours worth (estimated study time) of printed course materials.

Table 9–1.1 Enrolment figures, Bangladesh Open University

Programme	1992	1993	1994	1995	1996
Bachelor of Education (ex BIDE)	5,125	4,542	15,662	21,236	
Certificate in Management				1,256	
Diploma in Management					
Certificate in English Language Proficiency			4,997	5,586	
Secondary School Certificate				14,247	
Total actual	5,125	4,542	20,659	42,325	
Planned	4,000	13,000	24,500	42,500	54,500

Print is the core medium. Print is, of course, a highly flexible medium but it can be written in ways that students find hard to comprehend. This can reflect poor construction, or a poor fit between the text as it is written and the ability of the target audience to understand it. In a country where the adult literacy rate was only 36.6 per cent in 1992, the comprehensibility of the material is a significant factor. BOU surveys show that between 0.9 and 4.7 per cent of the students studying the first three books of the Certificate of English Language Proficiency found the texts difficult or very difficult, while between 7.9 and 11.9 per cent found the next three books difficult or very difficult.

Most national distance education systems using broadcasting, whether television or radio, are concerned about the quality of their access to transmission times and, assuming they aspire to be national organisations, to transmission networks that cover the whole country. Bangladesh Television (BTV) has provided BOU with 25-minute transmission slots from 6.55 to 7.20 p.m., Sundays to Wednesdays, and on Fridays, on terrestrial transmission networks that reach 85 per cent of the total population. The actual transmission times are felt to be reasonable. Having said this, BOU urgently needs to expand the numbers of broadcast slots available to it. It is currently negotiating for a few more slots on the existing terrestrial television channel, but only access to time of the proposed second, satellite-based channel, will give it sufficient airtime to meet its growing needs.

In Bangladesh there is an added problem: the relatively low level of ownership of receivers. A survey undertaken in late 1994 and early 1995 showed that nationally 8 per cent of households owned a television receiver, with a wide disparity between urban areas (40 per cent of households) and rural areas (3 per cent) (Mitra & Associates 1995). The same survey showed the extent of individual access to a television set (percentage of people who say they had the opportunity to watch if they wished) and individual reach of television (percentage of people who said they saw a programme at least once a week) with national figures for access of 38 per cent. During 1995, BOU also surveyed students on two of its programmes, the Bachelor of Education (BEd.) degree and the Certificate in English Language Proficiency (CELP), to see how many of them managed to watch the broadcasts.

As one would expect, reach is always going to be less than access, but what is notable about these figures is the very high level of reach and access relative to the actual ownership of receivers, bearing out the contention that where people do own a set, they are likely to let others watch it. So far as radio is concerned, Radio Bangladesh's medium wave transmission reaches most areas of the country with the notable exception of the Chittagong area, where there is a local radio station to which BOU does not currently have access. The same national survey as for television shows the proportion of households owning a working radio (Mitra & Associates 1995). What is surprising about this survey is that ownership of a working radio in urban areas is only on a par with television ownership, while in rural areas, while much higher than television ownership, it is still not that high. Again, access is higher than reach, with rural women at a distinct disadvantage. Both the general population and BOU student reach is higher for radio than for television in rural areas, but higher for television than for radio in urban areas. BOU broadcasts its radio programmes between 7.30 and 8.00 p.m. each day. The time of broadcast is not regarded as ideal – only one in five BEd. students ranked this as the preferred time, and only one in fourteen CELP students did so.

Audio-cassettes are used on appropriate courses, notably the Certificate in English Language Proficiency where they play an important role in language learning. There are some acknowledged production problems, with up to about 8 per cent of the tapes having faults on them. Access to audio-cassette players has not been identified as a problem.

The final 'medium' is that of face-to-face contact. Tutorials are held on Fridays (the national day of rest) in BOU's tutorial centres. Attendance is mandatory, and so high. The number of locations where tutorials are held varies from programme to programme: the School of Education supports the BEd. in sixteen centres, while the School of Business supports twenty tutorial centres across the country; on the other hand, the Secondary School Certificate (SSC) programme is delivered in each of the country's 460 Thanas (local administrative units). In a situation where attendance is mandatory, the paucity of centres in some programmes becomes a barrier to access. The number of centres is determined in part by the extent to which the University can contract tutors to teach its courses.

Credibility

It is unlikely that distance education would have been developed in Bangladesh but for the decision to establish a new distance-teaching university. The dual-mode option was not a feasible one, given the parlous financial state of the existing university sector, while the Bangladesh Institute of Distance Education (BIDE) lacked the resources, the mission or the credibility to act as a launching pad for the development of a new initiative. Legislative action and the support of an international aid agency (the Asian Development Bank) were necessary prerequisites to development of distance education within the country.

If, as with so many projects, the new university was initially regarded with a degree of scepticism, its course materials have rapidly established themselves as quality products. The BOU's texts are now being used as standard texts for students studying in the traditional system: thus, for example, the texts produced by the School of Business are being used as standard texts in the universities of Dhaka and Chittagong, while the School of Education's texts are used in the Teachers' Training Colleges. There is, however, some scepticism about the legitimacy of a university engaging in non-tertiary level activity. Currently, this focuses on the Open School, though it may well extend to the non-formal role that the University is adopting. Whether one gives credence to this criticism probably depends upon the view of the role of the university embedded in a particular socio-political system. The BOU will need to address this criticism robustly, by pointing out that its engagement in these activities is both justified in its own right, and has no deleterious effect of the quality of what it is doing at the higher education level. On the contrary, it ensures that the University remains in touch with the wider needs of the society and thus has positive benefits. It also provides BOU's students with a ladder of educational qualifications which will eventually stretch from Secondary School Certificate level to university postgraduate studies level.

Structurally, the development of the University was initially regarded as a project funded by short-term external aid. Recently, however, with the setting up under the Act of the University's own organs of governance, it has established the structures that help integrate it into the mainstream planning and funding of the country's higher education system. As a result, BOU is emerging as a properly constituted university in fact as well as in law, while shedding its project status.

Sustainability

Setting up an open university is an expensive proposition. Where projects are set up using foreign aid monies, there is a risk that, once the aid ends, the project will be unable to sustain itself. The issue of long-term sustainability is therefore crucial.

The total project cost was estimated to be US $43 million over the five-year period during which the project is being developed, of which 80 per cent would be met from the ADB's loan. While the government of Bangladesh is expected to meet some of the costs, in the long term BOU is expected to recover a substantial amount of its costs from student fees and other charges, including sufficient income to maintain and update its academic programme and infrastructure. The Project Appraisal (ADB 1992a: 35–6) suggested that by the sixth year of the project (1998/9) BOU should be recovering 98 per cent of its recurrent costs, rising to 100 per cent in the tenth year (2002/3).

BOU's costs are driven by three considerations: student support, driven by the number of students and decisions regarding the nature and quality of the services offered; materials development and production costs, driven by the size of the academic programme, the media chosen, the media mix in any one course and the length of life of courses; and the overhead costs of the infrastructure, driven by management decisions. BOU's 1995 operating costs are shown in Table 9–1.2 (based on Enamul Haque 1995: 25). This table

Table 9–1.2 Bangladesh Open University: operating costs by programme, 1995 (Taka)

Programme	Direct student support costs	Annualised course development costs assuming a 4-year course life	Total operating cost	Number of students (estimated)	Average operating cost per student
SSC	33,788,195	1,800,000	35,588,195	13,701	2,597
BEd.	32,287,833	1,440,000	24,626,833	5,708	4,315
Dipl.M/Cert.M	5,411,832	1,320,000	6,731,832	1,070	6,291
CELP	2,834,760	300,000	3,134,760	2,078	1,509

Source: Based on Enamul Haque 1995: 25.

Note
US $1.00 = Tk.41.00 (approximately).

shows the estimated number of enrolments in 1995 at the time the exercise was carried out.

It is intended that in the long term each academic programme should cover the costs of student support and the annualised cost of developing new and replacement courses, and make a contribution to overhead costs and the costs of renewing the infrastructure (including buildings, equipment and software-based systems). There will also be scope for profitable programmes to cross-subsidise those not covering their full costs. Thus it looks as if BOU will be financially self-sufficient. This compares well with traditional universities in Bangladesh, where fees meet about 15 to 20 per cent of operating costs. Current cost projections suggest that BOU will recruit sufficient students to enable it to recover most of its operating costs and make a contribution to overheads, at fees that the students will be able to afford. It is thought that a 20 per cent increase in fees would make the University self-financing, and that the target population would be able to meet such an increase, though this remains to be tested.

Conclusions

The beginning of this article spelt out the specific objectives of the BOU project at inception (ADB 1992a: 14–15, 33, 37). To what extent, then, is BOU:

* meeting a wide range of identified educational needs, both formal and non-formal? Existing higher and professional education and training opportunities were deemed to be inadequate. BOU was set up to provide higher education and professional training in selected areas, and to strengthen informal and non-formal educational programmes aimed at the

general population. It has introduced a range of programmes at higher education level (including certificates, diplomas, Bachelor's and Master's degrees), at secondary level, and in the non-formal area. The last two in particular are aimed at the general population, both rural and urban.

- assisting national development and meeting the needs of the national economy? BOU was set up to strengthen human resource development in Bangladesh. Particular targets included adults who had to work to support their families; and people in work who needed retraining, professional upgrading, and personal development, including untrained teachers at primary and secondary level, and extension agents in agriculture, family planning, health and rural development. There are specific programmes for untrained teachers. A number of its other programmes are aimed either directly or indirectly at developing professional and vocational skills (management education, nurse education, computing, agriculture and rural development).

- reaching large numbers? The University's student numbers are rising rapidly. Some care needs to be taken in assessing the figures, because the gross enrolment figures published by the University do not reflect drop-out and hence are not an accurate measure of number of active learners in the system. The Open School programme, supported by the regular school teachers, is proving to be a significant programme in its own right. The non-formal programmes are also reaching very significant numbers of viewers, notwithstanding the relatively low ownership of television and radio receivers in rural areas.

- helping democratise education? The University was set up primarily to serve those sectors of the population who were currently excluded from the traditional education system and those who, for one reason or another, had dropped out of traditional education. Particularly targets included students in rural areas, and in particular women and out-of-school youth. In the main, BOU's higher education programmes are reaching urban populations. In direct contrast, the Open School's SSC is available nationwide, in both rural and urban areas, through over 500 tutorial centres. The SSC is also the programme that has had the greatest impact in increasing the opportunities for girls and women to participate in education. The non-formal programme is also countrywide and is likely to have a real impact on rural areas, once it is fully developed.

- reaching the masses through the use of technology? BOU is using broadcasting to deliver non-formal programmes to the rural and urban masses. At the higher education level, it has developed a second-generation distance education system (Nipper 1989: 63), based on print, correspondence tuition, audio-visual materials, broadcasting, and face-to-face tuition. Distance educators in the West are currently focusing on the possibilities of the new interactive technologies. There is little possibility that the truly underprivileged will be able to access these technologies. There are, however, more accessible, lower cost technologies. The use of lower resource-intensive technologies such as those adopted by the Bangladesh Open University should not be seen as a second rate alternative to the newer technologies being explored in the West, but as a wholly rational strategy to deal with situations arising in countries where resource is scarce. BOU's approach to distance education is emerging as an attractive and sustainable model for the use of distance education technologies to meet the challenges faced by Third World countries.

• being cost-effective and more cost-efficient than traditional educational systems? It looks as if BOU will be able to sustain itself financially, with a high proportion of its costs (and perhaps all of them) being met from fee income. How cost-efficient and cost-effective it is in comparison with conventional higher education in Bangladesh has yet to be determined. Drop-out rates are unclear, but significant numbers of students are graduating from its programmes: of the 11,195 students who enrolled on the BEd. programme in 1992 and 1993 and who therefore have had time to graduate, 5,401 (48.2 per cent) had graduated by early 1996; and of the 7,333 students who had enrolled on the Certificate in English Language Proficiency in either 1994 or 1995, 3,841 (52.4 per cent) had gained their Certificate by early 1996. These figures compare well with the graduation rates achieved by the UK Open University.

• helping avoid the opportunity costs of taking people out of their normal employment for training (e.g. in in-service teacher education)? This is one of the routine benefits of using distance education methods. Many of BOU's students are in employment.

• raising educational standards through the use of high quality materials? BOU was specifically charged with enhancing the general quality and relevance of educational programmes. The quality of its printed and audio-visual and broadcast materials is generally rated to be excellent with many of its texts already being used in other universities in the country.

There are undoubted teething problems, and several challenges to meet, before success can be assured. The project has a number of technical problems around materials distribution. More significantly, it has yet to develop and successfully deliver a non-formal programme that will make a real contribution to development in Bangladesh. There are also some worries about the ability of some members of the targeted population to access some of the formal programmes. Two issues in particular are important here. First, the University needs access to more broadcasting time. Second, there is the University's reach. If the University cannot find the tutors and cannot set up local centres that are accessible to the students, its reach in some subject areas, at least, will remain limited. Nevertheless, BOU's experience to date suggests that it is possible to create an effective distance-teaching system that will meet mass needs without recourse to high technology solutions. The Delors report (Delors *et al.* 1996) indicates the massive scale of the educational problems facing the world, and particularly Third World countries, if underprivileged people are to have access to educational opportunities. Distance education offers one way of confronting the demographic and financial challenge facing educationalists. Within Bangladesh, the BOU is beginning to make a real contribution to meeting the country's educational and training needs.

References

Asian Development Bank (ADB) (1992a) *Appraisal of the Bangladesh Open University Project*, ADB, June 1992.

Asian Development Bank (ADB) (1992b) *Project Proforma*, ADB, May 1992.

Bangladesh Gazette (1992) *Bangladesh Parliament: The Act no. 38 of 1992. The Act Made for the Provision of Establishment of the Bangladesh Open University. English Version* (registered no – DA – 1).

Bates, A.W. (1995) *Technology, Open Learning and Distance Education*, London: Routledge.

Compton, J.L. and Timmons, M.C. (1993) 'Distance education and rural development: the challenge and the promise', in B. Scriven, R. Lundin and Y. Ryan (eds), *Distance Education for the Twenty-First Century*, Red Hill: Queensland University of Technology and International Council for Distance Education.

Delors, J. *et al.* (1996) *L'Éducation: Un Trésor est Caché Dedans*, Paris: Éditions UNESCO and Éditions Odile Jacob.

Enamul Haque, A.K. (1995) 'Economic feasibility of Open University', *The Guardian* (Dhaka, Bangladesh), November 1995, special issue *Open University: A Silent Revolution in Education*, 24–6.

Huq, S. (1995) 'Beneficiaries of Open University', *The Guardian* (Dhaka, Bangladesh), November 1995, special issue *Open University: A Silent Revolution in Education*, 22–3.

Mitra & Associates (1995) *Access to Media in Bangladesh: The 1995 National Media Survey*, Johns Hopkins University, Center for Communication Programs, Social Marketing Company, Population Services International, and Unicef.

Nipper, S. (1989) 'Third generation distance learning and computer conferencing', in R. Mason and A. Kaye (eds), *Mindweave: Communication, Computers and Distance Education*, Oxford: Pergamon Press.

World Bank (1994) *World Development Report 1994: Infrastructure for Development*, Oxford: Oxford University Press.

Distance education in China

Xingfu Ding

Since the end of the Cultural Revolution, China has carried out a range of socio-economic reform and a policy of increasingly opening the door to the outside world. In the next century it is anticipated that China will play a more active and important role in the international community and particularly the Asia-Pacific region. In the process of China's modernisation, distance higher education has made a special contribution to both higher education and more generally to socio-economic development. This chapter provides a broad overview of China's distance higher education and some major implications for Chinese society.

The political, economic and educational framework

Since the end of the 1970s, China, unlike Russia, other newly independent states of the former USSR, and Eastern European countries, has entered a new historical era of modernisation under the leadership of the Communist Party. In 1978, at the Third Plenary Meeting of the Eleventh Central Committee of the Chinese Communist Party, the centre of the Party and national agenda moved from class struggle and political movement to economic construction and social development. Since then, China has achieved significant progress in its process of modernisation. In 1997, at the Fifteenth National Conference of the Party, Secretary General Jiang Zeming presented a report entitled *To Comprehensively Take the Cause of Socialist Construction with Chinese Characteristics into the 21st Century by Holding High the Great Banner of Deng Xiaoping's Theory*. The Report has set an overall goal for social-economic development for the first half of the next century; by the middle of the twenty-first century, China will reach the medium level of developed countries and achieve the rejuvenation of Chinese civilisation (Jiang 1997). In fact, from 1978 to 1996, the Chinese GNP per capita has doubled twice over. This had been the principal aim of social-economic development for the last two decades of this century and was achieved four years earlier than the expected target year of 2000.

According to *The Governmental Working Report*, presented by former

Premier Li Peng to the First Plenary Meeting of the Ninth China National People's Congress in 1998, the GNP reached 7,477.2 billion RMB yuan (around US $900 billion or over US $700 per capita) in 1997, an increase of 8.8 per cent from the previous year. Based on comparative prices, the average growth rate of GNP per capita has been 11 per cent over the past five years (1993–7) (Li 1998: 7). According to *The 1997 World Development Report* issued by the World Bank, the DNP per capita for China in 1995 was US $620 and the average growth rate in the period 1985–95 reached 8.3 per cent (World Bank 1997: 214).

The Report of the Party's Fifteenth National Conference pointed out that 'The progress of Chinese modernisation mainly depends on the advance of personnel quality and the development of human resources across the nation' (Jiang 1997). From the end of the 1970s to the beginning of the 1990s, Deng Xiaoping continuously emphasised the significance of developing education, sciences and technologies in Chinese socialist modernisation. Since the Party's Fourteenth National Conference in 1992, education has been designated as a strategic priority area for development. The Central Committee of the Party and the State Council developed *The Outline of Innovation and Development for Chinese Education* and *The Executive Recommendations for the Outline* in 1993 and 1994 respectively. The *Outline* and the *Recommendations* formulated a framework of innovation and development for Chinese education in the 1990s and the early twenty-first century. A strategy entitled *Developing the Nation Through the Promotion of Science and Education* was proposed at the Sixth Plenary Meeting of Fourteenth Central Committee of the Party in 1995 and *The Ninth Five-year Plan and Developing Program for Chinese Education in 2010* were developed along with the overall national social-economic development plan in 1996. More recently, the Party's Fifteenth National Conference has reconfirmed these policies and guidelines, drawing up a blueprint for further innovation and development in Chinese education approaching the twenty-first century. In addition, the current Premier Zhu Rongji of the newly elected State Council has declared that his government will strengthen the strategy of *Developing the Nation Through the Promotion of Science and Education*. Accordingly, the past five years (1992–7) since the Party's Fourteenth National Conference has been one of the most significant periods in the development of Chinese education.

The major achievements and features of Chinese education and its development during the past five to ten years can be appreciated through an examination of some fundamental statistics. National education in China can be defined as a binary system. One subsystem is regular (pre-employment) education for the young generation, and the second is adult education. In 1996, there were 934,432 regular schools with total enrolments of 234.4 million. Among them, 740 institutions were for postgraduate study with enrolments of 162.3 thousand; 1,032 regular higher education institutions (RHEIs) with enrolments of over 3 million for undergraduate study;

98,665 regular secondary schools with enrolments of 68.3 million; 645,983 regular primary schools with enrolments of 136.2 million; 1,428 special education schools with enrolments of 321.1 thousand; and 187,324 kindergartens with enrolments of 1.2 million. There were 617,498 adult schools with total enrolments of 69.6 million. Among them, 1,138 adult higher education institutions (AHEIs) with enrolments of 2.7 million; 453,221 adult secondary schools with enrolments of 60.2 million; 163,139 adult primary schools and literacy classes with enrolments of 6,731.4 thousand (DPC of SEdC 1997: 2–3). These statistics demonstrate that Chinese education has reached new levels of scale and speed in its development. Gross entrance ratios for primary, junior secondary, senior secondary schools, universities and colleges were 98.5 per cent, 78.4 per cent, 33.6 per cent and 6.5 per cent in 1995, increased from 96.3 per cent, 66.7 per cent, 21.9 per cent and 3.4 per cent in 1990 respectively. The illiteracy rate for young and middle-aged people dropped to 6 per cent in 1997, down from 10 per cent in 1992 (Zhu 1998). Promotion rates for junior secondary, senior secondary, universities and colleges were 92.6 per cent, 48.8 per cent and 32.1 per cent in 1996, increased from 74.6 per cent, 40.6 per cent and 19.8 per cent in 1990 respectively (DPC of SEdC 1997).

An overview of open and distance learning for higher education

In 1996, President Jiang Zeming pointed out that 'There are two critical issues in our educational work which need to be more effectively addressed. One is that education has to adapt itself thoroughly to the task of training various kinds of personnel required by modernisation construction, and the other is that educational quality and effectiveness should be improved integrally'. In relation to the strategy of *Developing the Nation Through the Promotion of Science and Education* and the strategy of sustainable development, the Report of the Party's Fifteenth National Conference pointed out that:

> Science and technology are the major forces in production, the advance of science and technology is the determinant element of economic development. We need to pay much more attention to the future development of science and technology, especially high technologies and their significant influences on the overall power of the nation, its economic structure and social life. It should be assigned a key place in socio-economic development to accelerate the advancement of science and technology and to move economic construction on to a path based on the advance of science and technology and the enhancement of the quality of work.

Concerning guidelines for educational innovation and development, the

Report said: 'Developing education and science is fundamental in the engineering of cultural construction. To train high quality workers in numbers of hundreds of millions and a wide range of professional personnel in the tens of million which are required for modernisation, and to take full advantage of the huge human resources of our nation, all of these are relevant to the overall destiny of socialist construction in the twenty first century. We should make sure that education is made a strategic priority for development' (Jiang 1997: 40). These policy statements present the broad governmental priorities for national education, especially for higher education moving into the twenty-first century. Higher education has developed steadily during the last five years. On average, the number of new entrants and enrolments in higher education institutions increased by 8 per cent and 10 per cent each year. In 1997, the total number of enrolments reached 6.08 million, an increase of 62 per cent from 3.76 million in 1992. Among these were 0.18 million postgraduates, an increase of 85 per cent; 3.17 million undergraduates in regular higher education institutions, an increase of 45 per cent; and 2.73 million undergraduates in adult higher education institutions, an increase of 84 per cent (Zhu 1998).

Due to its features of openness, economy of scale and flexibility, open and distance learning has made a special and significant contribution to Chinese higher education, and more broadly to socio-economic development. First, distance higher education has widened opportunities for access to higher education, especially for employed adults, school leavers, and some disadvantaged groups. Second, it has improved the geographical distribution of higher education across China, by creating and developing educational provision for advanced study in remote, mountainous, rural and minority nationality areas where economy, science and technology, education and culture are underdeveloped. Third, distance higher education has improved the structure of higher education in particular disciplines and fields of study, and in professional areas of training personnel, as well as by providing programmes, curricula and courses urgently demanded by national and local labour markets and various groups. Fourth, distance higher education has achieved higher economy of scale and cost-effectiveness that has been recognised by governments and by the general public (Ding 1998).

China has a triple national system of distance higher education, consisting of correspondence education, radio and TV education and state examinations for self-study (Ding 1994a, 1996). Except in the case of four independent correspondence colleges, correspondence education mainly offered by regular higher education institutions and is recognised as dual-mode provision. China's radio and TV universities (RTVUs) system, a national single-mode provision, has been identified as the largest of today's eleven mega universities (Daniel 1996). The state examinations for self-study system has been classified as a 'quasi-mode' provision because it is really a state examinations system and not institutionalised education with full teaching, learning support and student management functions (Ding 1995, 1996). Concerning the funding mechanism of China's higher education sector, most regular higher education institutions are funded by national budget at central and provincial levels. However, for distance higher education (e.g. the RTVUs), there are four quite different sources of funding: government funding (51.6 per cent of the total funding) (at three levels: central – 3.6 per cent, provincial – 20.3 per cent and local – 27.7 per cent); funding from various organisations, mainly work units (40.0 per cent); funding from students themselves or their families through student fees (5.1 per cent); and a mix of other sources (3.3 per cent). (The figures came from an evaluation project conducted at the end of 1980s, see Ding 1994b.) Concerning educational cost, various researches in the 1980s (Ding 1994b) have shown that the average institutional cost of the RTVUs, including all fixed costs consumed by RTVUs and broadcasting organisations at various levels and variable costs consumed by TV classes in both recurrent expenditure and capital depreciation, was only about one-fourth of the average recurrent expenditure of the regular higher education institutions. Excluding capital depreciation, the average recurrent expenditure of RTVUs was only about one-fifth of that of the regular higher education institutions. The on-time graduation rate was more than 70–80 per cent in the RTVUs, so the annual cost per graduate of RTVUs was about one-third to two-fifths of that of the regular higher education institutions (about 30 per cent for humanities, 35 per cent for economics and 40 per cent for sciences and engineering courses respectively) (Ding 1998). From the viewpoint of demographic statistics, there have been some changes in the characteristics of undergraduate students of China's RTVUs in the past two decades (see Table 9–2.1). Basic facts and figures about distance higher education in China are shown in Tables 9–2.2 and 9–2.3.

Critical issues for distance higher education in the future

Concern for future options first arises from the awareness of changing societal context by the end of the twentieth century. In Western developed countries, modern industrial society has begun to give way to an information society with many postmodern and post-industrial features. In Eastern developing countries, though modernisation and industrialisation are still a significant task, along with the progress of economic globalisation, the information revolution is knocking at the door of many Eastern nations. Not only science and technology, but also social structures, change rapidly in an information society. All of these factors have very important implications for the future of distance higher education. The future concern also derives from changing educational circumstances during the intersection of the two centuries. An information society is a learning society. Post-compulsory education, especially mass higher education and continuing education for

Table 9–2.1 Characteristics of undergraduate students in China's RTVUs

	Entrants in 1979–82		Entrants in early 1990s		Free entrants in 1996	
	Sample data		Sample data		114,080 Entrants	
Sex	Male	72%	Male	65.3%		44%
	Female	28%	Female	34.7%		56%
Nationality	Minority	2.5%	Minority	4.2%		4.6%
Age	Average	24.9	Average	22.8	21–30	61.7%
	Maximum	53	Maximum	46	31–40	21.1%
	Minimum	15	Minimum	16		
Geographic distribution			Rural areas	32.4%	Rural areas	43.6%
					Cities	39.8%
					Major cities	16.6%
Educational qualification	SHS and above	82.4%	SHS and above	92%		
	JHS and below	17.6%	JHS and below	8%		
Employment	Average years	5.8	n/a		Employed	91.3%
	Maximum years	34				
	Unemployed	7.5%			Unemployed	8.7%

Source: Adapted from Huang and Zhao 1990; Huang et al. 1996; and Sun 1997b.

Table 9–2.2 Main features of China's national triple system of distance higher education

Correspondence education	Radio and television education	Satellite TV teacher training[a]	State examinations for self-study
	Radio and TV universities education		
Foundation date 1953 First correspondence division was set up by People's University of China in 1953	1960/1979 First group of metropolitan TV universities set up in the 1960s China's national RTVUs system was founded in 1979	1986/1987/1993[a] China began to transmit satellite TV education programmes in 1986 China's TV Teacher Training Institute was set up in 1987	1981 State examinations of higher education for self-study were first introduced in several metropolises in 1981
Provision in 1997–8 635 regular higher education institutions have built up their correspondence divisions/schools 4 independent correspondence colleges	1 Central Radio and TV University 44 Provincial RTVUs 823 branch schools 1,713 work stations Over 13,176 TV sites (classes)	China's TV Teacher Training Institute Various education colleges Teacher training schools The national RTVUs system	National Guidance Committee Provincial Guidance Committees Various examinations held in regular higher education institutions Various learning support units
Student numbers in 1996–7 Enrolments: 896,300 Entrants: 286,400 Graduates: 212,300	Enrolments: 526,600 Entrants: 197,100 Graduates: 187,900	(Not calculated independently)	In 1997 Enrolments (unit: person-course): 5,000,000 Graduates: 300,000

Programmes			
Normal undergraduate studies awarding university diploma and degree	Short-cycle undergraduate studies mainly awarding college diploma	Normal undergraduate studies for senior highschool teachers	Normal undergraduate studies awarding university diploma and degree
Short-cycle undergraduate studies awarding college diploma	Normal undergraduate studies awarding university diploma and degree	Short-cycle undergraduate studies for junior high school teachers	Short-cycle undergraduate studies awarding college diploma in both fundamental and specialised programmes
	Various non-diploma programmes awarding certificates only for adults	Various non-diploma programmes for in-service teacher training	
Curricula and courses			
Most fields of study and disciplines in universities	Most fields of study and disciplines in universities	Teacher training courses	Most fields of study and disciplines in universities
Target groups in 1996–7			
Adults mainly	Adults mainly (School leavers: 35% of total)	In-service teachers in senior and junior high schools	Any applicants by independent study without limitation
Types of enrolment and learning strategy			
Part-time and spare-time	Full-time, part-time and spare-time	Spare-time	Spare-time
Group based: correspondence, classes in work places	Group based: TV classes in work places of RTVUs	Group based or individually in the schools	Individually in most cases and in groups occasionally
Compulsory pace of study	Compulsory pace of study	Compulsory pace of study	Flexible pace of study

Table 9–2.2 contd

	Radio and television education		
Correspondence education	Radio and TV universities education	Satellite TV teacher training[a]	State examinations for self-study

Educational technology and instructional media

Printed course materials	Printed course materials	Print course materials	Printed course materials
A few audio-visual materials	Nationwide and local radio and television programmes by satellite, cable and microwave networks	National television programmes by satellite	A few audio-visual materials
Correspondence tutorials		Other audio-visual materials	Face-to-face tutorials by various kinds of institutions and organisations
Face-to-face tutorials, regular and at semester-end	Other audio-visual materials	Face-to-face tutorials	
	Face-to-face tutorials		
	A few CAI and multimedia courseware		
	A few initiatives using computer and telecommunications networks		

Model of organisational and administrative structure and function[b]

Separated model of dual mode	Hierarchical multi-bodied model of single mode	Course transmission centre model of quasi mode	State examination model of quasi mode

Source: Ding 1996: 329–30; DPC of SEdC (1997); ICEM of CRTVU (1998).

Notes
a   China's TV Teacher Training Institute (CTVTTI) has become a part of China's Central Radio and TV University (CRTVU) since 1993.
b   Refer to Ding 1995, 1996.

Table 9–2.3 Time series of the development of distance higher education in China (unit: ten thousand)

	1982	1985	1988	1990	1991	1992	1993	1994	1995	1996	1997
New entrants											
Higher education	58.92	140.68	136.80	110.13	108.54	134.59	179.17	168.48	183.97	191.10	n/a
Adult higher education	27.42	78.78	69.83	49.24	46.55	59.17	86.27	78.50	91.38	94.52	n/a
Distance higher education	22.04	45.23	38.66	27.22	23.91	32.69	47.56	57.28	47.68	41.84	n/a
Correspondence education	3.54	17.92	19.47	16.00	13.56	18.33	25.70	34.06	27.62	21.23	n/a
RTVUs education	18.50	27.31	19.19	11.22	10.35	14.36	21.86	23.22	20.06	20.61	20.03
Graduates											
Higher education	68.41	66.33	130.74	110.24	123.47	112.20	101.19	109.26	144.15	161.01	n/a
Adult higher education	22.69	34.70	75.39	48.88	62.04	51.78	44.12	45.52	63.61	77.15	n/a
Distance higher education	14.26	21.69	43.97	24.77	32.53	29.16	23.82	23.08	32.07	40.24	n/a
Correspondence education	5.06	5.17	16.47	12.72	16.24	17.06	14.02	13.02	16.29	21.23	n/a
RTVUs education	9.20	16.52	27.50	12.05	16.29	12.10	9.80	10.05	15.78	19.01	18.71
Enrolments											
Higher education	232.70	342.80	379.36	372.94	351.71	366.31	439.84	515.65	547.65	567.685	n/a
Adult higher education	117.30	172.50	172.76	166.64	147.31	147.87	186.29	235.17	257.01	265.57	n/a
Distance higher education	42.39	104.81	94.36	97.02	82.73	82.69	103.20	133.20	140.01	143.25	n/a
Correspondence education	16.54	37.45	48.98	56.25	49.26	49.65	59.34	78.41	85.48	89.63	n/a
RTVUs education	25.85	67.36	45.38	40.77	33.47	33.04	43.86	54.79	54.53	53.62	51.64

Source: DPC of SEdC (1984, 1991, 1992, 1993, 1994, 1995, 1996, 1997); Sun (1997a); ICEM of CRTVU (1998).

adults, will become a significant part of all national educational systems. The ongoing growth of adult education and lifelong education, and the development of various kinds of resource-based teaching and learning, will continuously change traditional educational philosophy and pedagogy. Distance education and open learning will make significant contributions to and will benefit from such general developments and changes. With these contextual changes in mind, the critical issues for educational development in the early twenty-first century worldwide could be summarised as follows.

- Conventional education will maintain its position as the mainstream form of provision. Advanced technology will make inroads into traditional instruction. A significant proportion of instruction in higher education on campus will be carried on through information technology in addition to the face-to-face oral interaction process. Gradually, there will be an increasing convergence between conventional and distance education. Eventually, conventional instruction will evolve from a pre-industrial (handicraft) form to a post-industrial form (information technology intensive, with high levels of academic responsibility and a learner-centred approach).

- All distance education systems need to improve further in the open learning dimension, that is, to make continuing efforts not only in openness and equity of access, but also in openness and flexibility of teaching and learning. Conventional educational institutions can also make a great contribution in developing open learning initiatives. They may offer open learning courses independently, jointly and/or collaboratively with distance education provision. Open learning will be the most significant development in the sector of continuing education and in-service training.

- Distance-teaching universities will continue to develop early in the next century. However, for most dual-mode universities, distance education or off-campus studies will continue to be treated as second rate by the institutions and as a marginal job by academic staff. Most campus-based universities, especially the best-known ones, will not convert themselves into dual-mode universities. Nevertheless, there will be a growth in the number of campus-based universities converted into dual-mode universities, and an increasing number of dual-mode universities where on-campus and off-campus studies operate in an integrated way. In the next century, distance-teaching universities, dual-mode universities and various kinds of multi-institutional models of provision will face more competition, and will need more collaboration in forming various national systems and in becoming part of the globalisation process.

In the Chinese context, during the intersection from the twentieth century to the twenty-first century, three significant historical shifts are expected to be achieved in a single jump: from agricultural society to industrialised society, and then to information society, and from planning economy to market economy. The development of education, including higher education and adult education, has been planned on a strategic basis for this commitment. Due to its huge population and vast territory, and the weak and unbalanced development of its higher education system, distance higher education for adults will have great strategic significance for Chinese modernisation in the next century.

- China will maintain a national binary system of higher education consisting of regular higher education institutions and adult higher education institutions. In the early twenty-first century, China's conventional higher education will retain its handicraft, elite and closed features: residential full-time studies on-campus for young school leavers who pass the National Unified Entrance Examinations successfully. Nevertheless, along with the economic development and technological advance in Chinese society, China's conventional higher education will gradually carry out a series of reforms and innovations moving towards a more open, cost-effective and technology-based system.

- China's adult higher education will continue to develop in two sectors: campus-based and distance provision. In the Chinese context, distance higher education will develop more rapidly. China's national triple system of distance higher education with single (RTVUs), dual (correspondence education) and 'quasi' (state examinations for self-study) modes will develop further. Competition needs to be balanced and coordinated, and collaboration must be encouraged and developed by formulating new policies, a funding scheme, and evaluation by the government, and by encouraging various initiatives by institutions.

- China's RTVUs should and could develop more rapidly in the early part of the next century. Some recent innovative trends will develop further:
    - efforts to meet the needs of changing markets nationally, locally and individually;
    - efforts towards a more open and flexible learner-centred learning policy and strategy;
    - encouragement of innovation in the use of educational technology and improvement in the instructional design of course materials; and
    - continuing to construct and improve the infrastructure for student learning support services.

In this way, the national RTVUs system will continuously shift from a highly centralised Fordist paradigm into a more decentralised and flexible neo-Fordist and then post-Fordist model.

• In the Chinese context, the regular higher education institutions will continuously make their contribution to adult higher education in the form of running evening schools, higher correspondence education and state examinations for self-study. More and more RHEIs will convert themselves into dual-mode providers with both on- and off-campus studies for young school leavers and employed adults.

China will continuously share experiences and perceptions of distance education and open learning with other nations in the world, especially with developing countries in Asia and with some Western developed countries (Ding 1996).

Abbreviations

CRTVU   Central Radio and TV University
CTVTTI   China's TV Teacher Training Institute
DPC   Department of Planning and Construction, SEdC, China
ICEM   Information Center of Educational Management, CCRTVU
PRTVUs   Provincial Radio and TV Universities
RTVUs   Radio and TV Universities
SEdC   State Education Commission, China

References

Daniel, J. (1996) *Mega-Universities and Knowledge Media: Technology Strategies for Higher Education*, London: Kogan Page.
Ding, X. (1994a) 'China's higher distance education – its four systems and their structural characteristics at three levels', *Distance Education*, 15, 2, 327–46.
Ding, X. (1994b) 'Economic analysis of the radio and television universities in China', *Open Praxis*, 1994, 2, 14–21.
Ding, X. (1995) 'China's higher distance education – its system, structure and administration', in AAOU, *Structure and Management of Open Learning Systems. Proceedings of the 8th Annual Conference of the AAOU, New Delhi, 20–22 February 1995*, New Delhi: Indira Gandhi National Open University, 1: 260–74.
Ding, X. (1996) 'A Comparative Study of Higher Distance Education Systems in Australia and China', unpublished PhD thesis, Murdoch University, Australia.
Ding, X. (1998) 'Evaluation of distance teaching universities: Chinese perspective and experiences', in *Keynote Papers and CD-ROM for '98*, Shanghai International Open and Distance Education Symposium, 15–17 April 1998, Shanghai, China: Shanghai TV University.
Department of Planning and Construction of State Education Commission (DPC

of SedC) (1984, 1991, 1992, 1993, 1994, 1995, 1996, 1997) *Educational Statistics Yearbook of China*, Beijing: People's Education Press.

Huang, Y. and Zhao, Y. (eds) (1990) 'Report on first trace study of graduates for China's RTVUs', *China's RTVU Education*, 1990, 9, 13–48 and 10, 42–8.

Huang, Y. *et al.* (eds) (1996) *Method and Practice of Comparative Study for Education: A Chinese-Japanese Joint Project on Comparative Study Between Radio and TV Higher Education and Conventional Higher Education in China*, Beijing: CRTVU Press.

Information Center of Educational Management of CRTVU (1998) 'The '97 communiqué of basic statistics of China RTVUs education', *China RTVU Education*, 1998, 3.

Jiang, Z. (1997) *To Comprehensively Take the Cause of Socialist Construction with Chinese Characteristics into the 21st Century by Holding High the Great Banner of Deng Xiaoping's Theory*, Beijing.

Li, P. (1998) 'The Governmental Working Report', in Office of Standing Committee of National People's Congress (ed.), *The Documents of the First Plenary Session of Ninth National People's Congress in People's Republic of China*, Beijing.

Sun, L. (1997a) *1996 Education Statistics Yearbook of Radio and TV Universities in China*. Beijing: CRTVU Press.

Sun, L. (1997b) 'A pilot program of enrolling "free entrance students" in China's RTVUs and its quality assurance', in P. Chooi *et al.* (eds), *Quality Assurance in Distance and Open Learning*, conference proceedings for the 11th annual conference of the Asian Association of Open Universities, Putra World Trade Center, Kuala Lumpur, Malaysia, November 11–14, 1997, 1: 245–50.

World Bank (1997) *The 1997 World Development Report: The Governments in A Changing World*, Chinese version, Beijing: Chinese Finance and Economics Press.

Zhu, K. (1998) 'The Speech at '98 Educational Working Meeting by State Education Commission', *China Education Daily*, 11 February 1998.

The Open University of Hong Kong

David Murphy and Yvonne Fung

It may be difficult to imagine why Hong Kong needs distance education. After all, with its 6 million or so people living in such close proximity to each other, distance surely is not a problem. However, 'distance' can take on many forms, not just geographical, and for such reasons distance education has taken firm hold in Hong Kong, and continues to grow and flourish. This chapter outlines this growth, focusing in particular on the establishment of the Open University of Hong Kong, and highlighting emerging issues, particularly those relating to the offering of overseas distance education courses.

The major development in distance and open education in Hong Kong over the past decade has thus been the establishment and steady growth of the Open Learning Institute of Hong Kong, more recently known as the Open University of Hong Kong. Clearly differing from its university counterparts in Hong Kong with respect to its student base and its mode of operation, an additional identifying feature of the OUHK is that it is the only university in Hong Kong which does not receive government funding through the University Grants Committee. Fundamentally, it is self-funding, having been provided with seeding money to get started and left to fend for itself in Hong Kong's highly competitive distance education market-place.

The Hong Kong context

Hong Kong is the vibrant and prosperous home of about 6.3 million persons and, as is well known, has recently changed status from that of a British colony to a Special Administrative Region of the People's Republic of China. Although affected by the Asian economic crisis of late 1997, it continues to act as a regional financial hub, and is emerging relatively unscathed from the economic crisis. Hong Kong's population in general enjoys a high standard of living, with the per capita GDP being higher than most of its regional neighbours, including Australia.

As far as education is concerned, nine years of free and compulsory education for children between ages 6 and 15 has been available since 1978. Over 85 per cent of the young people continue with full-time education to Secondary 5 after compulsory schooling and most of the others enrol in full-time vocational training of one sort or another for another one or two years (Education and Manpower Branch 1994). Entry to tertiary education was very competitive until the 1990s. In the mid-1980s, there were only two universities and one polytechnic, providing 2.2 per cent of the 17 to 20 age group with a local first degree programme (ibid.). A review of the education system by overseas consultants recognised that Hong Kong people had a great need for tertiary education, but the panel was conservative in suggesting the expansion of higher education provision. The main concern at that time was the availability of sites for new universities and the foreseeable difficulty in recruiting qualified and motivated university staff (Llewellyn *et al.* 1982). However, there was growing demand for higher education to cater for the increased need to have a better qualified workforce, in both government and non-government sectors, as Hong Kong's economy moved from manufacturing towards services and finance.

The Hong Kong government, in meeting this demand and the aspirations and needs of Hong Kong people, decided in 1989 to expand access to full-time undergraduate education to 18 per cent by 1994 (University Grants Committee 1996). This was made possible by the inception of a third university in 1991, the expansion of the existing two universities, the offering of more degree programmes in the two polytechnics and the two other tertiary institutes. With the later attainment of university status by the polytechnics and another tertiary institution, Hong Kong's tertiary sector expanded to include six universities and one degree-offering college providing full-time degree programmes for secondary school leavers. All of these tertiary institutions are government funded. Since the expansion of places in higher education, the government has focused on enhancing the quality and cost-effectiveness of higher education. This year it has proposed the development of centres of excellence in its universities, for improving the quality and relevance of teaching, learning and research.

Knowledge of the major issues that have faced the ongoing development of educational provision in Hong Kong can be gleaned from the periodic Education Commission Reports, which began in 1984. These reports, along with earlier White Papers, have been highly influential in determining government policy and direction with respect to education. However, in recent years implementation of recommendations has become less effective (Cheng 1995), particularly as the government tries to address the thorny issue of quality. Initiatives such as the Target-oriented Curriculum and the School Management Initiative have not been able to achieve their initial aims, and the issue of language proficiency continues to defy easy solution.

A history of open and distance education in Hong Kong

As early as 1979, the Working Group set up by the Hong Kong government to reassess the 1977 Green Paper on 'Senior Secondary and Tertiary Education' mentioned possible development of open learning as one of the options for the development of tertiary education (Government Secretariat, Hong Kong Government 1981). However, the government considered technical and vocational education to be more important in meeting economic demand, and decided that this, and general education, should be the target of expansion at that time. The report by the overseas visiting panel in 1982 considered the introduction of a 'university without walls' using the mass media as an attractive idea but was sceptical about its viability and credibility (Llewellyn *et al.* 1982). It described this kind of university as a 'surrogate form of higher education' (ibid.: 64), not really based on the principles of continuing education. Hong Kong's neighbour city – Macau – had just established a university with an Open College. It was reported that the Executive Council of Hong Kong at that time decided that the Open College of Macau should not be permitted to operate study centres in Hong Kong to support its distance-learning programmes, but rather a public-sector open university-type institution for Hong Kong should be considered (ibid.).

In 1984, the Education Commission Report No. 1 (ECR1) devoted one of its nine chapters to discussion of the advisability of setting up an open university in Hong Kong. It defined an open university as 'a dedicated institution which provides part-time higher education for adults in full-time employment or working in the home using distance-learning techniques' (Education Commission 1984: 73). Although the Education Commission recognised the value of open education as a means to remove access barriers and its possibility to extend education and training opportunities to a wider population, it endorsed the recommendation of the then University and Polytechnics Grants Committee that an open university, along the lines of the UK Open University, should not be set up for three reasons: the worry that there might not be enough students; the potential difficulty in recruiting qualified tutors; and the lack of study space at home for most Hong Kong people. Rather, the Commission recommended that there should be development of open education based on all existing tertiary institutions.

Though ECR1 did not support the establishment of an open university in Hong Kong, the Education Commission, in its second report (ECR2), revisited the issue of setting up an autonomous open university based on the British model. Again, the Education Commission (1986) confirmed the value of open education at post-secondary level for providing a second chance for those who were denied the opportunity to pursue further education earlier on, and for a more educated workforce for maintaining Hong Kong's economic, educational and social development. In proposing a framework for

Hong Kong, ECR2 studied the relationship between open education and distance learning, and recommended the adoption of a distance-learning approach consisting of pre-prepared course materials. Possible future development included the use of advanced techniques such as teleconferencing and cable television. Taking into consideration the recommendation of ECR1 that it was not practical to set up an autonomous open university, ECR2 proposed a consortium approach in which all five publicly funded tertiary institutions should be invited (but not forced) to participate as core members of the consortium. ECR2 also made further recommendations as to the organisation of the consortium, the mode of course delivery, and quality assurance and validation mechanisms. Significantly, it recommended that the open education institution should eventually become self-financing, with students meeting the direct costs of the courses which they took.

A year after the release of ECR2, the government set up a planning committee for establishing a degree-granting distance-learning institution with open access – the Open Learning Institute of Hong Kong (OLI). Although ECR2 recommended the development of open education through a consortium approach, when the OLI was established it was an independent autonomous institution. Its council did, however, include representatives from other local tertiary and overseas distance-learning institutions. This variation of the original intention is not surprising, given the poor track record of universities worldwide to work collaboratively. Resistance to formal collaborative arrangements, along with the lack of substantial progress towards ECR2 aims, meant that the establishment of an autonomous institution could be more quickly achieved. By mid-summer 1989, legislation for the OLI's establishment had been passed in the Legislative Council, with a role to provide higher education opportunities for adults by distance-learning methods. Hong Kong's universities provided, and continue to provide, informal collaborative support, mostly through the use of their academic staff as contracted course writers of open learning materials.

Initially, and necessarily given its funding and short establishment time, the OUHK was openly 'parasitic', drawing on course materials from around the globe, with the main supplier being the UK's Open University. Within a short time, however, it began developing its own courses, so that currently the majority of OUHK students are studying locally produced learning materials (or materials adapted from overseas courses) in both English and Chinese.

Following the CNAA panel's advisory visit in 1989, the OLI sought an institutional review in 1990 and, in 1992 all of its eighteen degree programmes at that time were validated by the Hong Kong Council for Academic Accreditation (HKCAA). With another institutional review by the HKCAA in 1995, OLI was recommended to attain self-accredited status by 1996. Then, in May 1997, it gained university status and was renamed the Open University of Hong Kong (OUHK). Though the former OLI achieved its self-financing goal in 1994, the Hong Kong government continued to make contributions to facilitate its development by providing it with special funds for course development, a new campus, an electronic library and a student financial-assistance scheme. Although the OUHK continues to operate outside the financial provisions of the University Grants Commission, financial support from the government is a clear indication of the acknowledgement of the contribution of OUHK to the community and a recognition of its quality and credibility. The significance of OUHK as a distance-learning university for Hong Kong working adults has been recognised by the Hong Kong Special Administrative Region government. In the first policy address of the chief executive – made in October 1997 – HK $50 million was granted to the Open University, chiefly for its development as a centre of excellence in adult and distance learning.

Today the OUHK is a financially viable institution providing open education to tens of thousands of part-time adult students. Overall figures relating to the University's operation and student numbers are shown in Table 9–3.1.

Issue – overseas courses

The Open University of Hong Kong is not, however, the only institution offering distance education courses in the Special Administrative Region. Most other tertiary institutions, along with dozens of minor private providers, offer such courses, but almost always through a cooperative arrangement with an overseas provider. The quality of the courses is highly variable, especially those associated with private providers, and many of them do not strictly adhere to normal definitions of distance education. This will be further discussed in the next section.

As well, a small number of distance education courses have been developed in Hong Kong by other universities. For example, the Hong Kong Polytechnic University has run a Certificate in Textiles and Clothing Manufacture for over a decade (offered in both English and Chinese), along with a Certificate Course in Pre-primary Education (in Chinese) for untrained kindergarten and nursery teachers.

It is difficult to obtain precise figures on the numbers of Hong Kong students studying with overseas institutions. While numbers who leave Hong Kong to study overseas can be found (it peaked at over 20,000 in 1990–1) (Lee and Lam 1994: 31), the numbers living in Hong Kong who are enrolled with an overseas institution are not easily accessible. What is clear is that the numbers exceed both the number who study overseas and the number enrolled with the Open University of Hong Kong. A further compounding problem is one of classification, in that it is not always clear whether or not a particular offering can be labelled a distance education course. Many of the courses are offered as a combination of self-learning materials (from the

Table 9–3.1 Basic data on the Open University of Hong Kong

	No
Programmes	
Master's degrees	3
Bachelor's degrees	36
Sub-degrees	24
Short courses	16
Students	
Male	11,654
Female	11,250
Total	22,904
Full-time equivalents	9,937
Age profile	
Below 22	7.4%
22–25	15.4%
26–30	22.2%
31–35	26.3%
Over 35	28.7%
Average age	32
Graduates	6,000 (approx.)
Staff	
Full-time	380
Part-time	980
Distribution of full-time staff	
Academic	22%
Administrative	26%
General support	52%
Finance (HK$Million, 96/7)	
Total income	337
Tuition fee income	314
Government subvention	nil
Others	23
Total recurrent expenditure	323
Academic	167
Administration	156
Capital (including course development)	21
Average unit cost per student (HK$)	$15,805

Source: Open University of Hong Kong statistics (December 1997).

overseas institution) and face-to-face teaching (provided by local academics or visiting academics from overseas).

At least 319 tertiary institutions from seventeen countries advertise their courses to potential students in Hong Kong (Lee and Lam 1994). Many of these institutions offer distance education programmes, sometimes through a local institution or agent. The areas of business and commerce are particularly popular, with a choice of around sixty MBAs available to Hong Kong professionals (Carr 1997). A large proportion of the distance education programmes from overseas are offered collaboratively with Hong Kong tertiary institutions, usually through continuing education centres. The largest of these is The University of Hong Kong's School of Professional and Continuing Education, with around 18,500 enrolments in degree and postgraduate distance education courses, as well as tens of thousands of other students enrolled in sub-degree and short courses (Cribbin 1997).

Until recently, there was little regulatory control by Hong Kong authorities of overseas distance education courses. Any non-local institution could introduce its programmes to Hong Kong without any intervention by the Hong Kong government. However, concerns have been voiced over many years about the provision of distance education courses at the tertiary level. In particular, there was a perceived case for establishing public safeguards, as 'the public needs to be protected from the incompetent and the substandard' (Pagliari and Frost 1987). Such concerns are certainly valid, as over the years there have been regular cases of Hong Kong students being cheated by unscrupulous local agents of sometimes equally unscrupulous overseas operators. The aim of government policy and intervention should then be, as propounded by government officers Pagliari and Frost (1987: 512), '*first*, to ensure that what is offered is of a satisfactory standard and *second*, to encourage the external institution to involve Hong Kong post-secondary institutions where possible'.

It took some years, but the situation with respect to regulation changed with the introduction of the Non-Local Higher and Professional Education (Regulation) Ordinance, passed on 18 July 1996. The upshot of the Ordinance is that all non-local distance education programmes and their agents/operators have to be registered. The aim is to ensure the standard and academic level of such programmes. Under the regulation, all institutions offering non-local university distance education courses conducted in Hong Kong must apply for registration. The major criteria for registration are that the institution must be recognised in its home country, and that the course offered to Hong Kong students must be at the same level as the equivalent offered in the country of origin. It is significant, though, that courses offered in collaboration with local institutions of higher education are exempted, the local institution being required to provide the registrar with certification of the collaborative arrangement.

Costs of registration are significant, and potential penalties for offences or non-compliance with certain provisions are severe (including forcible police entry to premises, personal detention, seizure of documents, and possible fines and imprisonment). There is an initial payment required of HK $33,200 for degree-level and HK $16,600 for professional-level courses, with annual reregistration fees of HK $18,200 and HK $2,300 respectively. In addition, the regulation requires the use of safe premises for conducting tutorials and other student support activities. Many commercial buildings currently used by overseas institutions and their local agents do not comply with the fire, building safety, approved planning and land use provisions for educational purposes. This may shift tutorials to hotels, which may be used for educational purposes under an exemption clause, and consequently increase costs for overseas providers. The overall effect is thus considerable pressure for overseas providers to work in collaboration with local institutions of higher education, so as to secure exemption from the regulation. The future of independent local operators and agents is thus questionable.

Conclusion

Distance education has experienced rapid growth in the past decade or so, and demand seems likely to continue. The Open University of Hong Kong has evolved rapidly into a viable self-financing institution, and its future appears secure, especially with its development of courses in Chinese, clearly with an eye to enhancing links with the rest of China. The Hong Kong government, with its introduction of regulation of course offerings, has given tacit approval for overseas institutions to continue offering their distance education courses to local students, albeit with certain safeguards.

References

Carr, R. (1997) 'Cultural relevance as a quality issue', in Chew Poh Chooi *et al.* (eds), 11th annual conference of the Asian Association of Open Universities, *Quality Assurance in Open and Distance Learning*, Kuala Lumpur, 11–14 November.

Cheng, K.M. (1995) 'Education: crises amidst challenges', in Y.L. Cheung and M.H. Sze (eds), *The Other Hong Kong Report 1995*, Hong Kong: The Chinese University Press.

Cribbin, J.A. (1997) 'Opportunities for international cooperation', in Chew Poh Chooi *et al.* (eds), 11th annual conference of the Asian Association of Open Universities, *Quality Assurance in Open and Distance Learning*, Kuala Lumpur, 11–14 November.

Education and Manpower Branch (1994) *A Guide to Education and Training in Hong Kong*, Hong Kong: Government Printer.

Education Commission (1984) *Education Commission Report No. 1*, Hong Kong: Government Printer.

Education Commission (1986) *Education Commission Report No. 2*, Hong Kong: Government Printer.

Government Secretariat, Hong Kong Government (1981) *The Hong Kong Education System*, Hong Kong: Government Printer.

Kember, D., Lai, T., Murphy, D., Siaw, I. and Yuen, K.S. (1992) 'Demographic characteristics of Hong Kong distance learning students', *International Council for Distance Education Bulletin*, 29, 24–34.

Lee, N. and Lam, A. (1994) *Professional and Continuing Education in Hong Kong: Issues and Perspectives*, Hong Kong: Hong Kong University Press.

Llewellyn, J., Hancock, G., Kirst, M. and Roeloffs, K. (1982) *A Perspective on Education in Hong Kong: Report by a Visiting Panel*, Hong Kong: Government Printer.

Open Learning Institute of Hong Kong (1995) *Opening Doors to Learning: The First Five Years of the OLI*, Hong Kong: Open University of Hong Kong.

Pagliari, M. and Frost, J.A. (1987) 'Distance education in Hong Kong', in Asian Development Bank, *Distance Education in Asia and the Pacific*, vol. 2, Manila: ADB.

University Grants Committee (1996) *Higher Education in Hong Kong: A Report by the University Grants Committee of Hong Kong*, Hong Kong: Government Printer.

Developments, networking and convergence in India

Santosh Panda

Context

India has had a democratic government of its own since 1947, when it got independence from British Rule (and when the greater India was divided between India and Pakistan, and later in 1971 Pakistan being divided between Bangladesh and Pakistan). Its planned mixed economy (with co-existence of public and private sectors) is in order since 1951 when the first Five Year Plan was prepared and implemented; and its present educational structure is an outcome of continuous experiments of scholarship and perseverance since the ancient times.

As a developing democracy, its GNP per capita stands at US $329 (1996–7) and GDP per capita is US $358 (1997–8), and during the last decade due largely to economic liberalisation the disparity between rich and poor has increased, and the public control on the production and distribution system has been reduced considerably. Out of a total population of about 966 million, about 40 per cent (386 million) live below the poverty line, and about 60 per cent (580 million) belong to the disadvantaged group (scheduled caste, scheduled tribe, rural poor, urban poor, women in villages and small towns, and handicapped) (Gandhe 1998); and while the Constitution recognises fifteen major languages, as many as 1,652 dialects and languages are spoken. The government spends about 2.5 per cent of GDP on defence; the expenditure on education stands at 3.4 per cent of the GNP (about 21 per cent of the total budget). Since education is in the concurrent list (of both central and state governments), the state governments on an average spend about 22 per cent of their budget on education annually (Mukhopadhyay 1994). Six per cent of the GNP for education recommended by the Kothari Education Commission in 1966 and promised by the last two central governments has not yet come into force, nor seems to be so in the near future.

The structure of education is such that a student enters grade 1 at the age of 6 and continues until grade 12 without any diversification, after which varieties of specialised areas of study begin. The 10 + 2 + 3 system of education (ten years of secondary, two years of higher secondary and three years of graduation) is in operation in all the twenty-six states and six union territories in the country. Higher education starts after 10 + 2 education, and a Bachelor's degree is earned after three years of study in liberal arts, four years in the case of most professional colleges, about four-and-a-half years in the case of medicine and five to six years in the case of law.

The constitution of India guarantees free compulsory (universal) elementary education (up to grade 8, age of 14). A 1994 Government of India document (GOI 1994) shows that since independence the number of elementary schools and enrolment of children have increased from 234 thousand and 22.28 million to 725 thousand and 144.1 million respectively in 1992–3. About 243 thousand non-formal education centres enrolled about 5.3 million school drop-outs in 1993–4. While every child is expected to get enrolled in grade 1 (about 153 million in 1991, comprising 18 per cent of the total population), this is not always the case; and the drop-out rate is 46.97 per cent in grades 1 to 5 and 62.29 per cent in grades 1 to 8, and about six out of 100 enrolled at grade 1 pass out grade 10. At the secondary level, only 35 per cent of children of the relevant age group attend school which comes down to about 6 per cent for higher education. Out of 190 million children to be enrolled for 1997 in formal and non-formal schools/schooling centres (which had capacity to enrol about 150 million), about 40 million children were yet to be provided with school education which the National Open School and State Open Schools are expected to cater to (besides their secondary, higher secondary and need-based programmes). A gigantic task indeed!

Starting from just twenty universities (seventeen before, three in the same year) at the time of independence, there has been a transition from an elite system to a mass system of higher education which has been marked by a twelvefold increase in the number of university-level institutions, and about twenty-eightfold increase in the number of students. India has the second largest higher education system in the world comprising 237 universities, about 9,000 colleges, 7 million students, and above 0.30 million teachers. The annual growth rate of students in universities and colleges which was as high as 10 per cent in the 1970s and 4.2 per cent in the 1980s has now stabilised at 4.5 per cent. This is just 6 per cent of India's population in the relevant age group of 18–23 (5.5 per cent for Sri Lanka, 3.8 per cent for Bangladesh, and 2.8 per cent for Pakistan), which is abysmally low compared to the gross enrolment ratio of about 99 per cent in Canada, 76 per cent in the USA, 40 per cent in Western Europe and 18 to 20 per cent in Southeast Asia (UNESCO 1994). During the last fifty years, male:female ratio has come down from 8.29:1 to 1.69:1 and the general and scheduled caste and scheduled tribes ratio has increased from 6.27:1 to 7.16:1 (though in absolute terms the number of the latter has increased about three-and-a-half times).

The government expenditure on higher education under various Five Year Plans has come down from 25 per cent in the Fourth Plan of 1969–74 to 8 per cent of total educational expenditure during the Eighth Plan of 1992–7. Expenditure of central and state governments put together was 10.09 per cent in 1995–6.

As higher education shifts from elitism to massification additional resources are sought through cost recovery from students. India is no exception to this; and the recent discussion paper of the Government of India (1997) clearly classified education (other than elementary and agricultural education) as a non-merit service for which subsidies may be reduced so as to further reduce the overall subsidies which constitute 14.4 per cent of the GDP. The end result would be further increase in student fees which are, however, very low in colleges and universities.

Distance education: development and status

Government support for higher education after the Fourth Plan period (1969–74) has decreased considerably. There is an increasing rush of students at the doors of colleges and universities which the mainstream sector cannot accommodate. There has been a tremendous increase in the number of institutions, but it could not keep pace with the increasing number of students. The Private Universities Bill which is lying for long in the Parliament when implemented may take care of the number especially in professional education, though this would be on the basis of increasing cost recovery from students. There are private colleges in almost all the states in the country, and in some they outnumber government supported colleges. At the university level only a few reputed institutions like Birla Institute of Technology and Science, Manipal Academy of Higher Education, Bharati Vidyapeeth have been accorded the status of deemed-to-be universities. For obvious reasons, therefore, distance education was considered as a viable supplementary mode.

Though there have been reports pointing out that Ekalavya (the disciple) studied the art of archery from the Guru at a distance in ancient times or that Loka Siksha Sambad (Council for People's Education) initiated in 1937 in Visva-Bharti (central university) by Nobel Laureate Tagore made 'best use of distance education as a tool for continuing and further education' (Mukherjee 1997: 21), it was in 1962 that distance education in the form of correspondence courses at undergraduate level with 1,112 students was started at the University of Delhi in response to the recommendations of the committee of the Central Advisory Board of Education, Government of India headed by Dr D.S. Kothari (GOI 1962). The initiation of correspondence education was broadly aimed at providing higher education opportunities to those who could not make it to mainstream colleges, could not afford regular education and could not attend classes regularly due to social, family and employment constraints.

The government sent three delegations to the erstwhile USSR during 1967–71 to study their evening and correspondence courses. Though the

University Grants Commission (UGC) had agreed in principle to set up a
National Institute of Correspondence Courses in 1972, it was never established. A national seminar on 'open university' was organised by the union
Ministry of Education and Social Welfare in collaboration with the UNESCO
in 1970 in which detailed recommendations for such a university were made.
This is to point out that the deliberations and developments towards open
distance education in India were in conformity with such contemporary
developments elsewhere in the world, though the then scepticism and political
elephant-walk slowed down the process of both reforming the existing correspondence education and establishing independent open universities in the
country. By 1970, nine universities were offering correspondence courses.

The Fifth Plan (1974–9) had expected about one-fourth of university
enrolment in correspondence courses which might comprise about 600 thousand students. On the basis of the 1970 seminar, the government of India
constituted a working group to deliberate on the establishment of an open
university, though no progress could be made afterwards. The government of
the state of Andhra Pradesh appointed an expert committee with Professor
G. Ram Reddy as its Chairman on 25 May 1982, to look into the establishment of an open university in the state. It is a sort of record that the report of
the committee was submitted and the Andhra Pradesh Open University
(APOU, renamed as BRAOU) established within about two-and-a-half
months through an Act of the State Legislature in August 1982. By that time,
thirty-four universities had introduced correspondence education, and about
6.16 per cent of students were pursuing higher education at a distance.

With the enduring efforts made by academicians, APOU leadership and
the government of India, IGNOU was finally established by an Act of Parliament on 20 September 1985. By that time, the student enrolment had
increased to 9.04 per cent (Table 9–4.1) and only five more universities
started correspondence courses during 1982–5.

Table 9–4.1 Enrolment in higher education 1975/6 to 1994/5

Year	Conventional universities/ colleges	%	Open universities	Other distance education	Total distance education	%	Total enrolment
1975–6	2,426,109	97.42			64,210	2.58	2,490,319
1985–6	3,570,897	90.96	27,629	327,461	355,090	9.04	3,925,987
1986–7	3,681,870	91.14	28,745	329,046	357,791	8.86	4,039,661
1987–8	3,814,417	90.45	36,448	366,272	402,720	9.55	4,217,137
1988–9	3,947,922	89.68	77,748	376,495	454,243	10.32	4,402,165
1989–90	4,246,878	88.84	66,265	467,176	533,441	11.16	4,780,319
1990–1	4,425,247	88.72	75,417	487,397	562,814	11.28	4,988,061
1991–2	4,611,107	87.18	122,531	555,532	678,063	12.82	5,289,170
1994–5	5,310,753	86.86	n/a	n/a	803,176	13.14	6,113,929

Source: Various UGC Annual reports.

Subsequently, student enrolment increased with simultaneous increase in university correspondence institutions. By 1998, fifty-eight mainstream universities have institutes/departments of correspondence/distance education, and there are nine open universities in the country (Table 9–4.2), all with a cumulative enrolment of about 20 per cent of the total students in higher education.

In 1997–8, six out of seven functional open universities (Table 9–4.3) enrolled 339,780 students, and their cumulative enrolment stands at about 988,000 which is nearly one-and-a-half times the total number of students in university correspondence course institutes. Data on six functional open universities given in Table 9–4.3 indicate tremendous growth of the open university system in the country. Moreover, many universities have initiated action on establishing centres for distance education, and as per the recommendations of the Central Advisory Board of Education (highest educational policy making body of the central government) each state should have one open university and one open school. With this recommendation, at the dawn of the next century, Indian higher education would have 25 per cent of its students studying through distance education.

Organisational structure and funding

For the fifty-eight university correspondence courses institutes (CCIs), the mainstream universities have full control over all the aspects of the institutes including the financial income. Therefore, it has become well-nigh impossible

Table 9–4.2 Open universities in India

Name	Year of establishment
Dr. B.R. Ambedkar Open University (formerly Andhra Pradesh Open University) (BRAOU)	1982
Indira Gandhi National Open University (IGNOU)	1985
Kota Open University (formerly Directorate of Correspondence Courses, University of Rajasthan) (KOU)	1987
Nalanda Open University (NOU)	1987
Yashwantrao Chavan Maharashtra Open University (YCMOU)	1989
Madhya Pradesh Bhoj (Open) University (MPBOU)	1992
Baba Saheb Ambedkar Open University (BSAOU)	1994
Karnataka State Open University (formerly Institute of Correspondence Courses and Continuing Education, University of Mysore) (KSOU)	1996
Netaji Subhash Open University (NSOU)	1997

Table 9–4.3 Open university statistics

Details of information	IGNOU (1998)	BRAOU (1998)	YCMOU (1997)	KOU (1995)	MPBOU (1998)	KSOU (1998)
Programmes on offer	39	19	42	13	16	37
Courses on offer	4,816	303	173	120	172	250
Students registered	162,540	73,397	59,596	8,557	8,614	26,222
Students of rolls	394,388	253,000	249,819	20,120	–	46,636
Regional centres	17	12	8	6	89	5(UP)
Study centres	268	116	800[a]	24	8	90(UP)
Academic counsellors	16,364	3,215	3,798	1,914	1,982	1,500
Students awarded	16,150	27,932	6,877	–	1,932	400
Audio programmes	659	1,900	260	–	UP	nil
Video programmes	606	182	110	–	UP	nil
Staff strength	1,286	688	240	373	267	184
Academic/professional	236	98	43	45	22	62
Administrative	819	370	167	254	15	118
Technical production	231	7,200	30	30	18[b]	4
Others	–	–	–	44	212	nil

Source/courtesy: IGNOU 1998; VC, MPBOU; Rector, BRAOU; VC, YCMOU; Registrar, KSOU.

Notes
UP = under process.
a   Including 350 centres for computer programme.
b   Out of which 15 are production staff.

for the CCI faculty to think about any curriculum reform; and in many cases they had to fight in various university statutory bodies to start a new programme non-existent in the parent university. On the other hand, the parent university treats the CCI as the major source of income (as fees from large number of students) to the tune of meeting in some cases about half of the expenditure of the parent university each year. Therefore, it is not surprising that the quality of correspondence education has been low in terms of course lessons, teacher input, student support and student learning. In some instances, though, correspondence students have topped the university merit list. This is important since students of both the streams study the same syllabus, sit for the same examination and are evaluated by a common pool of evaluators. During the past few years, some correspondence institutes have been granted faculty status, or department status with some financial, administrative and academic autonomy.

The organisational structures of open universities are more broad, diversified and conform to the industrial system of education. Being independent universities, they enjoy considerable autonomy, occasional state and central government interferences notwithstanding. The academics in open universities enjoy reasonably high autonomy in formulating, designing, developing, implementing and evaluating academic programmes, though within the boundary of institutional mission, national development priorities and available resources.

While IGNOU, as a central university (directly associated with the central government, and not the University Grants Commission) with dual responsibility of offering open distance education programmes and coordinating and maintaining standards of distance education institutions in the country, receives direct budgetary grants from the central government, the state open universities get grants from state governments, and only developmental grants from IGNOU through its Distance Education Council. IGNOU has been able to generate about 35 to 40 per cent of its expenditure from student fees and other sources, and the plan grant from the government still remains high at 40 per cent. On the other hand, BRAOU, the first (state) open university in the country, generates about four-fifths of its income from student fees and gets state government grant to the tune of only about 22 per cent (Srinivasacharyulu and Rao 1998). The university spends about 30 per cent more on students than it receives from them. In a recent study based on 1989–90 data (Pillai and Naidu 1998), it has been pointed out that in comparison to open universities, conventional university distance education institutions show considerable variance in student fees as a source of income. For instance, while Madurai Kamraj University gets public subsidy up to about 52 per cent (48 per cent student fees), SNDT Women's University generates up to 92 per cent from student fees, and universities like Sri Venkateswara and Kerala generate all the resources from students. On the other hand, conventional university colleges get about 95 per cent public subsidy and generate only 5 per cent of income from students.

Nature of learners and unit cost

All open universities had been established with the prime objective of providing educational opportunities to the disadvantaged sections of society (besides offering need-based and job-oriented programmes to all). These include women, those from rural and far-flung areas, economically and otherwise handicapped, and those from scheduled and backward castes and tribes. The nature of students on some selected indicators for some selected OUs and CCIs is indicated in Table 9–4.4. These data may be compared with the situation as obtains in mainstream higher education. For general higher education, in 1996, women and scheduled castes/scheduled tribes constituted 37 per cent and 12.25 per cent respectively, the figures of which were 24.11 per cent and 10.30 per cent for professional higher education (Powar 1997). In the case of professional distance education offered at the Birla Institute of Technology and Sciences (BITS), only 10 per cent and 5 per cent were women and rural students respectively (Table 9–4.4). The study by Singh et al. (1994) on twenty-nine university CCIs reveals a better picture with regard to enrolment of women, employed students, and rural students.

Table 9–4.4 Nature of audience (%)

Variables	IGNOU (1996–7)	BRAOU (1994–5)	YCMOU (1990–3)	BITS (1992)	Singh et al. (1994): 29 CCIs
Gender					
Male	77.18	72	78.28	90	60.4
Female	22.82	28	24.72	10	39.6
Residence					
Rural	16.48	–	23.39	5	39
Urban	83.52	–	42.49[a]	95	60.2
Employment					
Employed	67.54	34	–	100	42
Unemployed	32.46	66 (men)	–	–	56
Social status					
SC/ST/BC	6.01	55	28.68	–	12.3
General	93.99	45	71.32	–	87.7
Age					
Under 25	9.02 (<21)	80	64.72	–	–
26–30	58.21 (21–30)	11	19.13	–	–
31–50	31.31	8.9	15.05	–	–
Above 50	1.46 (1991–2)	0.2	1.10	–	–

Notes
SC = schedule caste; ST = scheduled tribe; BC = backward caste; BITS = Birla Institute of Technology and Sciences (deemed university).
a   Information for 6,602 students not available.

For BRAOU, during the last ten years, enrolment percentages for women and disadvantaged castes have increased from 15 and 39 to 28 and 55 respectively which is a positive indication. In the case of IGNOU, during 1991–7, the percentage enrolment of women, disadvantaged castes and rural students has decreased considerably: 24.91 to 22.82, 8.18 to 6.01, and 38.39 to 16.48 respectively, though the percentage of employed students has increased from 52.67 to 67.54. While it is widely believed that the national open university which accounts for about 30 per cent of all students on rolls in distance education in the country needs strategically to extend education to those who are otherwise deprived of mainstream higher education, the consolidated picture shows that distance education has moderately significant achievement in providing post-secondary education, especially in professional areas and to those who are either in employment or who wish to be professionally prepared to take up employment in a variety of areas.

It was pointed out above that student fees contribute about 14 per cent to higher education expenditure, while its share is only 5 per cent for unit operating expenditure. For distance education, it varies from 35 per cent

(IGNOU) to 78 per cent (BRAOU), 92 per cent (SNDTWU) and 100 per cent (Kerala, Sri Venkateswar). On the other hand, the unit cost of distance education as a whole, on an average, is about one-third of conventional education. While, for instance, the annual recurrent costs per student at BRAOU, IGNOU, YCMOU and conventional universities (CUs) for 1991–2 were Indian rupees 777, 2,046, 2,214 and 5,746 respectively (varying from 14.2 per cent to 40.4 per cent), the unit costs for the three-year undergraduate programme at IGNOU and CUs were Indian rupees 6,000 and 16,428 respectively (Naidu 1993).

Teaching and support systems

The university CCIs follow procedures of course design, development and offer as determined by the authorities and bodies of the parent universities. As noted earlier, the correspondence students study the same courses and sit for the same examination as their mainstream counterparts to be awarded the same degree.

Most of the open universities follow distance education methodologies (and with the objective of practising open learning), though in most cases may end up using an upgraded correspondence education. The BRAOU was established on the model of OUUK; so also IGNOU, especially the latter has highly been influenced by the OU model of the UK. The open universities are autonomous institutions and therefore free to innovate. State open universities have students enrolled from within their respective state, and use expertise and other resources available within the state (except occasional assistance provided by IGNOU). The IGNOU, as a COL Centre of Excellence in the region, has national and international jurisdiction, human and other resource networking all over the country, and the responsibility of coordinating and maintaining standards of distance education systems in the country.

The OUs largely follow the industrialised system of mass education, variations of the course team approach for material design and development, and the system of regional and study centres for providing student support and administering academic programmes. The offer of programmes is at non-credit, certificate, diploma, degree, Master's and doctoral levels, and most of the OUs have expanded professional and job-oriented programmes for both economic and national development reasons. Programmes cover such areas as management, computer education, surgery, nursing, library and information science, food and nutrition, mother and child health, tourism studies, water resource management, construction management, creative writing, rural development, child care and education, teacher education, journalism and mass communication, agriculture, applied electronics, horticulture, and the like. Students are provided with printed self-instructional modular packages, supported by assignments, projects, practicals, counselling, audio and video programmes, libraries, intensive workshops (all usually provided at study/work centres) and teleconferencing (telecast at the headquarters of IGNOU).

Other communication media like radio, audio, television, video and tele-conferencing are optional and supplementary to the printed course lessons. Only a few CCIs use these media for distance teaching, while most of the OUs use them extensively; and IGNOU provides regular two-way audio and one-way video teleconferencing every day through extended C-band for purposes of student counselling, orientation and training, and business meetings with the regional and study centre officers. CCIs of Madurai Kamraj, Panjab and Punjabi universities use radio broadcasts twice a week and some do it daily. IGNOU broadcasts three times a week and BRAOU programmes are broadcast daily from respective All India Radio stations. Telecast of television programmes is rare in the case of CCIs, while IGNOU programmes are telecast on the national channel Doordarshan each working day.

Unlike the PCPs of the CCIs, the open universities offer student support services through regional and study centres (data in Table 9–4.3). Regular (usually weekend) counselling, audio-video sessions and peer discussions take place at study centres (though it is not compulsory to attend), and students submit assignments there to be evaluated by the counsellors. Since every student registered on any course is allotted a study centre, it becomes the nodal agency for sharing information between the university and the learner. The centres situated at mainstream colleges/universities/industries/NGOs are run by part-time staff – coordinator, assistant coordinator, counsellors and support staff. The regional centres (for instance, of IGNOU) with full-time staff of the university act as the face of the university in the respective states/regions and liaise between the headquarters and study centres.

Both continuous and term-end evaluation systems are in practice in open universities. The CCIs have the practice of student response sheets attached to each course/paper which students are required to answer and submit to the institute for correction. Rarely these are scored and comments sent back to students. At BRAOU, students submit assignments and corrected response sheets are sent back to students without giving any weightage of scores. YCMOU has the provision of, besides semester/course-end tests, class tests in which a student has to compulsorily take two such tests the scores of which count towards final evaluation. IGNOU has the provision of assignments (tutor marked and computer marked) carrying 25 to 30 per cent weightage the grades of which are counted towards final grade and certification. Like IGNOU, other open universities also follow both the schemes of grading and marking.

Quality assurance and networking

The Distance Education Council (DEC), a statutory authority of IGNOU, looks into coordination of various distance-teaching institutions (DTIs), their quality assurance and networking, accreditation and provision of development grants for system development. Norms are developed and guidelines issued to all DTIs, though it has not become compulsory to follow. This voluntary strategy is extended to the latest attempt of offer of credit transfer and joint degree programme (between open universities, and between DTIs and mainstream universities). Since many distance education programmes, especially in professional areas, need to have recognition from the parent mainstream councils (like Medical Council of India, Indian Nursing Council, All India Council for Technical Education, National Council for Teacher Education), DEC has to negotiate and at times fight with such councils for their offer at a distance (an issue which needs to be resolved for successful collaboration and convergence of the mainstream and open distance education).

Possibilities of convergence

This chapter has highlighted the development of distance education and its contribution to national development and the new society. Two major regional developments within and around distance education – networked application of media and technology, and staff development – have facilitated the process of convergence of systems and methods, a case that was put forward in an earlier discussion (Panda 1996).

First, there have been developments within distance education which have influenced the functionaries and processes within mainstream higher education. The rigorous procedures of course design and development (and application of educational technology/educational development methods), the inputs provided in staff development (continuing professional development) programmes, and the structural and methodological inputs provided through institutional, individual and technological networking have all influenced higher education practices.

Second, there have been developments within distance education in the country responding to developments in distance education globally. The developments in technological media and the sustained reformative practices towards open learning are pointers to this trend. India has one of the most sophisticated state-of-the-art educational media production and (satellite) uplink centres in Asia at EMPC of IGNOU, and also the Commonwealth Educational Media Centre for Asia (at IGNOU), supported by the COL. Technological facilities and educational telecasts had been in operation much before open universities were established – the educational television programmes of the National Council of Educational Research and Training

(NCERT) for school students; the countrywide classroom television programmes of the University Grants Commission for college students. Agricultural universities and technological universities have their respective technological networks. The existing IGNOU network of about 160 teleconferencing centres is being expanded under the OPENET (open education network) of DEC to cover all the distance-teaching institutions in the country. There is a move to establish a collaborative telecast network of IGNOU (and all DTIs), UGC and NCERT at EMPC, IGNOU with direct linking facilities (without the existing facilities extended by ISRO) and have a full twenty-four-hour satellite channel for education.

There has been sustained collaboration in course design, course writing, course editing, assessment of student assignments/projects/answer scripts, student counselling and teleconferencing. For student support, study centres located in mainstream institutions and services of their teachers and other secretarial staff are being utilised on part-time and honorarium basis by the DTIs. On the other hand, many of the conventional university teachers and students find distance education course units handy for ready reference and further enrichment, and extensively use these (print, audio, video, telecast) materials.

A case in point is the medical programmes of IGNOU, more specifically the Postgraduate Diploma in Maternal and Child Health (PGDMCH), for doctors, in which three disciplines (community medicine, gynaecology and paediatrics) are involved, and for which student support to practising doctors is offered at twenty-four medical colleges/government hospitals of eighteen state governments. This model has enlarged the scope of medical teaching and curricular reforms; and distance education is helping non-medical college medical professionals like district hospital doctors to act as academicians and enhance their knowledge, which is not possible in the conventional system. This model has encouraged the mainstream medical education to adopt similar strategies and relook at medical education of today.

Third, distance education staff development, in the form of continuing professional development, has significantly contributed to higher education reforms and further convergence. In the open system, the role of the Staff Training and Research Institute of Distance Education (STRIDE) of IGNOU (further supported by the COL) has been to evolve strategies, methods and models of course design, development, implementation, evaluation and R&D for entire system development which is still unfolding. The role of teachers has been enlarged to areas which were never thought possible in the formal system.

Further, distance teachers have to innovate for what they have to practice, and have necessarily to get into all design and development issues in adult learning. On the other hand, the large number of mainstream teachers who have been participating in the need-based short-term orientation programmes of DTIs have eventually been equipped with skills that have high significance in their own teaching and research activities. While educational technology and distance education are converging, this has inevitably contributed to improvement in the practices of higher education in general and open distance education in particular, with distance education (enriched through staff development and other innovations) playing the lead role. In the whole process, however, the issue to be addressed and worked out by both the players is how to ensure interactivity in learning, active learning, and learning effectiveness. Finally, the debate on parity of esteem notwithstanding (which is gradually receding), within the framework of open learning, it is worth noting Smith (1987: 34): 'As distance education becomes more open, opportunities for the application of distance education methods in campus-based education will increase'. The convergence that is emerging in India would inevitably embrace the above and vice versa.

References

Gandhe, S.K. (1998) 'Access and equity: need of the disadvantaged', paper submitted to Asian Association of Open Universities 12th Annual Conference, Hong Kong.

GOI (1962) *Report of Expert Committee on Correspondence Courses*, New Delhi: Ministry of Education.

GOI (1994) *Open Schooling in India: Situational Analysis, Need Assessment, Strategy Identification*, New Delhi: Ministry of Human Resource Development.

GOI (1997) *Government Subsidies in India: Discussion Paper*, New Delhi: Department of Economic Affairs, Ministry of Finance.

IGNOU (1998) *Vice-Chancellor's Report* (Ninth Convocation), New Delhi: Indira Gandhi National Open University.

Mukherjee, N. (1997) 'Loka Siksha Sambad' (Council for People's Education), *Open Praxis*, 2, 13 and 21.

Mukhopadhyay, M. (1994) 'The unfolding of an open learning institution: the National Open School of India', in M. Mukhopadhyay and S. Phillips (eds), *Open Schooling: Selected Experience*, Vancouver: Commonwealth of Learning.

Naidu, C.G. (1993) 'Some economic aspects of conventional and distance education system in India', paper presented to Asian Association of Open Universities conference, Hong Kong.

Panda, S. (1996) 'Translating open university policies into practice in India', in T. Evans and D. Nation (eds), *Opening Education: Policies and Practices from Open and Distance Education*, London: Routledge.

Panda, S., Garg, S. and Khan, A.R. (1998) 'Growth and development of the national open university', in S. Panda (ed.), *Open and Distance Education: Policies, Practices and Quality Concerns*, New Delhi: Aravali Books International.

Pillai, C.R. and Naidu, C.G. (1998) 'Cost-effectiveness of distance higher education', in S. Panda (ed.), *Open and Distance Education: Policies, Practices and Quality Concerns*, New Delhi: Aravali Books International.

Powar, K.B. (1997) *Higher Education in India since Independence: Retrospect and Future Options*, New Delhi: Association of Indian Universities.

Singh, B., Mullick, S. and Chaudhary, N. (1994) *Correspondence/Distance Education in India*, New Delhi: Indira Gandhi National Open University.

Smith, P. (1987) 'Distance education and educational change', in P. Smith and M. Kelly (eds), *Distance Education and the Mainstream*, London: Croom Helm.

Srinivasacharyulu, G. and Rao, C. S. (1998) 'Dr. B.R. Ambedkar Open University: a critical profile', in S. Panda (ed.), *Open and Distance Education: Policies, Practices and Quality Concerns*, New Delhi: Aravali Books International.

UNESCO (1994) *Statistical Year Book, 1994*, Paris: UNESCO.

Contemporary distance education in Taiwan

Hung-Ju Chung

The government of Republic of China (ROC) relocated in Taiwan in 1949 after moving out of mainland China. During the following half-century, distance education has contributed to the national rise in the quality of human resources. The National Open University is the main provider of distance education.

Context

Taiwan, ROC, comprises a major island called Taiwan (394 kilometres long; 144 kilometres wide; and 36,000 square kilometres in area, less than one-sixth of the UK), of which about two-thirds is covered with forest peaks, and a number of surrounding small islands situated in the Pacific Ocean. The country is the second-most densely populated area in the world with 601 people per square kilometre. Over 21.7 million people were registered in January 1998 (Government Information Office, 1998c).

The last decade of the twentieth century has seen a major transformation in Taiwan, ROC. Taiwan has enjoyed economic prosperity for some time. As one of the four 'little tigers' of Asia, its per capita GNP reached US $13,233 and the average national income increased to US $12,019 in 1997. Taiwan has a very low unemployment rate, at 2.35 per cent in April 1998 (Government Information Office 1998a). Moreover, the country had one of the largest foreign exchange holdings in the world, US $84.03 billion in January 1998 (Government Information Office 1998a). However, there is a decline in the economic growth rate, dropping to 6.81 per cent in 1997. Owing to the country's shrinking trade surplus and south-east Asia's financial crises, financial markets have begun to sink. Maintaining existing economic achievements and further development are major concerns.

Political reforms in Taiwan, ROC, over the last decade, referred to as the 'quiet revolution', have rapidly accelerated. In particular, the abolition in 1991 of the 'Temporary Provisions Effective During the Period of Communist Rebellion', the legal basis for the enforcement of martial law in the country for over three decades, marked a significant move towards democracy.

The other milestone is the fundamental change in the presidential election system of the country. In 1996, for the first time people were able to elect their president by majority vote. A third remarkable political development is the opposition parties gaining more say in the country's political affairs. In 1997, Taiwan's largest opposition party (formed in 1986) won the majority of votes and the majority of seats in the election of county magistrates and city mayors (except in two special municipalities). It appears that the ROC in Taiwan is heading towards democracy.

Media markets in Taiwan also underwent dramatic changes. Radio broadcasting markets have grown more than threefold following the recent release of frequencies for radio broadcasting. In 1993, there were only thirty-three radio broadcasting companies; by the end of 1997, 118 radio broadcasting licences had been issued (Government Information Office 1998b). Regarding television, the fourth terrestrial television station was launched in 1997 – the first one affiliated with the opposition party. After the Cable Television Law was passed in 1993, all television stations faced severe threats from cable television. There were 150 cable television systems in 1997, offering around sixty channels including satellite-based programmes from overseas (Government Information Office 1998b). In addition, following the Public Television Law in 1997, a public-interest television station is planned to go into service in July 1998. At the end of 1997, about 99.3 per cent of households had colour television sets; about 28.6 per cent owned a second colour television set; and about 58.6 per cent had VCRs. By March 1998, about 65.5 per cent of households were connected to cable television (Directorate General of Budget Accounting and Statistics 1998).

As for telecommunications, both the National Information Infrastructure and Taiwan's ISDN local commercial service were launched in 1995. About 27 per cent of households had home computers in March 1998. With respect to the newspaper industry, after the removal of the restriction on newspaper licensing and the number of pages per issue in 1988, the number of newspapers increased tremendously from thirty-one in 1987 to 341 in 1997 (Government Information Office 1998b). The Taiwan public has access to information transmitted through a range of different media.

Compulsory education lasts for nine years, comprising two stages. Six- to 11-year-old children study in elementary schools for six years; 12- to 14-year-olds study in junior high schools for three years. Those who qualify enrol in secondary education. For those not going into secondary education, the government in 1983 introduced a one-year vocational education programme, extending compulsory education to ten years. In 1995, this system was renamed the 'Practical Technical Programme'. In the school year (SY) 1996 (the school year is the twelve-month period from August to July), the net enrolment rate of students was 96.06 per cent (Government Information Office 1998b).

Secondary education is multilateral, with a variety of different kinds of schools and colleges. Students take examinations to enter secondary schools. In SY 1996, about 90.7 per cent of junior high graduates continued their studies in secondary education institutions (Government Information Office 1998b).

Higher education has been the focus of educational development in Taiwan for the last decade. The number of universities and independent colleges boosted to eighty-eight in 1998 (Ministry of Education 1998). Among them, there are forty-one universities. In 1997, the Joint University Entrance Examinations enabled 61.6 per cent of those who took the examination to enter universities and independent colleges in SY 1997, up 11.2 per cent from the previous year.

In SY 1996, the enrolment rate of the population aged 6 to 21 in education was 84.96 per cent; more than a quarter of the total population was in an educational institution of some type (Government Information Office 1998b). The national literacy rate in 1996 was 94 per cent. Generally speaking, the focus of contemporary education rests on openness.

Provision of distance education

In the early days, distance education provision was very much based on educational broadcasting. After the ROC government moved into Taiwan, the Ministry of Education set up an educational radio station in 1960. The educational television station was later established, which broadcast educational television programmes for an experimental on-the-air supplementary senior vocational school. In 1970, it was restructured to become the Chinese Television System (CTS), a VHF broadcast system. Since then, the scope of distance education has been enlarged; developments include on-the-air supplementary senior vocational schools, senior high schools, junior colleges, supplementary instructional television programmes for conventional junior high schools, and on-the-air university-level courses. The on-the-air junior colleges, or 'open junior colleges', which the government categorises as institutions for 'supplementary education' are still functioning. The establishment of the National Open University (NOU) is the major landmark in the development of distance education in Taiwan. Following a revision of the University Law in July 1982 and a Ministry of Education experimental project involving the provision of several university-level distance courses between 1983 and 1986, the NOU was established in 1986, with first-year courses starting in November 1986. Before 1994, the NOU did not initially have the power to offer Bachelor's degrees; its graduates could only receive certificates of graduation.

Organisation and staff

NOU comprises thirty working units, some with sub-units. The major units comprise teaching, administrative and support units and regional learning centres. Seven teaching units include six academic departments (humanities, social sciences, business, living sciences, public administration and management and information) and one academic group (general studies). The administrative units are similar to those in other universities (personnel office, budgeting and accounting office, and departments of academic affairs, student affairs and general affairs). The supporting units – the publishing centre, library, computer centre, and departments of educational media and of research and development – and thirteen regional learning centres, have undergone changes owing to the need for reorganisation and expansion. The heads of these first-level working units report to the President of the University. Within this organisational structure are nine committees overseeing the functioning of the University and contributing to policy developments. An open junior college called the 'Open Junior College of Public Administration' was affiliated to NOU in 1992.

NOU had 234 full-time and contract staff in SY 1995, comprising eighty-nine academics, four research staff, sixty-four clerks and administrators, thirty-seven contracted workers, and forty other types of staff in SY 1995 (National Open University 1996b). Most full-time academic staff members are required to take administrative responsibilities either in the headquarters or in the regional learning centres.

Students

NOU has three categories of students: 'regular', 'non-diploma' and 'auditing'. Before SY 1998 a regular student must pass an entrance examination, be at least 20 years of age, and hold a high school graduate diploma or equivalent, and may apply to graduate. Students not fulfilling these requirements or simply wishing to study with NOU, may become non-diploma students. Non-diploma students, who must be at least 18 years old, may receive certificates of course credit for individual courses, but are not usually eligible for graduation. Non-diploma students can overcome the barrier of not having a high school graduate diploma or equivalent by accumulating forty course credits and applying to become regular students. Auditing students, who study NOU courses without informing the University, do not receive certificates.

Since SY 1990, NOU has recruited regular students once a year and non-diploma students three times a year. In SY 1996, there were 38,053 students (both regular and non-diploma) in the first semester; 34,969 in the second semester; and 23,153 in the summer semester (National Open University, 1997). Regular students make up the largest proportion, 77 per cent in the first semester of SY 1996. The percentage of female students is usually higher than for males; 68.9 per cent in first semester of SY 1996. The 25 to 34 age group is often the largest in the student profile, 45.5 per cent in the first semester of SY 1996. In terms of students' previous educational qualifications, senior high school and senior vocational school graduates form the biggest group (52 per cent in the first semester in SY 1996). Civil servants make up the largest occupation group (29.2 per cent in the first semester of SY 1996).

NOU produced its first group of ten graduates in SY 1990. The first graduation ceremony for fifty-eight graduates was in September 1991 (National Open University 1996b). The Legislative Yuan afterwards passed a bill enabling NOU to grant Bachelor's degrees in April 1994, a significant event in its public recognition. The number of graduates has rapidly increased to a total of 5,865 by the end of SY 1996, with 1,815 graduating in SY 1996 (National Open University 1997).

Courses and teaching methods and media

NOU operates a semester system, with eighteen-week first and second semesters and a nine-week summer semester. Only undergraduate courses are provided. Each course lasts one semester. There were ninety-two courses in SY 1996; twelve courses in the summer semester, thirty-nine in the first and forty-one in the second semesters (National Open University 1997).

Broadcasting, print and face-to-face tutoring are the three main methods used for teaching at NOU, with the broadcasting component used as a measure of the course-load. One course credit is equal to eighteen broadcast episodes, each episode being 30 minutes. The majority of courses comprise three course credits, although courses with two or four course credits are also offered. There were, for instance, 2,502 episodes broadcast in the second semester of SY 1996 (National Open University 1998b).

Television is the main broadcasting medium. In the second semester of SY 1996, 1,746 television episodes were broadcast, 69.8 per cent of total broadcasting in the semester (National Open University 1998b). Radio is used in some courses. Television episodes are broadcast through UHF. Television programmes are directly used to make video cassettes; sound tracks of radio programmes are used to make audio cassettes for supplementary material for students.

Each course has a printed textbook which has been developed and edited in-house. Additionally, a student newsletter is published twice per month, which contains broadcasting schedules, university announcements, assignment questions, and a range of supplementary readings. Moreover, the NOU collaborates with two newspapers which publish NOU columns.

Face-to-face teaching, once per month and four times per semester, is the third element of all courses (except for those offered in the summer semester). Laboratory hours in regional learning centres are included in computing courses.

Student assessment is through assignments and examinations. Students submit several assignments and sit mid-term and final examinations to earn course credits. Regular students can take up to a maximum of five courses per semester. In order to graduate, regular students need to both accumulate at least 128 course credits and fulfil certain regulations.

NOU is in the process of transformation, particularly in management, recruitment of students and use of media. These changes are triggered by a range of external forces, of which the main one is the threat posed by other higher education institutions.

New developments – threats and changes

Having served more than a decade as the major distance education provider to Taiwanese society, NOU increasingly realises that its educational territory is being invaded by other higher education institutions. There have also been other change factors in politics, media markets and educational policy. These recent developments and threats to NOU reflect the country's pursuit for openness, flexibility and decentralisation. NOU's own initiatives in these areas have been undertaken in response to the changes in the society of Taiwan.

The threat posed to NOU by increased competition from other higher education institutions emerges from current educational developments in Taiwan (see Table 9–5.1). Competition stems from two sources: the emergence of municipal open universities and developments within conventional higher education institutions.

First, the basis of the municipal open university system is in amendments to the University Law in 1994. One municipal open university is already established and another is in the planning stage. The first municipal open university, the Municipal Kaohsiung Open University, was established in

Table 9–5.1 Threats to NOU

Threat	Nature of threat	Contextual influence (developments in Taiwan, ROC)
Invasions by other HE institutions	Emerging municipal open universities	Educational development
	Developments in conventional HE institutions: • computer-based distance teaching • expansion of extension education • 'pre-study' scheme	Educational development

1997 in Kaohsiung City (the second biggest city in Taiwan). It plans to recruit a maximum of 10,000 students, of which 1,150 enrolled in its first year (Municipal Kaohsiung Open University 1997). There are five academic departments at the University (law and politics, industrial and business management, mass communication, foreign languages, and culture and art). The University emphasises teacher–student interaction in both the city and surrounding areas. The media it has selected are cable television, radio and computer (for Internet-based teaching). The only entrance criterion is that of age, 18 years or more. Taipei City, the capital and the largest city, is in the process of planning its own municipal open university. Since these cities are the two largest student markets, NOU's greatest concern is how to survive in competition with these two municipal open universities.

Second, rapid developments in conventional higher education institutions in relation to distance education provision also challenge the survival of NOU. Three main developments are: computer-based distance teaching, the expansion of the provision of extension education, and introducing a scheme of 'pre-study'.

As in other parts of the world, conventional higher education institutions in Taiwan have entered distance education via the use of information technology. In 1994, the government launched the first scheme to promote computer-based distance teaching in conventional higher education institutions. Since then, the provision of this type of teaching has increased rapidly in conventional educational institutions. In SY 1997, about a hundred courses which comprise synchronous group broadcasting computer-based distance-teaching were already available from seventy-one conventional higher education institutions (Chen 1998)

The expansion of extension education in conventional higher education institutions derives from the notion of expanding opportunities for higher education and the advocacy of lifelong learning. The new feature of extension education provided in conventional higher education institutions is that students completing courses in the extension education programme can now receive certificates of course credit. If students pass the entrance examination for higher level education, their certificates enable them to waive courses.

An experimental scheme of 'pre-study' in conventional higher education institutions was announced by the Ministry of Education in May 1998 to reduce the pressure on students from the Joint University Entrance Examination (China Times 1998). Under this scheme, those who fail the entrance examination can still enter conventional higher education institutions. On passing the entrance examination, course-credit certificates will be accepted. These two schemes are similar to NOU's policy enabling non-diploma students to accumulate credits as a step towards becoming regular students. In this respect, NOU has given a lead, but this scheme will push the University into a much more competitive environment.

Changes within NOU

Changes fall into three areas: (1) the promotion of university autonomy; (2) multiplicity in the use of media; and (3) greater openness (Table 9–5.2).

Promotion of university autonomy

The promotion of university autonomy at NOU was influenced by educational and political developments in Taiwan. The final report of the Commission on Educational Reform in the Executive Yuan (1996) recommended that education in Taiwan be deregulated, an action with implications for university autonomy. Two recent events, the establishment of the University Affairs Funding Foundation and the launch of an electoral system to appoint university managers, signify increasing autonomy at NOU.

Table 9–5.2 Changes within NOU

Changes in	What changes lead to	Actions by NOU	Contextual influence (developments in Taiwan, ROC)
Organisation and staffing	Promotion of university autonomy	Part self-financing: setting up of the university-affairs foundation	Educational development
		Election system to appoint university managers	Political development
Teaching methods and media	Multiplicity in the use of and production of media	Selection of more non-broadcast media	
		• packages (including a textbook, specially designed audio and video cassettes, floppy disks and CD-ROMs)	Economic development
		• use of communication media: telephone; on-line tutorials	Developments in media
		Call-in and call-out television and radio programmes broadcast	Development in the design of broadcasting programmes
		Contracting multiple production companies Linking cable television services	Political development
Student recruitment	Greater openness	Abolishing the entrance examination	Educational development

New Additional Articles in the 1997 ROC Constitution required the Ministry of Education to shift its financial focus away from higher education to compulsory education so that national universities were now compelled to raise part of their own funding. In response, NOU established its University Affairs Funding Foundation, although the University has been to some extent self-financing from its inception. The two major implications are that the University now has more control over its finances and that the concept of cost-effectiveness is now in the minds of NOU's management. The University is now aware of the need to take more responsibility for the success and failure of its educational provision.

The introduction of an electoral system to appoint NOU managers is in accord with the move towards academic autonomy in conventional universities, sought for many years and finally brought about by the revised University Law in 1994 which gave universities the right to run their own elections to select deans/directors of teaching units and university presidents. NOU's first election for President was held in June 1998.

These developments in university autonomy at NOU signify a move away from complete government control. Academics are becoming much more influential in the running of the University.

Multiplicity in the use of media

The growth in the economy, developments in media, and educational political development in Taiwanese society have all contributed to NOU's decisions on the use of media for its teaching. On one hand, high incomes enable Taiwanese people to buy communications media and appliances, together with communication services. On the other hand, Taiwanese people are becoming more and more eager consumers of information provided by the media. NOU has to calculate the best means of using media for educational provision. There have been four major developments in NOU use of media.

First, NOU has introduced more non-broadcast media into its teaching. An example is the recent production of study packages comprising a textbook, specially designed video and audio cassettes, floppy disks and CD-ROMs (National Open University 1998a). The use of non-broadcasting media for delivering teaching signifies the liberation of NOU from the hegemony of television, which apparently suited the contemporary lifestyle of Taiwan. Another example is the experimental use of both telephone and computers to replace the supplementary face-to-face tutorials. The experiments in group telephone tutorials and computer-mediated tutorials were intended to reduce travel problems and to enhance existing face-to-face supplementary tutorials. The launch of computer-mediated tutorials marked the beginning of computer-based teaching at NOU although it followed in conventional universities' footsteps. While the use of study packages and group telephone tutorials are not new for a number of distance-teaching institutions around the world, it took a decade for NOU to enter the arena.

Second, live call-in and call-out communication between teachers and students was made available in NOU's broadcast programmes. This was influenced by recent changes in commercial television and radio programmes in Taiwan which have made audiences and students accustomed to making telephone calls to television and radio stations. This helps interaction between teachers and students.

Third, NOU's television programmes have ceased to be produced solely by the CTS – NOU's own studio was set up on the campus in 1992 (National Open University 1996a). There is increasing involvement of several production and broadcasting companies since SY 1995. Historically, the CTS and its predecessor monopolised both the production and broadcasting of educational television programmes. Influenced both by political reforms and by the active television market, NOU has already found a way of contracting other television production and broadcasting companies, another example of decentralisation in practice.

And fourth, as part of their competitive strategy for survival, cable television service providers broadcast NOU's UHF programmes on their channels so that students can now watch these programmes on a local cable channel. This helps NOU come to the attention of more potential students and to receive more feedback from the general public.

More open access

NOU's policy of greater open access, from SY 1997, is also a response to the educational reforms in conventional education. For a long time, a major criticism of education in Taiwan has been that the highly competitive examination system places enormous stress on students. The government has thus, especially in the last decade, tried to reduce the pressure. The recent implementation of pluralistic channels to enter schools for secondary education and institutions for higher education has provided students with other means to advance their study without having to rely solely on entrance examinations. Affected by the changes in recruiting students in conventional education, the NOU as an institution for both higher education and adult education could not but discard its independent entrance examination. In the SY 1998 student recruitment scheme, anyone fulfilling two conditions – to be aged at least 20 and to be a high school graduate or equivalent – can become a NOU regular student without being constrained by a quota limitation. In May 1998, nearly 28,000 people applied to become NOU regular students (National Open University 1998b). NOU is striving towards greater openness.

Conclusion

The last decade of the twentieth century has seen significant progress in distance education in Taiwan, ROC. The establishment of NOU more than a decade ago was a major milestone, followed by two new municipal open universities (one in planning), and conventional higher education institutions entering the field. The most recent developments in distance education in the country are influenced by the developments in media, and by economic, political and educational developments. It is evident that distance education in Taiwan, ROC, is currently moving towards openness, flexibility and decentralisation. Contemporary distance education in Taiwan, ROC, demonstrates a current phenomenon common in distance education around the world, that the demarcation between conventional education and distance education is becoming very blurred. For NOU as an institution, these new developments mean more competition. NOU has to consider its position seriously; it is in a position to face these threats and still lead the way by attempting to build on its own expertise on teaching at a distance, using a more research-based approach and by exploring the use of new learning technologies to supplement and improve its traditional methods of providing education at a distance.

References

Chen, L.C. (1998) 'Current situation of accelerating long distance teaching and life long learning by Ministry of Education, ROC' (in Chinese), in *Proceedings of Life Long Learning and Distance Education Symposium, National Open University, ROC, 12th–13th May 1998, Taipei County, Taiwan, ROC*, Taipei: NOU, 7–14.

China Times (1998) 'Those who have failed in the Joint University Entrance Examination can enter universities by participating in the experiment of the system of pre-study starting from this year', *China Times*, 22 May 1998 (in Chinese).

Commission on Educational Reform in the Executive Yuan, ROC (1996) *The Final Report* (in Chinese). Available HTTP: *http://www.edu.tw/eduinf/change/5/index5.htm*

Directorate General of Budget Accounting and Statistics, ROC (1998) *The General Situation of People's Culture and Leisure Life in Recent Years* (in Chinese). Available HTTP: *http://www.dgbasey.gov.tw/dgbas03/bs3/analyse/new87121.htm*

Government Information Office, ROC (1998a) *The Republic of China at a Glance.* Available HTTP: *http://www.gio.gov.tw/info/nation/en/glance/index.html*

Government Information Office, ROC (1998b) *The Republic of China Yearbook 1997.* Available HTTP: *http://www.gio.gov.tw/info/yb97/html/content.htm*

Government Information Office, ROC (1998c) *Statistical Data on the Republic of China.* Available HTTP: *http://www.gio.gov.tw/info/98html/stat-e.htm*

Ministry of Education, ROC (1998) 'Department of Higher Education'. Available HTTP: *http://www.edu.tw/eduinf/now/moewww/md12/college/index.html*

Municipal Kaohsiung Open University, ROC (1997) *Introduction to the Municipal*

Kaohsiung Open University (in Chinese). Available HTTP: *http://web.twart.com/~airuni/*

National Open University, ROC (1994) *Introduction to the National Open University, the Republic of China*, Taipei: National Open University.

National Open University, ROC (1996a) *National Open University in Ten Years*, Taipei: National Open University (in Chinese).

National Open University, ROC (1996b) *Statistics Information from SY 1986 to SY 1995*, Taipei: National Open University (in Chinese).

National Open University, ROC (1997) *Statistics Information in SY 1996*, Taipei: National Open University (in Chinese).

National Open University, ROC (1998a) *Notification of NOU Campus* (in Chinese). Available HTTP: *http://www.nou.edu.tw/~nouwww/course/dept3.html*

National Open University, ROC (1998b) *Various Statistics Tables, Unpublished Internal Information*, Taipei: National Open University.

Chapter 10

Europe

The European distance education scene is extraordinarily active, even more so since the political events which led to the disappearance of the Soviet bloc. The region's five open universities, in Germany (not strictly a national institution although it operates outside its own *Länd*), the Netherlands, Portugal, Spain and the United Kingdom, are well established, as Baumeister's chapter attests, but they were preceded by a number of Scandinavian correspondence colleges, which have now transcended that title, have degree-level courses among their offerings, and use technologies every bit as advanced as those of any other higher education institution.

Europe is one of the world's regions where the trend towards dual-mode provision is most pronounced. This applies across both Western and Central and Eastern Europe. Szücs and Jenkins describe the experience of Hungary, where distance education centres have been set up in a number of universities in preference to the establishment of a national single-mode institution. The trend is also strongly reflected in the United Kingdom, where a majority of universities now operate distance education programmes. These tend to originate from initiatives of individual faculties or departments. Open learning programmes, which may or may not include a distance component, are also very common in the United Kingdom and across Europe, but they tend to be developed most frequently at sub-degree levels. Flexible learning is another term which is frequently encountered, sometimes associated with the increasing tendency towards modularisation of degree-level and other courses.

The European Commission is very influential in open and distance education in Europe in a variety of ways, as a note about its work indicates. Current programmes such as SOCRATES and Leonardo da Vinci, and earlier programmes such as DELTA, have been heavily subscribed by higher education institutions with an involvement or an interest in involvement in open and distance learning. Szücs and Jenkins also describe Commission programmes which operate in Eastern and Central Europe. The Commission has encouraged cooperation both across national boundaries and across sectors, so that educational institutions cooperate with private organisations as well as with peer institutions. Another characteristic of the Commission's promotion of open and distance learning has been an emphasis on applications of the latest computer and telecommunications technologies. There has even been an effect on current terminology; the favoured term in Commission documents has been 'open distance learning', which concertinas two terms whose distinct identity has long been debated in the literature.

A great deal of information on the European scene can be found in the database of the UK Open University's International Centre for Distance Learning (http://www-icdl.open.ac.uk). Another regular source of current information on new developments across the whole of Europe is the annual conference of the European Distance Education Network (EDEN), for which a conference volume is always published. EDEN's Web site is at http://www.eden.bme.hu/. Many European countries have also formed their own national associations; ICDL is a good source for further details of these, as is *Distance and Supported Open Learning Worldwide*, a directory published in Cambridge, United Kingdom, by Hobsons Publishing, based on ICDL's resources. The journal *Open Learning*, which is international in scope, frequently contains informative articles on developments in Europe and more specifically on the United Kingdom.

Distance education in Central and Eastern Europe

Andras Szücs and Janet Jenkins

Political and economic change and educational development in Central and Eastern Europe in the 1990s

The process of political and economic change in Central and Eastern Europe in the early 1990s was met by the academic community in these countries with overwhelming enthusiasm and great expectations concerning the opening of their societies towards Western countries, and particularly towards European integration. Higher education seemed especially well positioned to play a flagship role in the development of East–West cooperation and European integration: the difference between the university spheres of developed countries and Eastern Europe was certainly less than, for example, differences between the industrial or commercial sectors in these countries. The countries of the European Union were quick to offer support, to be delivered under a multi-sector programme known as PHARE. The first assistance projects within PHARE started in the field of higher education cooperation (TEMPUS). The projects were successful in rapid mobilisation of partnerships and the establishment of several substantial inter-institutional educational development programmes.

These developments sent the message to the higher education sector in Central and Eastern Europe that the intention of the European Communities was that higher education should take the lead in cooperation with European Union member-states and that universities could be expected to play an outstanding role in the transformation of society and economy.

Distance education was clearly very appropriate for Central and Eastern Europe. Fast, flexible and efficient, it could be used to provide high quality training in a wide range of professional fields, for a large number of learners, including those in employment. Distance education – apart from a few isolated attempts – did not have a real background in the countries of the region, but has rapidly become well known among leading educationalists. The challenge to deploy it comprehensively has been a prominent theme in educational policy reforms during the last decade.

Despite its attractions, open and distance learning had serious barriers to overcome. The most critical was the legacy of the correspondence education still delivered by many higher education institutions in the countries of the region. The old-style correspondence programmes had long outlived their purpose. Their academic standards were usually questionable, their efficiency low, their political connotations unwelcome, resulting in serious reservations among lecturers and potential customers. Open and distance education has had to prove its superiority over this heritage.

By the mid-1990s, it appeared that the higher education sphere had reacted to the challenges of the new situation with its traditional conservatism, not really responding to social needs and also reluctant to embark on necessary structural transformations. One reason was that, under the previous political system, higher education at both individual and institutional level had developed a certain resistance and ability to survive in spite of unfavourable conditions and environment.

One major factor inhibiting change has been continuing underfunding of higher education, to an extent which has endangered and distorted the normal operation of many universities. In spite of early expectations, human resource development did not become a serious priority for most of the new governments. The poor financial situation of higher education and the chronic lack of resources improved little under the new political and economic system, and practical support for open and distance learning from government has been slow to materialise. Crucially, most countries are still engaged in the process of developing a coherent higher education policy.

Private educational institutions were quick to discover major needs and seize opportunities, particularly those exploitable via distance education. Some used courseware imported from abroad, translated and adapted, others – less desirably – courses hastily developed and offered with little regard for professional standards of distance education.

Despite these constraints, international cooperation and European Union assistance have had a considerable impact in supporting the establishment of basic national structures and creating a solid framework for the development of open and distance learning in the countries of Eastern and Central Europe. In a very short period, demonstration projects have been launched which will serve as models for the future.

Recent development in Central and Eastern Europe

One of the main factors underlying continuing change is the rapid development and expansion of the application of information technology. Education has been in the vanguard. It is only recently that commercial use of the Internet has overtaken academic. The efficient use of information technology in education requires the adoption of the underlying principles and methods of open and distance learning. Thus, the shift of open and distance learning towards the centre of human resource development is not primarily the consequence of development of open and distance learning as a methodology, but rather mainly due to change in regional and national education policies, as they react to rapid technological changes and the arrival of the information society.

Increasing use of advanced information and communications technology for teaching and learning, associated with international cooperation in education, creates the potential, for the first time in the history of human resource development, for global competition between universities which use transportable course materials to teach and trans-national communication to support learning. In the long term, such competition will contribute to improvement in quality, relevance and effectiveness of education and training. But now, the sudden development of a global market in open and distance learning materials and systems has presented an unexpected challenge. World-class institutions may use distance education to attract a significant proportion of the better students from less developed education systems. If the response to new demands for education and training within Central and Eastern European countries continues to be slow, the risk from foreign competition may turn into a present danger.

The general context

In addition to common global challenges, human resource development systems and organisations in Eastern and Central Europe have since the early 1990s faced special demands. Rapid change in these societies has created many overwhelming needs: to expand student numbers dramatically, to retrain employees and to educate people for democracy and social-political involvement. These needs provided a good platform for the wide-scale use of open and distance learning. The main challenges which distance education could address are as follows:

* access: a basic shortcoming in all higher and post-secondary education and training in the Central and Eastern European countries is its inability to accommodate enough of the population.[1] A particular bottleneck is presented by traditional, full-time education establishments which are characterised by a weak infrastructure; they are unable to expand at the pace required, while in the smaller countries there are shortages of qualified personnel to fill posts even if expansion were possible;
* flexibility and diversity: another common problem is the inability of systems to adapt to the needs of rapidly changing economies. The traditional, academically oriented, long-cycle type of higher education is not flexible enough to accommodate the new need for professionals. The more rapidly an economy and society changes, the more justified it is to

introduce short-cycle post-secondary education. This kind of professional education, oriented towards the job market, is largely missing in the countries of Central and Eastern Europe;

• continuing education: a further common shortcoming in the region is non-existent or out-dated adult education in its various forms and at various levels. The adaptation of distance education for continuing education could be an effective way to update professional knowledge;

• transfer of new knowledge and skills: the ongoing economic, social and political changes in the region need continuing enhancement, development and transfer of relevant knowledge and skills to the population at large. Associated with this is the need to strengthen the European dimension of education: languages, European studies, management, business administration, environmental factors, social studies, political sciences, advanced technologies. These needs cannot be met in the short and medium term within the framework of traditional educational systems.

An ambivalent predecessor: correspondence education

Under the previous monolithic political system, universities offered courses in three modes: face-to-face, through evening classes and through correspondence. This last usually meant printed lecture notes with tuition. Evening and correspondence courses undoubtedly had a strong political colour: their main task, especially in the first period after the Second World War, with the introduction of the Communist system, was to ensure the supply of graduate manpower, mainly in leadership positions, for the new political establishment. Later on, the function of correspondence education changed somewhat: it lost its strong political determination, and offered a possibility of complementary training and retraining to those who needed it for their job. It has remained an important route to post-school qualifications. Statistics indicate that, for example, in Hungary, as late as the mid-1980s, almost 40 per cent of all degrees awarded were issued on evening and correspondence courses.

Unfortunately the content of the courses and the methods of teaching used in correspondence education have usually not been of a high standard: they have frequently been criticised, student drop-out and failure has been high, and the prestige of correspondence education was low even within the providing institutions.

A common regional response

The region possesses a common heritage and a common need. Open and distance learning represented an obvious choice of response, but the form it should take was less clear. Open universities – autonomous distance-teaching institutions – were already established in many European Union countries.

But new institutions such as these might challenge rather than strengthen existing universities, just as they were reasserting their academic status nationally and internationally. Moreover, the resources required to establish such institutions were out of proportion to the size of population of several countries in the region. But the poor reputation of the old correspondence system meant there were dangers in relying on existing universities to give the lead.

In this context, a multi-country approach emerged. Established universities were encouraged to embark on new high quality distance education to gradually replace the outmoded correspondence courses. This was seen as a means to change and strengthen participating universities, counterbalancing possible apathy or resistance by stimulating change within. A common approach across the region would have many benefits, encouraging economies of scale through partnership, shared investment, shared courses, shared experimentation and technological innovation. It would enable new quality standards to be set, provide a common basis for evaluating their achievement, and introduce checks on inferior operations.

This approach is beginning to bear fruit, but there are many difficulties still to be faced. To illustrate, we offer next a brief account of what has happened in one country.

Distance education development: the Hungarian example

The internationalisation of a number of Hungarian universities was accelerated by processes which took place in the second half of the 1980s in the European Communities. A significant movement for reform in higher education has been a high priority for international (mainly European) cooperation. This movement has emphasised common values, structures and techniques among universities across Europe. In the second half of the 1980s, the political constraints on international cooperation disappeared almost completely. But important barriers remained, notably the bottleneck in finances (including availability of hard currencies) and insufficient command of languages.

A structural basis for open and distance learning

The National Council of Distance Education was established in 1991 by the Ministry of Education and Culture, as the advisory body to the Minister on open and distance learning issues. The Council has elaborated a national concept of the development of distance education. Its main aims are:

- to build upon the higher education institutions as the basis for distance education development, and
- to implement development within the framework of a regional structure which would be established.

The main items of the development process have been: institutional development, the establishment of basic elements of a national network, the training of distance education trainers, a low profile investment in infrastructure, and finally course development activities.

Six regional distance education centres were initially established by the Ministry, each hosted by a university or college. These centres have the task of coordinating the development of distance education in their region. Funds for basic infrastructure development and a small element for personnel were provided by the Ministry. But the universities became ambivalent towards their distance education centres when they found that no continuous further funding was assured by the Ministry. It is also worth noting that – particularly in the first phase – it was not always those universities with the highest academic reputation that applied and succeeded in becoming regional distance education centres.

In a second phase, in 1995/6, four more regional centres were established. In 1996, sixteen universities and colleges joined a national institutional framework, the National Association of Distance Teaching Universities. The creation of a National Distance Education Centre has also been envisaged. A new and substantial initiative for open and distance-learning development was made in early 1998 by the Ministry of Labour with the establishment of the Open Vocational Training Foundation.

Problems and experiences of implementation

The development of open and distance learning had a very promising start in the early 1990s. Innovation was considerable, and ambitious concepts of structural development were elaborated and implemented on a national scale. These achievements served later on as the basis for the regional PHARE distance education development programme, which in turn gave a further boost to developments in Hungary.

It is still too early to evaluate the impact in terms of student throughput and performance. There has so far been insufficient time to plan and develop many new courses. Of those available currently, only a few, particularly in the higher education sphere, are regarded as reaching a high standard. Only a small number of universities offering distance education are systematically operating quality assurance and appropriate student support services. A couple of private educational companies – typically, with courseware and technology adapted from abroad – offer good quality distance education courses, but for groups of not more than a few hundred students.

In public higher education, the chronic lack of resources and modest commitment of the host universities, further exacerbated by general management problems, has brought only limited results. In the private sector, the capital necessary to exploit modern communication and information technologies in education is lacking, and even in this sector distance education is far from reaching a critical mass. The lack of a supportive legal environment for open and distance learning, and the tendency of big companies in the corporate sector to develop their own in-house education and training has also played a role in slowing down development.

In spite of numerous initiatives including training of trainers projects, the number of distance education experts is limited, particularly in the higher education sphere. Scientific *ateliers* of higher academic standard have just started to develop, for example, fifteen students of distance education are at present studying for a PhD at the distance education centre of the Technical University of Budapest. But additional professional development in distance education is still high on the agenda.

The PHARE regional distance education programme

The PHARE programme of the European Union was initially established to support the eleven countries of Central and Eastern Europe as they emerged from Soviet domination. Concern to support economic regeneration led to an emphasis on education and training, and distance education was soon identified as a suitable methodology.

The pilot project and multi-country cooperation

In 1994, on the basis of a feasibility study to investigate the appropriateness of distance education development on a regional basis in Central and Eastern Europe, the European Commission launched a pilot project in distance education as one of the PHARE actions for regional cooperation.

Following the pilot project, the European Commission launched in 1995 a larger project for all PHARE partner countries. The Multi-Country Cooperation in Distance Education Programme continues under the European Commission, designed and managed jointly by a management committee representing the eleven beneficiary countries and making decisions on their behalf. The intention of the programme was the development of distance education through coordinated establishment of national structures and harmonised support to national policy development resulting in the creation of a genuine regional, multi-country network of institutions, which would ensure at the same time the involvement and contribution of local educational cultures, the maintenance of cultural diversity and the social relevance of course materials and delivery systems.

The programme objectives are to support the establishment of a trans-regional network of distance education study centres which are to be linked electronically, to develop distance education course modules in subject areas of relevance to socio-economic transition and to closer integration with the European Union, and to support the development of a long-term strategy for distance education.

By the end of the first phase (1997) forty distance education study centres had been established, staffed and equipped in the eleven participating countries, and a significant proportion of key personnel had received basic training. The programme has now entered a new phase which has two major components: supporting the development of exemplary high quality course material for the region, and further training of trainers, with a focus on learning support and delivery.

The impact of the PHARE programme – a preliminary assessment

The Multi-Country Programme in Distance Education has stimulated a unique situation, where the development of distance education has a shared purpose across several countries. The eleven countries in which distance education has been adopted under the PHARE development programme were, to a greater or lesser extent, all under the domination of the Soviet Union for the latter half of the century until the collapse of the Union in the late 1980s. They thus share a common thrust for renewal. They are all arranged in a single geographical cluster, with shared borders among themselves, with Western Europe, and with Russia and its Commonwealth of Independent States.

Differences in characteristics such as size, culture, language and state of development, mean that while the need for distance education is common, its specific purposes and organisation vary considerably from country to country. So far these differences have been largely expressed in variations in organisational arrangements; the purpose is generally the extension of traditional university courses to a wider public and the relatively small-scale introduction of business courses at university level.

In each country, government is expected to provide leadership. Since the purposes of the larger PHARE programme go beyond education and relate to economic and societal impact, the Ministry of Finance or Employment is usually involved in strategic decision-making, with the Ministry of Education responsible for overseeing implementation. The extent of active participation by government varies. In some cases, programme management is effectively devolved to a distance education centre within a university.

The main agents selected to implement the strategy are universities. They receive PHARE project funding directly, and are expected to build towards self-support in distance education. These new demands create considerable strain in universities with a highly traditional ethos and structure. Academic traditionalism and highly centralised financial management and administration have an untold negative impact on the growth and shape of distance education in many countries. Issues to be tackled include planning and organising resources, budget management, interfaculty activity, and relations between faculty and administration. There is little attempt generally to use resources outside the immediate university environment. There is little experience of using audio and video, for example, although there is some experimentation with videoconferencing, and attempts to use broadcasting are very rare, even though it may stimulate wider participation in learning.

There has so far been no attempt to start an open university or large-scale autonomous distance-teaching institution in any of the eleven countries. Traditional universities are encouraged to develop capacity in distance education and deliver programmes. One mark of the success of the strategy is the large proportion of universities which have shown interest in distance education and put their name to proposals for projects. The majority of universities in the region now have some involvement in a PHARE project. The twenty-eight projects funded from December 1997 include 130 private and public organisations from both PHARE and European Union countries, with the lead institutions and the majority of consortium members in PHARE countries. A few have considerable experience and are on their way to becoming centres of excellence.

This very high level of involvement in only a few years is an indicator of the high status that distance education has acquired right across the region. Undoubtedly the promise of financial support has been a major incentive, and it remains to be seen how much of what has been seeded will continue to grow. But the initial achievement is remarkable, against no tradition of public-funded distance education in any of these countries.

A further feature of the PHARE programme is encouragement to universities to work in partnership with others for distance programmes to be made available nationally, through cooperation with other universities or through joint delivery. Courses should also be offered across the region, and partnership internationally, for course development, is encouraged. Both types of partnership are unfamiliar to the universities. Most striking of all is encouragement to collaborate with the private sector, which is entirely new in the region.

The latest PHARE projects, for the development of distance learning modules, promote partnership by insisting that every consortium has at least two active partners from PHARE countries. Rather than seeing the specification of themes as a threat to academic freedom, universities were ready to compete to gain the contracts for these courses. Partnerships across national borders seem to be easier to forge than those between universities within countries. There is little partnership between universities and the non-university education sector, or other institutions of ministries of education. The strategy of building up and changing universities works against the development of such partnerships; as a result, plans for distance education programmes for the professional development of middle-level personnel are limited.

Distance education development: perspectives and barriers

The idea of comprehensive and coordinated development of distance education in Central and Eastern Europe has offered an exceptional challenge and opportunity for the large-scale implementation of new methods and structures, initiating and catalysing processes which could play a determining role in the development and transformation of not only the educational systems, but – through the intensive multiplication effect of the modern training methods, combined with latest information technologies and telecommunication – also of the societies and economies themselves. As up-to-date open and distance learning barely existed in these countries, there has been a unique opportunity to design national structures and create physical and human infrastructure for distance education in harmony with emerging national policies for human resource development, thus determining basically the direction and extent of future developments.

As our case study shows, Hungary is a nation that has advanced further than others in distance education. But it is also typical in that its activity has been small scale, falling short of the grand objectives of the early 1990s. At the same time the leap forward is significant, and typical of the region. A powerful dynamic for change underpins this development. The PHARE programme has been effective in providing support. It could have been even more effective with consistently stronger support from individual governments.

The advantage of latecomers has frequently been mentioned in connection with distance education in the Central–Eastern European region – the chance to shorten paths of development and implement new strategies without retreading old ground. In practice, distance education in Central and Eastern Europe has developed more slowly than expected. This is partly due to the need for time to respond to rapid change in distance education itself, particularly in the accelerated development of information and communication technologies and the convergence of traditional and open learning methods. It is also due to increasing recognition of the importance of a fully professional approach and methods, the need to introduce quality assurance, the arrival of new information and communication technologies, the need for professional marketing. There is an urgent need for a communication strategy regarding distance education, as it has begun to gather a number of negative connotations. The heritage of correspondence education persists, and the activity of some private educational institutions who use 'distance education' as a marketing keyword to label their courses, of sometimes questionable quality, has had a bad effect. Accreditation and legislation arrangements for distance education are still not in place, reinforcing ambivalence towards distance education.

Meanwhile, open and distance learning at higher education institutions, particularly traditional universities, has two essential and urgent tasks: to ensure widespread recognition of the methods of distance education and to harmonise its further evolution within and between the countries of the region.

Achievements, perspectives, failures

As the end of the 1990s approaches, and we begin to assess the impact of the European Union assistance programmes, particularly in the field of open and distance learning, some crucial issues stand out:

- the sustainability of the structures established;
- usage of courses developed (or adopted) within the framework of cooperation projects;
- clarification of copyright questions on course materials, usually not settled;
- marketing of the courses;
- general questions of economy, course development and delivery in distance education.

Future policy is likely to be affected by the way these issues are resolved. Continuing economic growth and accompanying emerging demand from the corporate sector and private consumers alike for quality education, in parallel with increasing spending power of individual learners on the educational market, may stimulate the organic development of distance education, help to create synergy and bind what are today more or less isolated achievements into an integral, self-sustaining and well-functioning system.

We remarked on the relatively slow pace of change. This could be beneficial, allowing time within universities for the gradual department-by-department transformation to dual-mode operation, with small groups of faculty becoming committed to distance education as they experience the professional satisfaction of working with and for distance learners. But this process could be too slow to meet the demands of government and public. It could offer the commercial sector an opportunity to move in and cut short the development of high quality distance learning that is under way. Will governments allow this to happen? Or will they give universities enough support over the long term to consolidate the work that has begun?

Is distance education sustainable?

Do results live up to expectations? At present it is easy to conclude that they do not. There is, first, low take-up. This is partly a question of the type of course offered: for example, in Bulgaria recently, twenty-five students embarked on a Master's programme in International Economic Relations, while 124 started a postgraduate credit course on Quality in Food and Drinks. Launching courses such as these is dealing with economic priorities in a highly appropriate way. But the relatively small scale of enrolment is typical. The notion that distance education, to be effective, must cater for mass markets as well as niche markets has not yet become embedded. The forty PHARE Distance Education Centres are only just becoming operational, they have few courses, and few students. They need rapidly to prove their value as part of public education systems.

In Central and Eastern Europe, as in the rest of the world, developments in the field of education – including open and distance learning and higher education – are to an increasing extent part of a competitive, market-determined environment, subject sometimes to excessive financial pressures and in some cases competing against the forces of wild capitalism. Governments have very limited control of this market and can do little to promote their political preferences.

It remains an open question how far finally open and distance education will respond to the emerging needs of society. That depends partly on attracting resources, from government sources (education, labour market development) or from the corporate sector. The institutional system which has been established has to prove its fitness in a market situation sharpening daily, in competition with other actors. A further crucial underlying question concerns policy. What will be the role of government? To what extent will individual countries seek the inputs and services of modern educational methods? How far will comprehensive national infrastructures be established and courses developed to support the establishment of open learning systems? Can universities and other public institutions deliver what is needed? Will distance education survive if they do not?

One striking feature of distance education in the region has been the success of some outside institutions. To 'kick start' distance education in the region, some of the major distance-teaching institutions of Western Europe, particularly the UK Open University and FernUniversität Hagen, admitted students from Central and Eastern Europe on some courses, particularly courses in business and management. This was often done by setting up national subsidiaries, which have become established on a regular basis. These subsidiaries operate commercially, with students paying full cost fees. In terms of national salary levels, the fees are enormous. Small numbers of individuals are making a huge investment in learning.

If over several years distance education has proved its worth by attracting students even at such high cost, the seeds of success are planted. And yet courses developed and offered by local universities, although far cheaper, do not appear to attract proportional interest. What can be done to break through the barrier?

Higher education development and Western assistance

What is the impact of Western assistance?

There is a feeling in some quarters that Western assistance to higher education has been a disappointment, and that it should have done more to introduce essential structural changes in higher education. Most universities in
the region retain an old-fashioned, conservative atmosphere. A good chance
has been missed to build on the innovative ambitions characteristic of the
first half of the 1990s.

The majority of the universities have yet to develop full strategic development plans. In some cases, higher education development plans have been
put aside at national and institutional level. Assistance projects such as
TEMPUS have had variable results in this unstable context. On the one
hand, TEMPUS has produced only a few good institution- or faculty-level
projects; most initiatives addressed general department-level development.
On the other hand, some good examples were presented, mainly by those
universities whose existence was endangered because of their small size
and/or obsolete field of education, or by flexible colleges, which have used
TEMPUS in an efficient and appropriate way, to provide the international
dimension in the implementation of their development plans.

It was hoped in the early 1990s that European Union resources would
provide a bridge until conditions for effective human resource development
in each country were assured. Little progress has been made, little action
taken to follow up statements about the importance of human resources.
The next step in this field may be taken by the corporate sector, which is
developing cooperation with universities.

Expectations for distance education may have been unrealistically high.
An additional factor which has limited the value of assistance from Europe is
the shortage of suitable models. Central and Eastern Europe has chosen the
dual-mode style of distance education – a traditional university offering both
distance and face-to-face courses. But until very recently the main exemplars
of distance education in the European Union have been the autonomous
open universities. These are in many ways not ideal models for development
of dual-mode operations. Many of the dual-mode universities in the rest of
Europe are as new to distance education as the universities in PHARE countries. They also face difficult issues of institutional adjustment in embedding
distance education within the traditional university environment. These
Western universities organise their distance education in a variety of different ways. Some are effective, in other cases they are feeling their way. They
are all different from the model offered by open universities. There is scope
for two newcomers to learn the techniques of distance education together, in
partnership.

Models for technology use are also limited. Despite strong links between the United States and many of the Central and European countries, the US approach to distance education has received little attention. There, the use of televised lectures (tele-courses) is well established. In Europe, the technique is little used, the main exception being the Europace 2000 consortium which promotes the use of non-traditional media in distance education. It is possible that the tele-course would be culturally attractive as well as effective in some Eastern and Central European environments.

Underlying these shortcomings is the lack of a common approach to distance education across Western Europe. While the European Commission is firm in its support for open and distance learning in principle, strategy for supporting its development across Western Europe is still emerging. This uncertainty has perhaps been responsible for what has sometimes appeared to beneficiaries in Eastern and Central Europe as wavering commitment.

However, West–East distance education projects of the 1990s have started the ball rolling in a meaningful way. They have ensured that an infrastructure is in place throughout the region. And they have certainly contributed to providing social and cultural impressions for a large number of personnel, including younger staff engaged in developing tomorrow's systems, who had the chance of contact with issues of quality, efficiency, culture and language during their study periods abroad.

Improving distance education: can new technology help?

In the face of increasing competition from the commercial sector, universities may be able to hold their own as leaders in the development of distance education. They have the advantages of academic status, the cream of national intellectual resources, and the authority to award qualifications. And they have a new advantage, their growing capacity to use new information and communications technologies for teaching and learning, underpinned by university expertise in electronic engineering and access to the Internet and associated technologies.

The opportunity to use exciting technologies such as multimedia is the inspiration for much new distance education. Technology-based learning is already routinely integrated into campus-based operations. Universities in Central and Eastern Europe, newly endowed with state-of-the-art information and communications technologies, have an opportunity to start afresh and move ahead of some of their Western partners.

But the problem of scale has yet to be tackled. There is difficulty in visualising and creating learner support in an environment where learners are widely scattered. In a few cases – such as on the off-shore islands of Estonia – adequate numbers of local centres have been established to reach a high proportion of potential distance learners. Learning support is a completely new concept, alien to an academic culture where professors control what their students do.

Distance education must prove itself superior to the old correspondence system. Its main weapon is the use of new information and communications technology – the chance not only to do something different but to do it differently. In their search for quality, several universities have shown themselves ready to experiment and explore the potential of the new technologies to a far greater extent than their Western partners. The challenge is to harness and use technologies in innovative ways in order to increase participation and improve quality.

Partnership across frontiers

International partnership has been a catalyst for change in breaking the academic mould, and creating environments where people from different institutions work together in teams.

Coming to terms with the idea of international partnership has been particularly difficult in the formerly closed societies of Central and Eastern Europe, and there is still scope for misunderstanding and unrealistic expectations. Positioning oneself securely in an international team at a time when culture is being redefined and national education systems reshaped is especially difficult. Language poses a major problem, with English often used as a neutral and shared tongue, with enhanced dangers of miscommunication when nobody is communicating in their mother tongue. On the other hand, working in a team is exciting. Once practitioners get together to develop course material, the result can be openness, enthusiasm, enjoyment of the experience of team work, and commitment to a learner-centred approach.

Collaboration on some other matters is much more problematic. For example, intellectual property rights are generally poorly understood in the academic sector, and particularly difficult to sort out in an international context. There is often a sharp difference of values between academic institutions in countries where a commercial orientation has taken root and those in countries which maintain a strong tradition of financial support for education as a public service. This sometimes results in one partner failing to understand the charges imposed by another. Other financial bones of contention derive from pay differentials reflected in project funding arrangements.

Qualifications and courses from the West have high credibility, which is why people spend so much in order to follow distance courses from Western universities. The universities of Central and Eastern Europe have to reposition themselves to compete. Paradoxically, distance education can be used as a means to transfer both courses and expertise from one university to another. For example, a foreign university can authorise a local one to provide a local centre and perhaps local tuition for a course. As it gains experience the local university takes on more responsibility, and the partners offer a joint award. The final stage comes when the local university takes over the course completely and offers its own award. Such arrangements are in use in other parts of the world but do not seem to have made any impact in Central and Eastern Europe. Western universities may be as reluctant to lose students as the host countries are to lose the cachet of a Western degree.

In Central and Eastern Europe, the notion of a market for learning is still new. By contrast, some Western European universities regularly advertise, and distance education courses in particular are heavily publicised. Advertising, aimed at providing sufficient information to potential students to attract them to try a non-traditional mode of learning, requires substantial investment. If universities ignore marketing, there is a risk that potential clients will turn to commercial operators that advertise aggressively, with undesirable results: unreliable quality standards, outflow of foreign exchange, and under-exploitation of national intellectual resources. Transfer of expertise in marketing intellectual products such as distance education would be a useful complement to existing activity, and could be an element of partnership activity.

The development of partnerships between the countries of Eastern and Central Europe is at the heart of the PHARE multi-country programme but has attracted little attention. A real effort to plan and implement modalities of collaborative working and sharing of courses must now be placed high on the agenda.

Conclusion

This chapter has outlined the birth and development of distance education in the region. We have drawn attention to the lack of strategic thinking and firm policy frameworks in the countries concerned. But we have also drawn attention to the positive. The final task is to draw together the discussion and suggest how the problems may be tackled.

The burden placed on universities to develop distance education seems in most cases to be out of proportion to the help offered them. The huge problems of changing both the perspective of academic staff and university administration have yet to be squarely faced. Specific difficulties include:

- marketing – universities are used to students arriving at the door. The idea that distance courses have to be advertised and distance learners persuaded to enrol is completely outside the culture. Without marketing capacity, universities are handicapped and cannot compete with the private sector;
- low funding – seed funds are not enough. Universities need to develop a strategy and action plan for distance education. In particular, learners normally want qualifications and universities need to offer a range of award-bearing courses and programmes. A long-term strategy is essential to achieve such objectives in a context of very restricted resources;

- learning support – there is no understanding of what a distance tutor does, and no tradition of collaboration between universities to make it possible to share tutors and premises for learning support;
- ownership – the establishment of distance education centres with a small dedicated staff aids commitment, but can also lead to distance education becoming marginal within the institutions and courses not seen as owned by the university concerned.

Good leadership in academic institutions is critical to overcoming these difficulties. Universities have the intellectual resource to deliver high quality distance education and the ability to design new courses and offer awards. But that alone is insufficient without government commitment and support over the long term. Once the universities are secure in the knowledge that they have such support, they will be better able to build on the foundations of distance education now in place and participate as equal partners in Europe-wide open learning.

Note

1 Comprehensive up-to-date comparative data on participation in higher education are lacking; however the 1997 Human Development Report gives 1994 tertiary net enrolment ratio (as percentage of ages 18–21) for Hungary (11 per cent), Poland (15 per cent) and Czech Republic (15 per cent), compared with 33 per cent for France and 35 per cent for the USA.

Western Europe

Hans-Peter Baumeister

This chapter presents an overview of distance education in Europe, followed by a discussion of new developments relating to student attitudes and the increasing use of new technologies in distance education and also in traditional universities. The once clear distinction between conventional studies and distance education is becoming progressively more blurred. Also discussed are the tensions between the centuries-old European university structure and distance education. The chapter ends with an analysis of the top-down European Union policy on distance education.

What exactly comprises Europe in the context of this chapter? From a geographical, historical or cultural viewpoint, it is clear that Europe is more than just the fifteen member-states of the European Union. But there are good reasons for restricting this chapter principally to the European Union and its policies:

- the major institutions and consortia of contemporary distance education are in the European Union;
- one of the fundamental changes in the countries of Central and Eastern Europe in 1989 was the disappearance of the former well-established system of distance education, which had a specific function within the socialist system and was rapidly replaced by the re-establishment of traditional university systems;
- because of its political and economic power, the European Union also sets the agenda for the development of distance education in European countries outside the Union, for example, through programmes such as PHARE or TEMPUS, which include substantial training activities for future distance education experts in Central and Eastern Europe. And in countries with which negotiations for full membership (Estonia, Poland, Czech Republic, Hungary and Slovenia) start in 1998, the main lines of European Union policy are already being followed.

Other countries like Norway and Switzerland are associated with programmes of the European Union promoting distance education. Only the former Yugoslavia (with the exception of Slovenia) is still a blank area on the map.

Often neglected in discussion of European distance education is the Turkish Anadolu Universitesi, the biggest European institution, with around 560,000 students. Its organisational model is dual mode; distance education activities are managed by a specific faculty of the university.

Two characteristics distinguish the Turkish institution from other European developments:

- the huge number of students is partly explained by the concentration in Anadolu Universitesi on teacher training, which is not such a major responsibility of other European distance-teaching institutions;
- in the second major area of activity, business administration, the curriculum is based on a US model since most of the Turkish lecturers were educated in US universities.

Despite these distinguishing characteristics, and the fact that Turkey is not part of European programmes in the field of distance education, representatives of Anadolu Universitesi have launched initiatives to bring them into contact with European development, and may become involved with European Union policy initiatives in the future.

Returning to the sphere influenced by European Union policy, formulated by the consensus of member-states, the working definition of distance education in this chapter is as follows:

> distance education comprises those teaching–learning processes in which as a rule teaching and learning are separated in both space and time. Bridging the distance and guiding the learning process is effected by means of specially prepared materials (media) and in the context of an organisation which steers and supports the whole process.

With this definition in mind, the following account of distance education in Europe follows the traditional distinction between single and dual-mode institutions.

The five single-mode institutions in the European Union have 500,000 enrolled students, whose average age is around 32 years. Overall, more men than women are studying at these institutions.[1] The biggest of the single-mode institutions is the UK Open University with around 257,000 students (1996) followed by the Universidad Nacional de Educación a Distancia (UNED) of Spain with 136,444. Both institutions also recruit overseas students. The other three universities – the FernUniversität, Germany, the Open universiteit, Netherlands, and Universidade Aberta, Portugal – have together approximately 100,000 students. The British, Dutch, Portuguese and Spanish universities are national institutions, whereas the FernUniversität is regionally based, operating nationally through bilateral agreements with different German *Länder* to, for example, set up study centres. Spain has a different study centre set-up from that of the UK since UNED's study centres are partly funded, too, by the regions in which they are based. All the above institutions also have study centres overseas. Comparison of the sub-ject areas covered by the five is very difficult because of the variations between their faculty structure. In general, law and business administration attract most students, followed by the humanities; but the fact that business administration is outsourced from the UK Open University – to the Open Business School, and that neither law nor business administration are offered by the Universidade Aberta, Portugal, illustrates the difficulty of comparison.

All these institutions are very active in the application of new technolo-gies, with a wide range of practice, from experiments through to regular on-line courses. In addition to capitalising on new developments and trying to react flexibly to the demands of students, European distance education institutions are also keen to take the lead in future innovative use of new technologies for teaching and learning for all (European Commission 1997) and to act as centres of competence in their own countries and more widely (van Dam-Mieras 1997).

A new Web-based institution, the University of Catalonia (Universitat Oberta de Catalunya[2]), has entered the scene. This is a regionally focused institution, based in Barcelona and supported by regional bodies and indus-try, offering courses in Catalan. A number of courses are being developed with the support of members of other universities. There is no single-mode institution in Europe outside the European Union which is of comparable size to the five described above.

In 1994, Desmond Keegan, while acknowledging the difficulty of provid-ing accurate data, quoted a total of 2,249,810 students enrolled for distance-taught courses within the European Union (Keegan 1994). The valuable perception stemming from that figure is that while most attention is generally paid to the single-mode institution, the majority of students are enrolled with dual-mode institutions. At the same time, the many and varied forms of teaching and learning which are evolving within dual-mode insti-tutions in between the extremes of traditional structures of study and traditional distance education render the definition of distance education quoted above more and more difficult to apply.

One of the reasons for this development is the use of new technologies in traditional universities. Another is the change in the social situation of stu-dents within the last twenty years which has had the consequence that in most European countries the number of *real* (in a social, not a statistical, sense) full-time students is under 50 per cent. The contraction of budgets for the financial support of students has led to a new situation where many students spend more time earning money than studying. Distance education is becoming more and more important in providing opportunities for individual flexibility in the organisation of study. New technologies will increasingly support such individual solutions. Together with other new challenges, for instance, those stemming from demands for professional training (OECD 1995) or for improvement in the quality of teaching in general, it is clear that many reasons point towards new structures in higher education; but the availability of new technologies alone, without changes in the structure of European societies, would not have had such an immense impact. Industry's demand to have better and easier access to courses for professional training and continuing education is not a minor issue. *Easier* means not only greater on-line provision so as to use the working place for training purposes and to restrict employees' absence to the minimum, but also more open access to universities. In some European countries, universities as well as particular disciplines experience difficulties in coming into closer contact with the actual labour market, and they maintain a reluctant stance (Baumeister 1997). And since these stances have some bearing on national or European policies, it is important to keep constantly in mind the fact that developments occur within the European educational system independently of one another. This background helps to explain the reasons underlying European Union top-down policy in that sector.

While the definition of distance education quoted above still holds even in the case of dual-mode institutions in order to maintain a clear distinction from on-campus as well as from self-study or autodidactic forms, it is true that more and more varieties of knowledge acquisition of students are met with (Laurillard 1993), and that conventional European universities are beginning to adjust to meet the new challenges and social realities. However, it is widely viewed that the traditional system of higher education in Europe has some difficulties – in particular due to internal resistance stemming from the classical understanding of the nature of a university – in reacting to the demands of modern societies in the industrial world. For example, it is not easy to step beyond faculties or departments and to build interdisciplinary course teams or to integrate experts from computer departments. In addition, we still often encounter the 'lone ranger', beginning to transfer his or her traditional teaching into a media-based form. At the same time we can study barriers and obstacles in European universities which stem from their centuries-old history while also noting the innovative spirit of many lecturers building up a growing internal pressure to achieve new forms of teaching by seeking European partners outside their own institution.

But, the current situation is no longer comparable with that described by Keegan and Rumble in 1982, when mixed-mode institutions were not to be found in Europe. Today, there is no longer a clear distinction between on-campus and off-campus students. Also, the availability of new technologies together with important social developments encourage a well-known trend in distance education for students enrolled in traditional universities to buy study packages from distance education institutions – to support their own study rhythm independent of the sometimes inflexible course structure of traditional universities and/or to have access to more learner-oriented teaching material.

The typology of distance education should therefore extend to include not only institutional structures but also modern forms of creating individual study programmes. Students are already studying 'multiple mode' by integrating traditional teaching and distance education provision at their own desks due to their social situation and with the support of new technologies. European students are acting more and more like regular consumers in their study attitudes: they are looking for quality *and* for the best service to support their learning. There is also a growing tendency to buy learning material in portions to create an individual programme. These attitudes will directly influence the future service-oriented organisation of higher education institutions in Europe. Interuniversity competition and the pressure to offer more learner-friendly courses will significantly encourage this development. And it appears logical that the consumer society will create its own appropriated styles of education.

From a cost perspective, it is difficult to draw a clear line between different kinds of study forms and to compare different institutions in relation to student success. That kind of accounting is to a certain extent 'old-fashioned'; it could historically be explained by the defensive position adopted in the past to justify distance education's reasonable funding. More interesting is the question of how to combine different methods of learning and teaching within an individual study programme in order to be effective in terms of costs. Unit costs to the student and also to society in relation to quality, completion time, and the adaptability of units to the new everyday life of students, are decisive parameters.

How does all this apply to distance education in Europe? Many of these topics have already been discussed and managed by distance education institutions, but poor communication between different types of European higher education institutions has resulted in little permeability in terms of teaching and learning methods across the whole system. There is a danger of time being lost through reinvention of the wheel at conventional universities, but in dual-mode institutions, where different forms of study are already being undertaken, the traditional parts of established institutions are also being currently influenced. European planning papers such as the UK Dearing Committee report (National Committee of Inquiry in Higher Education 1997) illustrate how far the terminology of distance education is already an influence: and concepts such as study packages, study modules and improving the technological skills of staff members, are all applied to the traditional system. But it is still unusual to find recommendations to improve the exchange between conventional and distance education institutions.

This survey of Europe ends by noting that European institutions as well as individual academics are also engaged in research on distance education. The Institute of Educational Technology at the UK Open University and the independent Deutsches Institut für Fernstudienforschung at the Universität Tübingen, Germany, are the major research bodies. Other single-mode institutions also undertake research on their own study programmes and increasingly on new technology applications. In Scandinavia, there is a well-established research tradition in distance education as well as in adult education.

The private sector has always had a limited role in higher education in Europe. Significant growth has been precluded in part because of the issue of granting degrees, and in part through the prevailing influence of traditional institutions. But there is currently interest in the possibility of cooperation among private and public institutions; for example, in public institutions validating private programmes by offering exams, conducting examinations, offering degrees, or providing other support, possibly across national boundaries, and creating joint ventures in the field of professional training and consulting. Major assets of private institutions include their flexibility to react to students' changing social situations and to new demands of companies in relation to professional training, and their familiarity with costs and profits. Though the question of individual costs is still a difficult one in those European countries where study fees are not usual as in Germany, the private market will grow because it will better serve the demands of students and companies in a consumer society. Discussion about fees for regular students has already begun in the few European countries where students do not already pay for their study programmes (Turner 1996). Cooperation with private institutions will open access for traditional institutions in to the market-place, and private partners will take advantage of the sound academic quality delivered by institutions of higher education.

There is also a growing technology market where institutions of higher education cooperate with private companies such as software or telecommunications companies to develop technical platforms for Web-based teaching and learning provision. This is also an important area of intersection where European Union policy of supporting distance education is a significant factor in the creation of new public–private partnerships in the sector of new information technologies. Although it is a unique challenge to mirror on a technical platform the complex structure of a regular university with all its forms of autonomy and its accepted duality of research and teaching, companies like IBM, Siemens-Nixdorf, Softarc or Cap Gemini have begun to work in some of these areas, either alone or partly in cooperation with distance education institutions.

To this point, the relationship with the European higher education system has been viewed from a distance education perspective. The view of distance education from a traditional university perspective offers some sharp contrasts:

- to a certain extent, distance education, in particular in its institutional-ised form, is not at all or is only marginally registered by the academic community (Gellert 1993; Scott 1996);
- from the viewpoint of political decision-makers, in particular within the European Union, distance education is one of the most important developments in the higher education sector (European Commission 1997).

Distance education is still ignored by the traditional university system in Europe to an astonishing degree. In the article 'Structures and functional differentiation – remarks on changing paradigms of tertiary education in Europe' (Gellert 1993), both the term 'distance education' and any mention of its role in a modern system of higher education are absent, though the text deals with '*functional* differentiation'. And in relation to continuing edu-cation, distance education is not always discussed as one of the most important developments in terms of methodological innovation (Teichler 1996). It is strange that distance-teaching institutions should be largely ignored, especially in view of their student enrolments and of their financial allocations from national budgets. Equally ignored are the new social devel-opments and the developments in the field of new technologies which have already affected the traditional system and will do so more strongly in the near future, more than any other previous developments in higher education.

This approach is equally astonishing with regard to a unique European prerequisite, namely Article 126 of the Treaty of Maastricht of 1992, the political basis of the European Union, where members agree to support the future development of distance education. This is unique because there is no other multilateral agreement creating a specific policy to improve one single form of education in all signatory states. European Union bodies implement this Article which is as far as European Union responsibility extends towards a common education policy, and millions of ECUs are spent on European development of distance education year by year.

Even where distance education institutions can point to successful histor-ies, it is still difficult to gain acceptance and respect. Van Dam-Mieras reports in relation to the Dutch Open universiteit that it is still difficult to cooperate with other institutions of higher education in an unbiased way (van Dam-Mieras 1997). Looking at distance education in the light of traditional higher education, the following reasons can be adduced:

- distance education is more associated with a teaching-oriented approach than other systems of knowledge dissemination in modern societies. This departs from the European conception of scholarship where more weight is placed on research. Therefore, distance education institutions have been seen for a long time as offering only 'lightweight' academic qualifications without any significant basis in research activities; in this view, *real* teaching is crucially dependent on the unity of research and teaching;

- delivery is not an abstract term in distance education but has to be managed in a concrete way. That includes new forms of organisation in an institution of higher education unknown to those who are used to thinking in terms of chairs, departments, faculties, library and central administration. Teamwork across the borders in these traditional institutions is still a word seldom heard;

- perhaps the most important reason is that distance education curricula are open (i.e. public), which means they can be read, discussed and criticised. But above all, to develop a curriculum in distance education means to structure an area of content in advance. To put the teaching task to the forefront and to deal with it in the academic spotlight is not, to put it mildly, one of the most popular tasks in the higher education system.

The European tradition in higher education is built on the authority of professors appointed to a chair undertaking research as well as teaching their students. This medieval structure of universities still operates, so that the university represents one of the few European institutions which can follow its roots back to the twelfth or thirteenth century. Professors and their students came together at real places at real times to undertake scholarship. These crucial conditions have determined *universitas litterarum*, the university. Distance education is breaking up the physical core of the European tradition of scholarship. While distance education in the 1960s, 1970s and 1980s remained within a fenced environment with its own institutions, no significant public discussion occurred on the organisational impact of applying media-supported learning.

The increasing use of information technologies in higher education, together with emerging new types of institution (polytechnics, Fachhochschulen, Instituts Universitaires de Technologie) without the same depth of history, along with the social and economic changes we have reported, are creating waves throughout the whole system.

It would be naive to ignore deliberations within the traditional university system concerning modern challenges to teaching and learning. But the discussion in general does not connect their current situation – which is often seen as deplorable – with experience already gained from distance education. When E. de Corte (1996: 113) states that 'research on learning and instruction has produced over the past decades an empirically underpinned knowledge base for designing more powerful learning environments', he is not referring to the results of relevant distance education research. Diana Laurillard, in *Rethinking University Teaching*, however, deals with exactly this issue, namely future perspectives of teaching and learning. It is clear that better penetration of the different systems is needed, which requires not so much an exchange of information but a change in attitudes. The last section deals with the work of European Union bodies drawing on the current situation as well as the follow-up from Article 126 of the Treaty of Maastricht. Distance education-related European Union policy is meanwhile influencing large parts of Europe and not only the narrow circle of the fifteen member-states.

For over a decade the European Union has significantly supported the development of higher education in Europe, including distance education. The overall concept was to develop – over and above national educational systems – something like a European dimension within the structure of higher education. This would be achieved by different programmes, of which ERASMUS (to support the physical mobility of students and lecturers in Europe) is probably the best known; but starting in the mid-1980s, distance education components have also been integrated in a number of different, mostly technologically oriented European programmes. Here the main aim was to use modern technologies for networking institutions of higher education and to create new types of learning environments as well as a technical infrastructure for disseminating knowledge. With respect to the latter it was also intended to improve public–private partnerships to support hard- and software engineering and to prepare the appropriate parts of European industry ready for global competition.

Looking back, the first approaches appear naive because the early programmes did not start from the actual educational system as it existed at the time. Instead, their starting point was the supposed potential of modern technologies not only to transfer the historically developed structures of the European educational systems on to a new level but to change most of these structures, a classical top-down approach. The belief in such a 'quantum leap' was supported to a large extent by the sectors of industry which participated in programmes like ESPRIT and DELTA. That approach repeated to a certain extent some fundamental errors from the end of the 1960s, when in the absence of convincing and properly evaluated ideas for systematic solutions as to how to integrate new hard- and software into a particular education system – people believed in the revolutionary possibilities of newly available audio-visual components. The background for such approaches can be traced back to the foundation of the European Union which was on an economic basis. Founded in 1957 as the European Economic Community, it has always put economic purpose to the forefront; this fact should not be forgotten when talking about educational issues because they have never been discussed at European Economic Community or European Union level in their own right but only as elements of an economic policy. This to a great extent explains the overwhelming interest of European Union bodies in the application of new technologies.

The current European Union funding system for a number of major programmes follows the principle of subsidiarity through which only such

activities are launched which are deemed necessary from a European perspective and which could not be undertaken through national initiatives.
Generally, only 50 per cent of a project's cost will be funded, on the assumption that the other half will be paid by the beneficiaries because of their own
interests in new developments. At the same time, this system of funding
should support the idea of sustainability; if institutions invest 50 per cent
into a budget, they have an interest in achieving substantial results and in
subsequently continuing the project or programme on a commercial basis. In
practice, this funding philosophy has failed in relation to sustainability
because applying institutions have often worked on the basis of obtaining
European Union funding for programmes and projects which were already
planned. European programmes have been more successful with regard to
networks both on a personal and institutional level (e.g. the 'Coimbra
Group'[3]). It would also be unfair to ignore the fact that European policy has
achieved raising awareness for the potential of distance education even in
those countries with a weak tradition in that area (MacKeogh 1997).

In the past, top-down approaches in the field of educational policy have
been observed to respond less to the interests of learners and teachers than
to those of more powerful lobbies acting on the European level. How might a
top-down policy within the area of higher education, including distance
education, be combined with more bottom-up elements?

First, the funding of projects is mostly short term, usually for one to three
years. In some cases this is sufficient but in others it is not. In particular,
where a programme aims at sustainability, short-term funding is problematic.
Existing experience has already been drawn upon to demonstrate why longer
duration distance education projects should be contemplated; one reason is
to enable projects to cope with or improve long-established university structures (Wilson and Baumeister 1998). It is also important to be aware that the
European system of higher education is not *per se* easy to handle in terms
of institutional cooperation. Different types of organisation, of academic
career paths, of funding and of relationships with the labour market,
complicate the definition of common aims and the establishment of
transnational working structures.

Second, both the time and effort necessary to develop distance education
materials are notoriously underestimated, particularly by newcomers. In
consequence, it is often the case that a major proportion of project time is
taken up with developing working structures within the complex European
university landscape for producing study materials, preparing academically
sound teaching material and finding a common platform for assessing its
quality. Quality is an issue of great influence on transnational production
strategies, but the criteria are related to individual national academic roots.

The development of European structures in distance education has many
facets. In particular, the new technologies offer important facilities for a
decentralised European dual-mode approach in distance education which

requires further investigation which could be undertaken through the agency of existing European Union programmes. In order to support these developments, European policy on education should be seen clearly in its own right and not only as an appendix of the European economy. This would facilitate studies of longer duration as well as the allocation of funding to support real European activities through a bottom-up approach.

This chapter has attempted to portray distance education in Europe within the context of the existing centuries-old higher education system. The tension which emerges is typical of the specific quality of current European scholarship. While the picture may not be optimistic enough for those believing in the bright future of higher education facilitated by new technologies, it may at the same time be too heretical for those believing in traditional European values of scholarship.

Notes

1 For further details concerning the institutions mentioned below cf. EADTU 1997 (also http://www.eadtu.nl).
2 http://www.uoc.es
3 http://www.coimbra-group.be

References

Baumeister, H.-P. (1997) 'Germany's place within the international discussion of standards and quality in open and distance learning: some unsystematic deliberations', in A. Tait (ed.), *Perspectives on Distance Education. Quality Assurance in Higher Education: Selected Case Studies*, Vancouver: Commonwealth of Learning, 9–17.

Baumeister, H.-P. and Hauck, P. (1997) 'International transfer of knowledge. Cultural context and pedagogic consequences in times of globalisation', in G. Miller (ed.), *Proceedings of the 18th World Conference of the International Council for Distance Education* (CD-ROM), State College: The Pennsylvania State University.

Burgen, A. (ed.) (1996) *Goals and Purposes of Higher Education in the 21st Century*, London: Jessica Kingsley.

de Corte, E. (1996) 'New perspectives of learning and teaching', in A. Burgen (ed.), *Goals ands Purposes of Higher Education in the 21st Century*, London: Jessica Kingsley.

European Association of Distance Teaching Universities (EADTU) (1997) *Mini-Directory 1997/98*, Heerlen: EADTU.

European Commission (1997) *Programme Technologies for Knowledge and Skills Acquisition. Proposal for a Research Agenda*, Brussels: European Commission. Available HTTP: *http://www2.echo.lu/telematics/education/en/interact/bul_5th2.html/*.

Gellert, C. (1993) 'Structures and functional differentiation – remarks on changing paradigms of tertiary education in Europe', in C. Gellert (ed.), *Higher Education in Europe*, London: Jessica Kingsley, 234–46.

Girod de L'Ain, B. (1997) 'The future of European universities. How should students earn their diplomas? Nine goals for renovation', *Higher Education Management*, 9, 1997, 85–104.

Keegan, D. (1994) *Distance Training in the European Union*, Hagen: Zentrales Institut für Fernstudienforschung der FernUniversität.

Keegan, D. and Rumble, G. (1982) 'Distance teaching at university level', in G. Rumble and K. Harry (eds), *The Distance Teaching Universities*, London: Croom Helm, 15–31.

Laurillard, D. (1993) *Rethinking University Teaching. A Framework for the Effective Use of Educational Technology*, London: Routledge.

MacKeogh, K. (1997) 'Distance higher education policies in Europe: cooperative and competitive approaches', in C. Olgren (ed.), *Competition, Connection, Collaboration: Proceedings of the 13th Conference on Distance Teaching and Learning*, Madison: University of Wisconsin, 203–11.

National Committee of Inquiry in Higher Education (1997) *Higher Education in the Learning Society*. Available HTTP: *http://www.leeds.ac.uk/educol/ncihe/*

OECD (1995) *Continuing Professional Education of Highly-Qualified Personnel*, Paris: OECD.

Rumble, G. and Harry, K. (eds) (1982) *The Distance Teaching Universities*, London: Croom Helm.

Scott, P. (1996) 'Unified and binary systems of higher education in Europe', in A. Burgen (ed.), *Goals and Purposes of Higher Education in the 21st Century*, London: Jessica Kingsley, 37–54.

Teichler, U. (1996) 'Higher education and new socio-economic challenges in Europe', in A. Burgen (ed.), *Goals and Purposes of Higher Education in the 21st Century*, London: Jessica Kingsley.

Turner, D. (1996) 'Changing patterns of funding higher education in Europe', *Higher Education Management*, 8, 1, 101–11.

van Dam-Mieras, R. (1997) 'European agenda for change for higher education in the XXIst century: the Open University of the Netherlands', unpublished paper given to the European Rector's Conference, Palermo.

Wilson, K. and Baumeister, H.-P. (1998) 'Knowledge exchange in Europe: the CEFES project', in A. Szücs and A. Wagner (eds), *Proceedings of the Seventh EDEN Annual Conference. Universities in a Digital Era. Transformation, Innovation and Tradition: Roles and Perspectives of Open and Distance Learning*, Bologna, 24–6 June 1998, Budapest: EDEN Secretariat.

The European Commission and open and distance learning

Corinne Hermant-de-Callataÿ

It took time for open and distance learning to be acknowledged as a specific domain for transnational cooperation within European programmes of education and training. In the past, projects that involved the use of open and distance learning techniques and/or the development of multimedia courses and materials had been supported at Community level through the ERASMUS, COMETT and LINGUA programmes. But it was only at the end of the 1980s that open and distance learning and the use of new technology in education started to be explored as a specific domain in the context of education and training policies at Community level.

Before then, cooperation in this field had progressed through several steps. Several seminars were held on the experience in distance education in the various member-states. The European Commission adopted a memorandum on 'Open and Distance Learning in the European Community' (European Commission 1991) which set the framework for cooperation and action at Community level in this field, and contributed to the inclusion of a specific line referring to the promotion of distance education within Article 126 of the Maastricht Treaty.

A series of activities was launched from 1983–90 for the exchange of information and experience relating to the introduction of new technologies in education. Twelve national reports were written in 1992 and 1993 describing the use of new information and communication technology within member-states. In November 1992, the Ministers of Education issued recommendations on cooperation in these fields. This whole process resulted in the integration of an action specifically addressed to the promotion of open and distance learning, within the SOCRATES Decision.

The concept of open and distance learning was felt as the most appropriate to embed the many dimensions of the integration of information and communication technology in the learning process, with a view to the learning process itself rather than technology. Since then, the concept of multimedia has made its official appearance in many areas, as another way to condense the innovations which are taking place in the educational world.

Open and distance learning involves the use of new methods, technical and/or non-technical, to improve the flexibility of learning in terms of space, time, choice of content or teaching resources, and/or to improve access to educational systems from a distance. In the action 'Promotion of open and distance learning', the concept of open and distance learning is explained in its broader meaning: the use of multimedia services and products in any existing or potential educational place, and the providing of distance learning services.

The Commission has now proposed a second phase of the SOCRATES programme, within which a specific action would be devoted to open and distance learning and to the promotion of a responsible and critical use of new technology in education. This action, still under discussion, is called ATLAS: Accessible Teaching and Learning Across educational and technological Systems. The following sections provide a summary of the observations which can be drawn so far from the open and distance learning action of the current SOCRATES programme.

A strong rationale for cooperation

New technologies today represent a compulsory route which all pedagogical itineraries appear to follow. And yet, in spite of the fact that pilot experiences have been undertaken in a number of different countries, and in spite of statements which appear in national and regional plans, actual employment of these technologies has not progressed as quickly as was originally foreseen. Teachers and trainers are for the most part not persuaded of the benefits of technology and of its advantages for their daily work. Moreover multimedia equipment, access to networks, and support services are still largely missing from places where training is undertaken. The most conclusive experiences frequently stumble on the capacity of institutions to integrate innovations. There is also hostility from many managers, uneasy at developments which they have not anticipated and which challenge the traditional organisation of training and the management of time and space.

There is a great deal to be done, and the role of the European Commission in this context could prove decisive, given the crucial importance of the exchange of experience and analysis. In this perspective, the SOCRATES and also the Leonardo da Vinci programmes have since 1995 facilitated the launch of a series of cooperative projects concerning the promotion of open and distance learning, including the employment of new technologies within traditional systems of training. One hundred projects have been financed within the SOCRATES programme and 150 within Leonardo da Vinci.

Around this concept, which includes educational multimedia, the Commission has gathered all those who work at the European level to explore the potential of information and communication technologies and to develop methodologies to exploit them for the benefit of the training sector. This European cooperation aims to stimulate innovative pedagogical and organisational processes. It concerns, for example, exploring the application of technologies to encourage collaboration between students, between teachers, and between trainers. It is also involved with supporting the training of teachers, trainers and managers. It also has to do with the question of developing strategies for improving the quality of multimedia products and services.

This cooperation aims equally at an improvement in access to education and to training for all those who are presently excluded. It must be concerned with those who do not have access to educational facilities or to traditional training because they live in rural areas or are far away from training centres. It is equally about those who are excluded because they belong to disadvantaged groups because of their social or working situation, or because of disability.

Projects financed since 1995 have been classified according to the following three perspectives.

Improving the understanding of innovations in progress

Action research projects, studies and pilot experiences have been launched under this heading. Through projects in this area, teams from several European countries collaborate to 'learn by working together' on a common project. Projects are mostly innovative; they bring some new element to the manner in which classical education systems approach one or other type of training. Such a project may for example bring into contact teachers and trainers from the agriculture sector from three different regions of Europe. Each team carries out a local study in its own country according to a predetermined approach. Then a videoconference is organised in such a way that everyone can reflect both on their regional practice and on the European dimension of problems which they encounter. In this type of experience, the accent is placed on processes rather than on the product. In analysing the processes, the projects work towards teaching the best means of training teachers and trainers in good technology application. Other projects set out to analyse the potential of virtual mobility. Here, the emphasis is on the way in which technologies supplement physical travel across Europe. In effect they are creating novel means of collaborating at a distance. In one project, dialogues are instituted between students and teachers, between Bergen and Bologna, in the context of a conference on Umberto Eco. In this process, the keys to a fruitful dialogue depend not on the technology but on the capacity of teachers as trainers to construct situations for dialogue and interaction.

Developing information and communication services

European cooperation depends essentially on the creation of human networks. To sustain this dynamic, the Commission has retained several projects which aim to collect, structure and facilitate access to information. An example of this approach is the BASE (Base de données des Acteurs et des Supports Educatifs multimédia) project. Five partners, two French, one Italian, one German and one from the UK have come together to design, compile and produce a database containing information on 756 operators and pedagogical resources in the field of multimedia for education and training. BASE intends to provide a global picture of supply in the domain of multimedia educational products, and aims to enable users to get answers to their questions conerning products, suppliers, customers and potential partners. The database is addressed to a variety of users, including national organisations, professionals and institutions. It will be developed through a questionnaire sent to relevant actors, and will give rise to a CD-ROM on products and to a directory of actors available both in printed form and through the Internet. In this example, the emphasis is on the products, but in other European-funded projects, it is information on the process (the evaluation of products, for example, training of teachers, or of multimedia trainers) which is structured and reported.

More and more, trainers and managers on the ground find themselves confronted with the same difficulties and the same opportunities wherever they are located in Europe. The role of European projects is to build bridges between actual practitioners in order to determine common approaches. Information and communication systems, which are so widely available, are an essential component in this.

Creating pilot modules and developing methods

The creation of pilot modules constitutes a third essential perspective for the SOCRATES and Leonardo da Vinci programmes in the area of open and distance learning. Nevertheless, it is fair to acknowledge the fact that, here also, attention is directed towards the professional training process rather than towards products. The support of the commission is for example linked to the quality of the collaboration which is constructed in order to develop multimedia products and services. In the educational domain, it is also the quality of the European process or the exemplary approach which are the determining criteria for European Union assistance.

Types of projects

In SOCRATES-ODL, there are two types of projects – European partnership projects and observation projects.

The purpose of European partnership projects is to foster synergy and exchange of experience and resources at the European level through the process of working on collaborative transnational projects. They frequently involve a significant number of partners and must, in any case, involve partners from at least three countries. They are intended to contribute to the development of cooperation and human networks between users, producers and providers of ODL products and services in Europe.

Such projects aim at creating the conditions for a sound integration and development of innovative models within the learning environment. How to find the right pedagogy? How to match it with the constraints of costs and organisation associated with the innovations involved? How to gain the users' and managers' acceptance of these innovations?

The purpose of Observatory projects is to produce a comprehensive picture of the state of the art of particular aspects of ODL or the use of new educational technologies across a broad section of the countries participating in SOCRATES. There are several ways that this might be achieved, for example, through surveys, development of databases, training and workshops, information seminars, development of new models, etc. Although it is not mandatory to have a minimum of three European partners, consortia involving organisations in several countries are better placed to achieve optimal coverage and validity of outcomes.

Conclusion

It is difficult in just a few lines to provide a full account of the wide diversity of experiences which are developing today locally or at European level within communities which are concerned with common questions across national frontiers.

The first conclusions which can be drawn are:

- the quality of the pedagogical approach is the essential criterion of experiences analysed or developed at the European level, no matter what the level of training;
- work in collaboration and training in collaboration are growth areas for the employment of technologies. Nevertheless, they assume a mastery of the processes of communication. The technology must be transparent to the user; social and organisational aspects must be to the fore;
- there are real gulfs between different types of available electronic resources. Activities such as consulting data, finding information, and acquiring knowledge and 'learning' involve different processes; some of these activities demand much more than on-line services simply being made accessible. There is a qualitative leap between using electronic means to transmit data to a user, and ensuring that the user learns. This distinction is not always fully perceived;
- the European dimension of experiences raises difficulties which are, in themselves, sources of analyses and recommendations: the diversity of languages and of cultures should perhaps be taken into account more seriously in the future;

- the production of educational multimedia by students or by adults in training, who register in a project, has proved very fruitful. Several models of this type have been developed within projects;
- finally, we can witness the breaking down of barriers between different participants through educational processes or training. All innovative projects involve the development of multilateral collaborations which challenge the traditional frontiers between schools, universities, associations, businesses, and local groups. Technology is not itself the originator of the processes of the breaking down of barriers, but it is one of the catalysing elements.

The fields covered by the pedagogic application of technologies and of multimedia in different countries constitute a series of icebergs of which it is only possible to see the small parts which emerge at the European level.

Ten or twenty years ago, many people thought that a critical mass of multimedia products would be required for the 'information revolution' to succeed. Today, the same people and others think that widespread access to the Internet can bring about 'the information society'. Our experience shows us that it is necessary to have a critical mass of experiences of applications of the technologies and of reflections on these applications so that a true 'learning society' can be successful.

Note

The opinions expressed above do not necessarily reflect those of the European Commission. This chapter is adapted from existing publications from DG XXII (Education, Training and Youth) of the Commission: *The Magazine* (1998 – Issue 9) and *ODL in action* (mimeo August 1998).

References

European Commission (1991) *Memorandum on Open and Distance Learning*, Brussels: EC.

European Commission (1997) *ODL in Motion: Current Trends and the Way Forward Within the Action Plan Perspective* (mimeo), Brussels: EC.

Chapter 11

Oceania

The Australian education scene has been subject to almost continuous change over the last decade, and distance education has been affected as much as any sector. King documents the sequence of political and organisational events which has led to the present situation where distance education and open learning provision are widely available from a high proportion of higher education institutions, and Moran and Myringer also discuss some of the current trends and issues within distance teaching institutions. The term 'external studies' has traditionally been widely used in Australia and neighbouring countries, but one of the symptoms of change has been in the emergence and use of additional terms such as 'open learning', 'flexible learning' and 'flexible delivery', which reflect not only a general conceptual move towards more student-centred provision, but also a demand for institutions to produce course materials very quickly utilising the whole available range of technologies.

The Open and Distance Learning Association of Australia (ODLAA) was renamed in 1993 from the Australian and South Pacific External Studies Association (ASPESA). The change in title, as well as acknowledging the need to recognise new terminology, incorporates a narrower geographical focus. ODLAA, whose Web site is at http://usq.edu.au/dec/decjourn/odlaa.htm/, continues to publish the journal *Distance Education*, whose focus is international, and a volume of papers to accompany its biennial conference.

The former South Pacific members of ASPESA have re-formed to establish their own association, the Pacific Islands Regional Association for Distance Education (PIRADE). For many years, the island nations of the South Pacific were served almost solely by the University of the South Pacific, which is a dual-mode institution. Matthewson and Va'a's chapter describes the changing situation in which a number of other institutions and organisations are beginning to provide their own distance-taught programmes and courses.

New Zealand is also well served by distance education providers. A decade ago, the pattern of provision was relatively clearcut. Although there were also some specialist providers, the principal actors were Massey University, at higher education level; the Open Polytechnic of New Zealand offering technical and further education; and the Correspondence School, operating at primary and secondary levels. There has been a steady proliferation of new distance higher education providers, most of which are conventional universities and polytechnics, exploiting new opportunities offered by advances in computer and telecommunications technologies. Massey and the Open Polytechnic have responded to the challenge, so that the New Zealand scene is quite dynamic. The Distance Education Association of New Zealand (DEANZ) is a good source of information, holding regular conferences and workshops and publishing its own journal. At the time of writing, a Web site is planned.

Distance education in Australia

Bruce King

The development of open and distance learning in Australian higher education over the last decade is inextricably bound to the changes which have
shaped the university sector in general. This results from the particular
model of distance and open provision which has characterised the Australian
higher education scene since the establishment of the University of New
England in the 1950s.[1] Those courses offered off-campus are simultaneously
run on-campus, by the same academic staff, and with identical curricula and
expectations of students wherever they study. Only the delivery mode is
different. This means that for the large part of its short history in this country, open and distance provision at university level has had characteristics
which distinguish it from experience elsewhere. Two examples will suffice to
make the point.

First, off-campus provision has been for one of two reasons: institutional
viability or considerations of access and equity. The connection between
these is sometimes blurred. This needs some explanation. Australian universities, many of which were established initially as colleges of advanced
education, have typically been commuter institutions. There has not been a
significant pattern of students relocating between towns and cities to pursue
study programmes. Further, a number of institutions were established in
regional communities by way of government support for politically sensitive
electorates. Unless those institutions were highly specialised (e.g. in agricultural studies) it was extremely difficult for them to establish a viable teaching programme in even a minimal range of discipline areas without recruiting
beyond their local communities. Not surprisingly, nearly all became significant distance education providers. Metropolitan-based institutions that
moved to off-campus delivery of some courses had more mixed motivations.
Course viability sometimes played a part, but a larger consideration was government and social concern about overcoming barriers to access in higher
education. Of course, one person's institutional viability can be another's
social justice. The latter has tended to dominate the consciousness of
educators.

Second, the Australian higher education scene is very much that of government-supported homogeneity. Of the thirty-nine universities in Australia, thirty-seven were established and continue to be largely supported by government. While there are differences both in specialisation and quality within individual discipline areas, the institutions are predominantly comprehensive and broadly overlapping in their course offerings. While not all universities offer distance or open courses, there is still sufficient duplication of provision for very few Australian university providers to achieve the economies of scale off-campus which characterise distance provision elsewhere. This has implications for quality. If an institution is unable to amortise the costs of production with a large student cohort over time, there is a resultant press to keep those costs at a minimum. One consequence of this is that many Australian universities have pressed academic staff to author distance course materials as part of their teaching responsibilities; preparation of distance learning materials has been equated with on-campus preparation for teaching.

In short, university-level distance or open education in Australia has typically been provided from dual-mode institutions, sometimes for reasons of institutional viability but justified on access and equity grounds, often to small groups of students in significant competition with other providers, without the advantages of economies of scale common in other countries, using development strategies which reflect resource constraints and low expectations of production quality.

The Dawkins' reforms

It is the dual-mode nature of provision which so strongly ties developments in open and distance education to those occurring in higher education generally and over the last decade these have been substantial. Because of the public nature of Australian universities, government policy can have profound effects on them and the ten years from 1988 begin and end with significant government intervention in the higher education sector.

John Dawkins, the Australian Labor Party Minister for Employment, Education and Training, initiated major changes to the sector in the Commonwealth government policy statement on higher education in July 1988. Specifically, Dawkins sought to create a unified national system by merging the previously separate college of advanced education sector with existing universities. New institutions were commonly formed through amalgamation, many of them very large and dispersed over sometimes distant campuses. An international review of tertiary education in Australia pointed to the success of government in achieving desired institutional course and student profiles across the new universities. These were tied to funding allocations, which gave government officials considerable leverage in negotiations with institutions, but the new profiles were really only possible because of conditions created by mergers (DEETYA/OECD 1997: 3).

Other characteristics noted include:

- leadership and management problems arising from restructuring of institutions;
- increases in workload, both administrative and academic;
- challenges arising from the increasing diversity of students;
- a system of deferred payment for tuition;
- one of the fastest growth rates of student enrolments among OECD countries;
- a robust national policy environment;
- a spirit of entrepreneurial adaptability within institutions.

The implications for open and distance education of these general characteristics have been significant, as the following examples indicate.

First, at the time of the Dawkins' reforms, the greater part of post-secondary distance education was provided in the college of advanced education sector. The move to university status carried with it new expectations in relation to research output. For many, these intensified the demands made upon them by the need to produce distance teaching materials.

Second, as student numbers increased, teacher : student ratios worsened and, in distance education programmes where assessment was substantially based on written assignments, marking workloads sometimes became intolerable.

Third, the increase in student numbers also carried a greater diversity in the enrolment profile and there was pressure to provide programmes for students from diverse backgrounds such as Aboriginal Australians and people for whom English was not their first language. Such expectations produced new sets of demands, both for teaching materials and assessment activities which were inclusive of the experience of such students and for additional forms of learner support to ensure parity of educational outcomes with others taking the same courses.

Finally, the Dawkins' reforms extended to off-shore education. What had been a long tradition of educational aid became educational trade. Australian universities competed intensively for overseas students, most of whom relocated from Asia to take courses in the cities of Melbourne and Sydney and later elsewhere. While distance education seemed ideally suited to delivering programmes to students overseas, there was initially slow acceptance of such programmes in South-East Asia, where the Australian commitment to identical content and standards in both on- and off-campus courses was unusual. However, the cost advantage of taking an Australian degree without relocating from home led to a significant take-up of distance programmes from one or two universities which aggressively marketed their courses overseas. Within three years, some 2,700 overseas students enrolled in distance education courses, adding $13 million to Australian export income (NBEET 1992: 10).

Distance Education Centres

Beyond the general changes to the university sector in 1988 there was specific government attention given to distance and open education.[2] There had been rapid growth in distance education enrolments during the 1980s. Typically,

> distance provision arose rapidly and unplanned from existing on-campus courses, often in business or teacher education, and usually in advance of the capacity or willingness of institutions to provide appropriate levels of infrastructure support. As a consequence, some of the courses available were of poor quality, duplicated provision elsewhere, and appeared to take little account of any sensible cost-benefit analysis.
>
> (King 1994: 6)

The Commonwealth was determined to improve distance education and had a particular strategy in mind. The government would use its funding power to limit access to the means of production of distance education courses to a handful of institutions designated as Distance Education Centres (DECs). Other universities would have to purchase production services and other expertise from the DECs using part of the recurrent grants they received for teaching external students. Special funding arrangements were developed by the Commonwealth government to ensure compliance with its strategy.

The selection of eight Distance Education Centres was competitive and based on written bids and institutional visits. The assessment team represented both the Minister's department and the national advisory body, the Higher Education Council. Selection was influenced by publicly declared criteria such as the number of distance students currently serviced, the range of course offerings, and the existence of appropriate production and delivery infrastructure within the institution. It would appear that other factors (e.g. reasonable distribution across the six states of the Commonwealth and some correspondence to population spread) also influenced the recommendations.

Overall it would be hard to argue that the DEC system worked as the government intended. One institution, the University of South Australia, was acknowledged as working exactly as the government's rationalisation of distance education provision had intended (NBEET 1992: 6). This was very much a matter of institutional policy. The University had the smallest number of distance students in the DEC group and, as a large metropolitan university with a predominantly on-campus enrolment, did not rely on distance students for institutional viability. It did, however, have a strong commitment to access and equity in its mission and believed DEC status would enhance its capacity to discharge part of that charter. Further, as a post-Dawkins' university, it realised that designation as one of the eight national centres would raise its profile nationally. Accordingly, the University sought assiduously to meet the expectations of government in this area.

Johnson was possibly the first to recognise that a significant contribution of the DECs was to a professional distance education ethos or DEC culture. He describes its elements as:

> a belief in distance education; an awareness of the techniques, the technologies and the production processes; a respect for expert advice and recognition of the need for it; a sense of precision and structure in development of course materials; and an awareness of a range of possibilities in approach.
>
> (NBEET 1992: 6)

This ethos remains strong today and in part explains what could reasonably be considered the disproportionately large contribution of Australians to the literature and discourse of distance and open education. For example, there has been a serious Australian commitment to improving the professional standing of distance educators. The world's first qualification in the field was the Graduate Diploma in Distance Education offered in 1983 by the then South Australian College of Advanced Education. As the College was accorded university status in 1991 following a merger under the Dawkins' reforms, it moved with Deakin University on another first, a Master's degree in Distance Education, developed and taught collaboratively between the two institutions from 1992. Deakin University also introduced the biennial Research in Distance Education Conference which moved conference presentations on open and distance education well beyond the unreflected descriptions of practice which so dominate other forums. More recently, the University of Southern Queensland, like Deakin and the University of South Australia one of the original DECs, has had considerable success in fostering research, scholarship, on-line teaching, and international relationships within the open and distance education field.

From the perspective of the late 1990s, the DEC system worked well for a time, but the arrangements established by government were out of step with the times and were criticised as unfair. This caused a change in official attitudes before sufficient information was available to make an informed decision. In fact, the turn-around in government thinking was breath-taking. To summarise:

> The DECs were established by government decision in late 1989 and became operational in 1991. Dissatisfaction with the new system was evident as early as the first quarter of 1991. The National Board of Employment, Education and Training (NBEET) recommended the

removal of the funding arrangements which underpinned the system in June 1992, and this recommendation [came] into effect at the end of 1993. In little over a year, the DEC system came into operation and was abandoned. Clearly, the DECs had not time to establish how they would operate to further government aspirations.

(King 1994: 1)[3]

Despite the winding back of the DEC system, the universities involved had some very real success, if not always in areas the government initially intended. Three are discussed below, involving professionalism, quality and innovation.

The DEC system was a strong signal that government took distance education seriously and the government-funded universities quickly followed suit.[4] The DECs were successful in improving the quality of course offerings. Increased scrutiny played some part in this, as did competition to attract both students and revenue-generating specialist providers. The tangible nature of distance-teaching resources meant that the quality of institutional offerings was open to the judgement of friend and competitor alike. Government interest in distance education was quickly mirrored by private enterprise and major corporations made initial overtures to the DECs for assistance with in-house training or, in the case of some professional associations, the continuing education of their members. Decisions with significant consequences for revenue generation frequently turned on the quality of course materials and of the support infrastructure available to students. Quality of provision became an institutional priority. This was in line both with the quality movement in industry and the decision of the government to establish a non-statutory body, the Committee for Quality Assurance in Higher Education, which both assessed and rewarded university performance. Institutions were quick to recognise that distance education could demonstrate achievement not only in relation to the standards of teaching resources and support available for off-campus students but also in the responses made to government-nominated access and equity targets.[5]

The Open Learning Agency

An innovation with which the DECs were centrally involved was the establishment in 1992 of a private educational broker, the Open Learning Agency of Australia (later Open Learning Australia and, commonly, OLA). OLA was a major innovation funded by the Commonwealth government with the intention of making university subjects available to anyone who wished to take them upon payment of a tuition fee. The subjects had to be accredited by the universities from which they were offered and permit those taking them successfully to accumulate sufficient credit to obtain a degree. OLA was a considerable force for change within participating universities, particularly in relation to recognition of, and credit for, studies taken elsewhere. It also provided a substantial challenge to conventional notions of university entrance requirements, particularly as OLA-enrolled students began to succeed in subjects for which the only prerequisite was a fee payment.

OLA could not have survived without the DECs. It had no production capacity, accrediting authority, student-support or resource-delivery infrastructure, or professional development expertise in relation to off-campus delivery. While other institutions successfully contracted to provide subjects for OLA (Griffith University being a good example) its initial success was due to the capacity of the DECs to rebadge existing distance education subjects under the Agency banner. It was not only their production, delivery, and student-support infrastructure that were the cornerstone of OLA operations. The capacity of the Agency to support new developments was limited. Unreasonably low tuition-fee levels insisted upon by government meant only those institutions that could marginally cost their involvement against existing distance education activity could contribute on more than the most limited basis. Further, only universities with significant distance education expertise had the capacity to create teaching materials with the high level of embedded teaching OLA offerings required, because of the Agency's incapacity to pay for tutoring or support services.

The DEC system ultimately failed,[6] victim of the government's own central tenet, that control over the means of production for teaching resources would lead, among other things, to an improvement in the quality of off-campus teaching across the Unified National System. Other universities argued that the DECs had privileged access to funds and government-supported technology that prevented non-DEC institutions – the large majority of universities – from pursuing excellence in teaching. This argument achieved greater force through changes in technologies with implications for university teaching.[7]

Quality and information technology

In the early 1990s, the quality movement that took such hold in commerce and industry in the 1980s was having an impact in universities. Driven by active government intervention, through the establishment of the Committee on Quality Assurance in Higher Education, all universities were seeking to demonstrate the value and innovative dimensions of their teaching programmes.

The increasing availability on-campus of new computer-based technologies afforded significant opportunities for both staff and students to engage in fast and effective communications, to identify and retrieve information sources, and to rehearse skills and apply new understanding. Bandwidth constraints in the wider community meant that some on-campus teaching was beginning to provide richer opportunities in resource-based learning than were available through conventional distance education where, for equity reasons, there was a strong commitment to eschewing delivery methods that could not be accessed by all students.

While experience varied between universities, in some DECs there were elements of a rearguard action against the increasing movement to what was being called 'flexible delivery'. This was not so surprising. The DECs had typically managed to establish production systems that afforded their institutions a degree of quality control over distance-teaching resources. These were seen as having implications for institutional reputation. The move to flexible delivery had the potential to avoid these systems. For many distance educators, it was a potential return to the cottage-industry model of earlier external studies programmes they had struggled to overcome. Further, resource-based learning on campus created a form of *de facto* distance student, but without access to the support systems commonly available to distance students. There were calls for greater use of distance-teaching approaches to improve on-campus delivery (NBEET 1992), and enthusiasts with technological expertise began to develop new approaches to computer-supported teaching regardless of the sensibilities of distance educators. The government recognised what was happening and broke its nexus with the DECs. The National Distance Education Conference became the National Conference on Open and Distance Education in 1994 and membership was opened to any institution with an interest in flexible teaching approaches.

Flexible delivery

The move to flexible delivery is discernible across the university system. By flexible delivery I mean the provision of learning resources and the application of technologies to create, store and distribute course content, enrich communication, and provide support and services to enable more effective management of learning by the learner. In particular, the concept involves a view of learning in which a teacher does not predominantly mediate the student's experience.

In Australia, flexible delivery appears to have its origins in the conjunction of three elements: first, the growth and acceptability of distance education which demonstrated the effectiveness of one form of resource-based learning in higher education; second, an increasing acceptance in educational discourse of notions of openness (i.e. an acceptance of the legitimacy of transferring significant control over the learning experience from teacher to student); and third, the increasing availability of technologies with the potential to improve both communication and access to information in educational contexts. It is the last of these which has been most significant in changing teaching practice in higher education, but the other two have provided the legitimacy for using new technologies in teaching.

In a significant study of the introduction of information technologies to teaching and administration in twenty Australian universities, researchers from the Fujitsu Centre found 'almost universal agreement that information technology (IT) initiatives had both improved quality and reduced the costs in teaching and administration. But there was very little evidence . . . to support those claims' (Yetton & Associates 1997: xi).

The authors of the Fujitsu Report suggest that Australian universities will use different strategies to gain strategic advantage over their competitors in the way they apply IT to teaching and learning and argued that in the mid-1990s three generic strategies were evident:

*   Value adding – wherein traditional universities seek to provide high quality experiences for students as new members of a high service, high variety and high reputation educational community;
*   Mass customisation – typically where large devolved universities seek to employ IT through a low cost central infrastructure to empower inno-vation and a focus on student uses of technology in strong and relatively autonomous academic units (e.g. faculties);
*   Standardised delivery – typically where new universities use a separate, centrally resourced unit to build competencies across the institution such that IT-enabled learning can be used to delivery quality, standard-ised programmes to a large number of students (Yetton & Associates 1997: xii–xiii).

It is abundantly evident that most Australian universities are moving quickly to establish both an on-line presence and to employ flexible approaches to learning, although at different rates and not universally across all courses. This movement is typically presented as part of a global trend to which the institution concerned is making a serious response, as indicated in the following:

> The worldwide movement to employ flexible delivery has been stimu-lated by many factors . . . massive growth in number and diversity of student populations; career change as a normal expectation of each working life; commitment to equity of access; major developments in understanding of teaching and learning; a shift in focus from teacher-centred to learner-centred teaching; growth in distance education; the advent of new communication and information technologies; quality evaluation of universities; and a rapidly increasing competition among universities on national and global scales.
>
> (University of Newcastle 1997: 1)

For distance educators in Australian universities, there are thus two kinds of pressures: first, to maintain programmes to support students who wish to study at a distance, although increasingly in programmes directed overseas or to meet the training needs of corporate clients, and, second, to use their expertise and production facilities to provide more flexible learning opportunities for students generally within their institutions. There has been progress on both these fronts since 1988, but again, activity is being significantly shaped by government policy.

The election of the Liberal and National Parties in a conservative coalition government in March 1996 saw a dramatic increase in the intensity of commitment to the power of market forces in higher education. Bradley (1998: 4) argues that as a consequence, universities have had to respond to pressures resulting from the convergence of government policies and external forces in relation to the press to flexible delivery and, in particular, been required to:

• respond to changes in government policy and in funding priorities;
• absorb the effects of economic downturn and demographic shift;
• manage the impact of globalisation and technological change.

What impact this situation will have on open and distance education in the longer term is difficult to judge. The last decade, despite the structural difficulties described above and the pressure on distance educators to address the needs of on- and off-campus students, saw significant growth in distance education numbers. In 1997, distance education (officially, 'external') students comprised 13 per cent of total university numbers, but external enrolments had grown over the previous decade by 82 per cent compared with an increase of 57 per cent in the total student body (Gallagher 1997: 3).

The government predicts a further increase of 17 per cent by the year 2000 (Gallagher 1997: 5). What these numbers obscure – and it would be extremely difficult to obtain accurate figures – is the increasing number of on-campus students who are using resources developed with infrastructure initially developed for distance education. Some reasonable predictions would include:

• private providers competing with universities for distance students in areas of high demand, particularly where such providers use on-line methodologies in a limited number of teaching areas;
• increasing pressure from within universities for distance educators to deliver flexibly study options to students in ways that are more cost-effective than traditional approaches to on-campus teaching;
• expectations that distance education infrastructure and expertise will be used to generate revenue, particularly from corporate clients and in the delivery of programmes off-shore;
• growing tensions between the expectations of quality service with a strong customer focus in the provision of programmes and funding constraints, the substitution of technologically mediated delivery in areas

where there is an expectation of face-to-face interaction, and the need to meet revenue targets;

- increasing tension between the desire to employ new technologies in teaching and learning and the access and equity problems these generate for students in remote areas or from low socio-economic groups;
- growing requirements that expertise in the educational dimensions of resource-based learning be used to support academics as they seek to apply new technologies to on-campus teaching;
- pressure to reduce the number of offerings to students at a distance to enable greater economies of scale in the production of learning resources;
- attempts by management to buy-in distance education resources in areas of high student demand to release staff time for research and higher degree teaching.

Conclusion

In summary, the last decade in distance and open provision from Australian universities started with an attempt by government to bring order and quality control to what had been a significant proliferation of course offerings to external students. The specific structural solution adopted was quickly abandoned although the larger distance education providers continue to operate more or less as the government had intended. During the decade, there was a further significant intervention in the formation of the Open Learning Agency of Australia which was strongly supported by the large distance education universities but had only limited success. With the election of a Conservative coalition government in 1996, the decade ended with the removal of much of the policy framework which had been responsible for the reshaping of Australian higher education and much greater reliance on the power of market forces to shape provision.

Throughout the last decade, the boundary between conventional on-campus teaching and distance and open provision has markedly blurred, leading to the widely used redesignation 'flexible delivery'. This has built on the experience of Australian distance education expertise, the political imperatives of open education theory, and the increasing capacity of technological developments to improve access to content and the interaction between teacher and taught.

Notes

1 This is not true for the earliest phase of off-campus university education in Australia. From 1910, The University of Queensland offered a limited number of programmes from a discrete external studies section which employed its own teaching academics independently of the discipline groups constituting the University at large. The New England model came to characterise distance provision in

Australian higher education in its growth period during the second half of this century, however.

2 This is summarised succinctly in a report commissioned by the National Board of Employment, Education and Training principally authored by Richard Johnson who was a principal figure in much that is described.

3 There is much more specific discussion of the arguments for and against the DECs and the unrealistic expectations of government in an earlier paper (King 1994).

4 There are thirty-seven public universities in Australia, all with substantial government funding, and two private universities.

5 The University of South Australia reported to the Committee for Quality Assurance in Higher Education in July 1994 that its retention rate overall for 1993–4 was 83 per cent compared with the latest available national figures for 1992–3 of 82 per cent. Interestingly, however, the retention rate for Aboriginal and Torres Strait Islander peoples (who suffer massive educational disadvantage in Australia) was 70 per cent and about two-thirds of these studied at a distance. For distance education students overall, the retention rate was 88 per cent which was marginally better than for the on-campus students in the same subjects taught by the same academics.

6 The system failed in that the privileged relationship with government ended, but individual DECs continue to operate successfully. Many other universities, however, developed their own off-campus teaching infrastructure.

7 Ironically, the reasonably widespread view that DECs received privileged access to funds for educational technologies was not true, except in the one case of video-conferencing, which had very limited use as a teaching tool. Perhaps because of the long-standing Australian commitment to forms of distance education which value study opportunities free from the constraints of time and place, the synchronous communication of videoconferencing was seen as more appropriate for administrative use.

References

Bradley, D. (1998) 'Inventing the future: Australian higher education responses', in Indonesian Distance Learning Network, *[Proceedings of the] Third Indonesian Distance Learning Network Symposium, Distance Education and Open Learning: Future Visions, 17–20 November, 1997, Bali, Indonesia,* Jakarta: IDLN.

Department of Employment, Education, Training and Youth Affairs, Commonwealth of Australia, and Organisation for Economic Co-operation and Development, Directorate for Education, Employment, Labour and Social Affairs DEETYA/OECD (1997) *Thematic Review of the First Years of Tertiary Education in Australia,* Canberra: DEETYA. Also available HTTP: *http://www.deetya.gov.au/highered/oprations/thematic_review.htm*

Gallagher, M. (1997) *Current Approaches and Challenges in Higher Education,* Canberra: Department of Employment, Education, Training and Youth Affairs. Also available HTTP: *http://www.deetya.gov.au/highered/pubs/mgspch1.htm*

King, B. (1994) 'Whose future – the Government's, the Distance Education Centres' or the Open Learning Agency of Australia's?', in T. Nunan (ed.), *Distance Education Futures. Proceedings of the 11th Biennial Forum of the Australian and South Pacific External Studies Association, Adelaide, 21–23 July 1993,* Underdale, SA: University of South Australia.

National Board of Employment, Education and Training (NBEET) (1992) *Changing*

Patterns of Teaching and Learning: The Use and Potential of Distance Education Materials and Methods in Australian Higher Education, Canberra: Australian Government Publishing Service.

University of Newcastle (1997) 'Flexible learning: Improving student access and learning – a discussion paper'. Available HTTP: *http://www.newcastle.edu.au/flexintro.htm*

Yetton, P. & Associates (1997) *Managing the Introduction of Technology in the Delivery and Administration of Higher Education,* Sydney: Fujitsu Centre, Graduate School of Management, University of New South Wales, Evaluations and Investigations Programme, Higher Education Division, Department of Employment, Education, Training and Youth Affairs, Commonwealth of Australia.

The South Pacific: kakai mei tahi

Claire Matthewson and Ruby Va'a

It was fitting, twelve years ago, that Professor the Hon. Rex Nettleford of the University of the West Indies (UWI) and Marjorie Tuainekore Crocombe of the University of the South Pacific (USP) were members of Lord Briggs' group for planning the Commonwealth of Learning. The developing 'small states' of the Commonwealth were and remain central to the agency's mandate, and the regions served by UWI and USP include twenty-four of the smallest. In 1986, the higher education issues concerning 'small states' needed to have a voice. The voice still has much to say, but for reasons quite different from those of the 1980s.

Context

The region under review is that served by USP, a Commonwealth university for all twelve of its proprietors: Cook Islands, Fiji, Kiribati, Marshall Islands, Nauru, Niue, Samoa, Solomon Islands, Tokelau, Tonga, Tuvalu and Vanuatu.

Viewed from the outside, in simple land-mass terms, these are indeed 'small states'. Among their thousands of islands, islets and atolls, the largest land-mass of 10,429 km² is Fiji's Viti Levu. Tokelau's three atolls aggregate to only 12 km², the fifteen islands of the Cooks to 240 and Vanuatu's eighty-two to 12,189. National land-masses number from one (Niue) to 400 (Solomon Islands) and approximately 1,000 (Marshall Islands). Distances between the remotest community and its national urban centre range from 5 km (Nauru) to 3,500 (Kiribati).

However, viewed from the inside, these are not 'small states' at all. Lagoons and vast sea areas lie *within* their myriad national lands, just as prairies, deserts or tundra stretch between other countries' settlements. In these terms, Tokelau (the smallest) spans 290,000 km², Cook Islands 1.8 million and Kiribati (the biggest) 3.5 million. This largest of all oceanic and educational regions covers 33 million km², extending approximately W 155–E 150 longitude, S 25–N 17 latitude.

Communities variously inhabit four time zones (the dateline intersecting) and at least sixty distinct cultures. The ethnic heritage of its 1.4 million people is mainly Polynesian, Micronesian, Melanesian or Indian. An estimated 265 languages are spoken, with in-country distinct vernaculars ranging from one (Tonga) to around 105 (Vanuatu).

The majority of the region's population – up to 80 per cent – live in rural village communities that, in subsistence economy terms, have practised 'sustainable development' long before the phrase was coined. Within a global economic context and classification, however, all national incomes except Nauru's are aid-dependent or aid-augmented. Annual GDP per capita incomes range from 'not applicable' (Tokelau) and US $279 (Tuvalu) to US $1,550 (Fiji). The history of colonial intervention in the region is diverse, including the powers of Britain, Japan, New Zealand, Australia, Germany, the United States and France.

Pacific populations are becoming younger, approaching a majority under the age of 20. A commensurate educational phenomenon across the region comprises out-of-school youth. Majority access to a complete secondary school education is available in no country, with 'push-out' systems operating at various levels. In 1995, 'push out' affected 17,500 Solomon Island children from Forms 2, 3 and 5, with only 500 potential work places available (Treadaway 1996). In Vanuatu, approximately 80 per cent of children cannot progress to Class 7. While distance education has some role to play here, the questions of education for whom, and education for what, have no simple answers.

In senior secondary and pre-tertiary sectors, a regionwide challenge is the cost of establishing these higher educational levels for a minority at the expense of access and quality in basic education. At the pyramidal top, higher education in national and regional jurisdictions both inherits this dilemma and exacerbates it. Just as it is difficult to build an upper secondary system on the back of and at increasing cost to an underdeveloped lower system, it is even more difficult to build a higher education system on the back of and at increasing cost to an underdeveloped pre-tertiary system. Educational development in this context risks becoming educational drag: the top drawing off resources from the bottom which, in turn, undermines the top (Matthewson 1996: 23). Within post-secondary and higher education, the region's six largest countries, Fiji, Tonga, Solomon Islands, Kiribati, Vanuatu and Samoa, had capacity in 1992 for 4 per cent of the 18–25 age cohort (Fairbairn 1992: 6).

In the twelve states associated with USP, there are currently seven degree-granting institutions: USP; Pacific Theological College (PTC); Fiji School of Medicine (FSM); 'Atenisi Institute; Pacific Regional Seminary; College of the Marshall Islands and National University of Samoa. The nature of the degrees offered is not common, however, with only USP and PTC offering postgraduate degrees recognised throughout the Commonwealth. USP alone provides comprehensive discipline coverage and doctoral programmes.

Overview of developments

Government priorities for higher education broadly include:

- teacher education, especially for widening access to the school sector at all levels;
- public and private sector development;
- specialised skills to survive in a global economy;
- interfacing with rim country tertiary systems (in response to both internal and external pressure);
- political agendas for education development.

Distance learning's role in respect of these priorities has not radically changed since USP was planned in the 1960s as the region's premier institution of higher education. Reasons for the University's establishment of distance delivery within one year of receiving its charter included that:

- the region to be served is three times larger than Europe, with a diameter one-sixth of the earth's circumference;
- higher education in many areas vital to national human resource development strategies (HRD) had to be sought outside the region, mainly in Pacific rim countries;
- internal study within the region (but not locally) was not a general option for countries with 'low capacity to provide for expenditure on higher education' (Aziz et al. 1991: 3);
- expatriation for study by a relatively elite cohort also exacts social and economic costs within the community.

In brief, member governments applying precious resources to a university thousands of kilometres away expected it to reach their communities, have a strong in-country presence and contribute to their ongoing development as newly independent states.

This context for higher education has not basically changed. Three updating observations could be made, however. Higher education expertise in most key HRD areas has become available within the region and particularly within USP. Despite this, entrepreneurial developed country institutions have increased their in-region activities. At the same time, expanded capacity in many national school systems continues exponentially to be outstripped by increasing populations.

Within higher education, the current decade has brought dramatic developments in distance and open learning. These include the emergence of:

- new providers, removing USP's solo status;
- increasingly independent pathfinding;

- regional association and collaboration.

The USP, now in its thirtieth year, continues to expand as Oceania's premier provider of distance higher education. After twenty years as a solo voyager, it was joined by the Fiji School of Nursing (1991), SICHE (1993), PTC (1996) and FSM (1998).

Institutional structures

The USP and those who have joined it are dual-mode institutions. There is no single-mode open university. For USP, enrolment in the distance (Extension Studies) mode has become substantially larger than internal enrolment at its three campuses. Although developmentally important, distance education for the new providers is still a small operational component. All have chosen centralised coordination of distance education development and delivery, with academic content and support provided by teaching departments. All follow a team model for course development, comprising authors working in concert with designers, editors and media advisors. In contrast, each has structural aspects of interest to note.

The University of the South Pacific

The University adopted what was once the New England model of distance education. This comprises a centralised Extension Services to administer, develop and support distance programmes taught by dual-mode departments. Extension Services, renamed University Extension in 1992, also includes the staff, resources and activities of the University's respective national centres, the world's first satellite-for-teaching system (USPNET), and responsibilities for regional continuing education.

This 'mixed-mode, multi-departmental model' (Keegan and Rumble 1982: 27) remains both intact and strengthened. By the mid-1990s, the initial Extension staff of six had reached 160, about two-thirds of whom are located throughout the region in a network of centres and outer island sub-centres. This figure does not include local part-time tutors. Senior staff in the headquarters (management, instructional designers and editors) and lecturers in the centres have academic status. USP's five schools or faculties all teach distance-mode programmes (carrying identical credit with those internally taught) and as part of normal load. Policy decisions specific to distance education are the prerogative of the Distance Education Committee, chaired by the Deputy Vice Chancellor and comprising the Heads of School and University Extension Directorate. Contribution to distance teaching is a criterion for academic promotion.

Funding of distance education resides in USP's core budget, 72.3 per cent of which will be provided by its twelve proprietor countries in 1998.

Members' main contributions are levied on the basis of respective national full-time equivalent students (FTES). Distance students are included in the accounting (and substantially so). Countries also contribute relative to the value of USP human and capital resources located in their territories. In 1998, New Zealand and Australia will provide 8 per cent of the core budget. Fees, interest and revenue-generating activities provide the remaining 19.7 per cent. Across academic disciplines, students pay non-differential tuition fees that accrue to the University's general ledger.

Fiji School of Nursing

This is a dual-mode institution based in Suva, catering for approximately 120 students each year. Although nationally owned and funded, FSN regards itself as a regional trainer. FSN is unusual in the Pacific for its post-basic nursing education in distance mode. Now in its seventh year of offering, the Diploma in Nursing Management was launched with support from the World Health Organisation (WHO). The one-year programme, centrally coordinated and planned for enlargement, targets experienced professionals (Cava and Tuiloma 1994: 4–5).

Solomon Islands College of Higher Education

The College was established on Guadalcanal in 1983, amalgamating four government training institutions. As the national tertiary provider, SICHE was founded to meet lower and middle skills requirements. At that time, secondary school completion for higher education, and higher education itself, were locally available only through USP. SICHE offers programmes from middle secondary to advanced diploma level and, more recently, first-year degree provisions.

Distance development began in 1991 and has continued to grow in size and strength since then. Its first distance courses were offered in 1993.

Pacific Theological College

The College was established in 1962 in response to the social, economic and political changes evident within the post-war Pacific. PTC serves a total of eighteen countries spanning in excess of 45 million km^2. In its field, PTC is the region's premier institution of higher learning, with its graduates internationally accepted for doctoral studies.

Distance education beginnings date from 1989 and a Diploma in Theological Studies was launched in 1996 to reach the span of Polynesia, Melanesia and Micronesia.

Fiji School of Medicine

Although a national institution (since 1886), Fiji School of Medicine is a regional trainer, attracting students from fourteen Pacific 'small states'. To develop distance capacity, FSM initially entered into a joint arrangement with the University of Otago Medical School. Core delivery was provided at a distance from Otago by print materials and teleconference, with FSM providing local tutorial support (also by teleconference).

Institutional patterns

In the Pacific region, distance studies in higher education:

* are firmly in place (as they began) to address the practicalities of real distance: that is, they continue primarily for bridging vast geography and its related barriers of access, cost, and small, dispersed populations;
* exist only peripherally for personal convenience or choice of flexible delivery. They retain as their focus a distinct distance-learner profile and generally remain a single-access option for the physically distant;
* tend in their content to reflect and be demand-driven by national and regional HRD considerations rather than by an Anglo-American notion of individual career-path opportunity. (Resources are not the only determinant of this. Strong cultural values prioritise community needs over private benefit);
* are not developed for institutional profit or even cost returns, for they exist to provide contextually affordable education;
* with the exception of FSM, are characterised by providing also for their own preparatory or prerequisite levels of education. This additional 'up-and-down' responsibility of developing their own higher education cohort was noted in the COL review of USP as a feature of 'a new, third world university' (Renwick *et al.* 1991: 65).

Institutions of higher learning in developing regions of 'small states' far from denigrate themselves with sub-degree provisions. In these, they nurture their downstream cohort and thus pursue fulfilment of their higher education mandate. In Oceania, both are achieved largely in distance mode.

Teaching and support methods

In general, the teaching model espoused and consolidating in Oceania's 'small states' is print-based and locally developed:

* supported with tutorials, both face-to-face and via technology;
* augmented often with audio tapes (and occasionally with video);

- supported by human networks of full- or part-time staff;
- centrally coordinated;
- expanding in respect of all these.

Appropriate technology for Pacific 'small states' has as much to do with national resources and climate as with size. Public utilities such as electricity and telecommunications are not comprehensive. Humid salty air, particularly in atoll environments, is corrosive to technical equipment, and repair services may not be available. Traditional housing such as the Samoan *fale* and the Kiribati *maneaba* (which have no walls) or urban households of extended family that have no study space make personal use of some technologies difficult. 'Like the sirens with their enigmatic song in mythology, the technologies beckon, tempt, lure. . . . But we must also listen to another voice intoning . . . we must look at the technology not in the milieu of the siren but in our own context as a teaching institution' (Padolina 1998: 6).

Despite institutional use of Internet technologies, therefore, print remains the core instructional medium. Study guides are often accompanied by off-print readers to obviate the lack of local libraries. Expensive, foreign textbooks are avoided where possible. Audio tapes are common components, as even students without electricity can usually access batteries and a player. If video instruction is included, it is usually for courses whose students have access to a centre. Students are generally not expected to have access to computers. Colonialism, myriad languages and dialects determine English as the common language of instruction.

Distance education in the Pacific 'small states' is notable, however, for use of a particular technology: satellite for teaching support. From 1972 on ATS-1 (though PEACESAT), USP pioneered the sustained use of satellite technology for education delivery. After ATS-1 faded in the 1980s, USPNET moved to INTELSAT, where it has continued. In 1998, negotiations are confirmed for a multi-million dollar replacement system, with assistance from New Zealand, Japan and Australia. The dedicated system is used for tutorials, administration and liaison with university facilities in twelve countries.

Similarly, SICHE used satellite technology from its distance-mode beginnings. The Solomon Islands Distance Education Network (SIDEN), operating on DOMSAT, is a dial-up network administered by the College for tutorials, student support and liaison with provincial study centres. Fiji's schools of medicine and nursing have, from the outset, used teleconferencing as an instruction medium.

The networks characterising Oceania's distance education are, however, more human than electronic, and the two largest providers, USP and SICHE, continue to expand these. If the University of Papua New Guinea (UPNG) and PNG's College of Distance Education (CODE) were included, this Pacific characteristic is even clearer. The four institutions collectively serve almost 100,000 enrolments annually through physical centre and sub-centre networks across islands and remote provinces.

The largest model in the region is obviously USP's. In addition to its three campuses, in all twelve countries the University maintains national facilities for distance and continuing education. Typically, centres comprise management, academic and support staff, a library, computer room, science laboratory, USPNET and e-mail access. Some (Vanuatu, Tonga and Samoa) also have residential facilities. The majority now also have sub-centre outposts, ranging from substantial to agents and facilities in other establishments. The largest centre has thirty staff (Fiji), the smallest, three (Niue). Materials and assignment transport involves a weekly mailbag system now twenty-two years old and initially eight international airlines. Thereafter it involves a multiplicity of national sea and air carriers. Final transport may involve canoes or feet and much walking. In 1996, 84,751 course material items were despatched to centres from Suva. Examinations (common to both modes) are administered by centres simultaneously across the time zones. For access policy reasons, most USP courses (excepting science) have no mandatory face-to-face components. These are often available, however, from local or visiting tutors. Summer schools as an alternative mode are on the increase (thirty-four in 1997).

Audiences

Higher learning's distant audiences in Oceania reflect institutional founding roles and missions. This statement is not casually made, for it reiterates the points of:

- strong policy links between governments' HRD needs and provider concerns. (Indeed, USP's governing Council includes twelve Ministers of Education or their nominees and the institutional budget is set by the Ministers of Finance);
- education's focus on community rather than on private or institutional benefit;
- the challenge to meet the needs of excluded generations (now adult) and to decrease exclusion of increasingly youthful generations;
- westernisation issues relating to health profiles, environmental fragility, economic viability and culture conservation.

USP has distant audiences at senior secondary, vocational (professional) and degree levels. Programmes are completable partly, mainly or entirely in distance mode. Courses adhere to BA, BAg., BEd., BSc. and LLB degrees, to sixteen diplomas (comprising only degree-level components), nineteen sub-degree certificates, two senior secondary programmes and four non-credit continuing education certificates. Some diplomas and certificates are available only in distance mode. The postgraduate audience is served by summer schools. Items of note include that audiences:

- are more urban than rural, mature rather than young, and more male than female;
- include cohorts of full-time students, either in school or based at a USP centre, enrolled in the senior secondary (Preliminary and Foundation) programmes;
- include students of non-USP tertiary institutions that prescribe USP distance degree-level courses in their curriculum.

Of note, the University's distant audience at pre-tertiary level has not diminished. Preliminary and foundation (Years 11 and 12) provisions comprised forty-one courses in 1984, forty in 1989 and forty-two in 1997. Their percentage of the distant programme has altered markedly, however, as students thus prepared increase demand at higher levels. In 1984, 55 per cent of distant courses were pre-tertiary and 31 per cent were degree level. In 1997, 27 per cent were pre-tertiary and 63 per cent were degree. This pattern of a constant, narrow bridge but an increasing cohort demand across it is one that the new Pacific providers will likely share.

SICHE's initial audience was to be in-service teachers (most) without training or complete formal schooling. It then set up an Adult Education Proficiency award to provide access to higher level studies. SICHE's current development includes teacher education, agriculture and professional nursing awards. All schools (education, finance, humanities and science, industrial development, natural resources, nursing) are collaborating with the DEC.

FSM's audience is qualified doctors, especially those involved in surgery, anaesthesia, public health, child health, obstetrics and gynaecology. Graduate diplomas will bridge into Master's degrees with one year's standing. FSM plans also to apply distance methodologies to professional continuing education and consultation services. FSN's current audience is nurses in management positions. It plans to expand into midwifery and public health.

PTC's audience is crucial in the Pacific context. The church's role in social, political, educational and economic development cannot be undervalued, for there is no community issue that lies outside its capacity to influence. It addresses issues of gender equity, population, health, environmental degradation, youth, education and literacy, and participates widely in national and regional NGOs. In the Pacific, mature community leaders undertake theological studies, from the public service, private sector and government. PTC's distance programme provides ecumenical education for this wide audience and also a bridge to higher studies at PTC.

Enrolments

In 1971, USP offered its first two distance courses, attracting 154 enrolments. By 1984, enrolments in seventy-five courses comprised 25 per cent of the full-time equivalent student (FTES) roll. By 1993, 173 courses accrued 46.2 per cent of total course registrations. With a budget substantially allocated on an FTES basis, distance education represents viability for many academic departments (particularly for the School of Humanities with 66 per cent external enrolment in 1996 (5,104 of 7,738)).[1] This is, therefore, a dual-mode university with an interesting profile.

Overall, the male : female ratio in 1996 and 1997 was 56 : 44, identical to that of internal enrolment. National figures indicate lowest female enrolment in Solomon Islands (82 : 18) and the highest in Samoa (46 : 54) (Bolabola and Wah 1995: 176, 275). SICHE enrolments have been 115 in 1993 (two courses), 220 in 1995 (four courses), 870 in 1996 (four courses) and 1,200 in 1997 (six courses). The male : female ratio is 62 : 38. The programme's first full graduates emerged in 1995 and totalled 259 by 1997. In 1996, PTC's first three courses attracted fifty-six students (sixteen female), deriving from nine denominations in eleven countries. The number rose to eighty-four on six courses in 1998.

FSM has only just launched its first course. The postgraduate diploma in surgery has two enrolments, both male, in Tonga and Vanuatu. (Overall the school has a positive gender profile. In 1996, the ratio of male to female was 52 : 48. In the initial three-year tier of the six-year medical programme, it is 45 : 55.) FSN enrols twenty senior nurses each year. All have been female.

Table 11–2.1 Head-count enrolments in distance credit courses

	1989	*1990*	*1991*	*1992*	*1993*	*1994*	*1995*	*1996*	*1997*
Enrolment[a]	11,888	10,851	10,485	10,595	11,386	13,284	15,431	16,302	16,317
Courses	148	145	120	119	173	140	148	153	174

Note
a   *USP Statistics 1996:* 4–1 and *USP Statistics 1997:* 4.1.

Table 11–2.2 Country percentages of overall distance enrolments in 1996

CI	*FJ*	*KB*	*MI*	*NI*	*NU*	*SM*	*SI*	*TK*	*TG*	*TU*	*VN*
2.0	53.6	6.6	2.6	1.2	0.5	3.9	10.6	0.0	8.6	1.1	9.3

Source: Derived from *Annual Report 1996:* 22.

Measures of success

These include:

- student endorsement. Generally enrolments continue to rise, and ceilings constrain demand exceeding supply. Endorsement resides also in the hardships many students embrace for distance study;
- strong commitment in institutional budgets for programme growth;
- low attrition rates by international standards. This was variously noted in NZODA's distance education survey (Hendey 1994: 13).[2] In 1996, semesters one and two USP attrition rates were respectively 29.9 and 21.1 per cent (University Extension 1997: 20);
- ongoing donor support for expanding development;
- fees sponsorship from the private and public sector;
- external review. Successive University Grants Committees affirm distance education as lying 'at the heart of USP's role as a regional university' (Bhim 1990: 21; Kanaimawi 1993: 26);
- consultancy services. SICHE and USP attract external training contracts;
- survival itself. 'There can be no other part of the world with as many challenges to the development of effective distance education as the region covered by USP. . . . The problems that other institutions have to some degree, USP has on a massive scale' (Renwick *et al.* 1991: 41).

Assignment turnaround is not a success indicator in contexts of a monthly boat (Tokelau), erratic shipping and aircraft (Tuvalu) or frequent cyclones. Nor can completion rates be success indicators, for students in these truly dual-mode institutions move and graduate without transcript differentiation between modes. For this reason, true costs per 'distance graduate' do not exist either.

Themes

Throughout this account, the placing of 'small states' within commas has thematic reasons. The Pacific higher education sector, with multiplying voices, is challenging a worldview of its states as 'small'. Belittlement (of 'too small, too poor and too isolated') is increasingly eschewed:

> the peoples of Oceania . . . did not conceive of their world in microscopic proportions. Their universe comprised not only land surfaces, but the surrounding ocean as far as they could traverse [it]. . . . Their world was anything but tiny. . . . There is a gulf of difference between viewing the Pacific as 'islands in a far sea' and as 'a sea of islands'. The first emphasizes dry surfaces in a vast ocean far from the centres of power. . . . The second is a more holistic perspective in which things are

seen in the totality of their relationships. It was continental men, namely Europeans, on entering the Pacific after crossing huge expanses of ocean, who introduced the view of 'islands in a far sea'. . . . Later on it was continental men, Europeans and Americans, who drew imaginary lines across the sea, making the colonial boundaries that, for the first time, confined ocean peoples to tiny spaces.

(Hau'ofa 1993: 6–7)

What is the relevance of this challenge to social science hegemonics in a book on open learning and higher education for the new society? The authors contend that it addresses international issues in education, culture and technology, and particularly in relation to the themes:

- that the capacity for global perspectives on distance education trends may be inversely proportional to geographical size; if so, views held by 'small states' have issues of importance to share with larger states in times of accelerating change;
- that the paradigm shift being effected by technological advance could, if perceived as a global absolute, recast the north–south divide as one of virtual–real world divide and 'small states' as the residual champions of historical memory of distance.

Four matters are raised in relation to these themes. First, that education is the most powerful conduit of culture and its destruction (Goldsmith 1993: 285) is becoming acutely obvious and perceived in 'small states'. Culture is transmitted in what is taught (curriculum). Moreover, that it is transmitted in how the curriculum is taught (pedagogy) is also increasingly perceived (Matthewson and Thaman 1998: 119).

Second, increased flexibility or openness of delivery effected by convergent new technologies is regarded erroneously as having a culture-free value. Independent, self-paced learning is not an educational virtue regardless of context. Indeed, learner autonomy runs counter to some cultures and can impact on holistic value systems in complex ways (Va'a 1997: 85; Wah 1997: 80). That higher education solutions in Commonwealth 'small states' should lie in asynchronous, electronic delivery undertaken virtually alone is culturally questionable. Pacific providers expand their human contact and synchronous communication networks for reasons other than technology unfriendly conditions.

Third, belief by higher educators in convergent technology's eradication of distinctions between distance and internal modes risks losing some of the specific skills, resources and structures that champion the genuine distance learner. S/he still exists (in both the developed and developing Commonwealth) at distances remaining geographic and socio-economic and entrenching with the new distance between the information rich and poor. Large proportions of distance enrollees in North American universities are internal students. These audiences are not all those of the past, now progressed to a brave new world of pedagogical paradigm shift. These are new audiences to which distance mode resources are channelled.

Smallness, like a point in Darien, can afford wide perspectives as trends in 'larger states' impinge from many directions. Regarded at some remove and in their variations, these trends can be comparatively assessed for their contextual value, rather than confused with global absolutes. Belonging to the international higher education community, distance providers serving Pacific 'small states' do travel cybernetic and collegial highways with state-of-the-art technology. Firmly grounded, at the same time, in their national communities, they also strengthen and refashion models of delivery that increasingly are their own.

Finally, in the Commonwealth of Learning's decade, Pacific distance education has come of age in terms of recognising its own experience and expertise. The Pacific Islands Regional Association for Distance Education (PIRADE) was inaugurated in 1995, following the PNG Association for Distance Education's establishment in 1993. PIRADE co-hosted the Open and Distance Learning Association of Australia's 1995 Forum in Vanuatu. SICHE and USP jointly convened the largest ever gathering of Pacific Island distance educators in the 1996 Reaching Out Conference. Pacific institutions now look to one another for consultation and partnership, no longer only or first beyond. It has been a decade of increasingly independent pathfinding for *kakai mei tahi*, the people of the sea.

Notes

1 This only sounds like smoothly evolving history. The year that Lord Briggs' group submitted *Towards a Commonwealth of Learning* was historic for USP; 1987 brought Fiji's military coups, army forays on to the campus to decommission the USPNET satellite system, and Fiji's suspension from the Commonwealth. Fiji's currency devalued by 40 per cent, severely affecting the regional institution's budget and exacerbating an institutional funding freeze that was to last seven years. The fiscal constraints on USP overall impacted most severely on its distance activities. Between 1984 and 1989, USP's roll increased by 44 per cent, comprising a distance enrolment increase of 115 per cent (while internal numbers increased by only nineteen). Growth, currency devaluation and budget freeze decreased real funding per FTES over the period by 33 per cent. In 1990, further constraints were imposed. More recently, external registrations have slightly declined as a percentage of overall numbers. In 1997, they comprised 42.2 per cent as a result of fees increases, some scholarship withdrawal and greater relative growth in internal students.

2 Hendey (1994) cites (with references) attrition rates at Massey University as ranging between 30 and 40 per cent for introductory courses; the University of Papua New Guinea's (in rural areas) as 38 per cent, and rates having been as high as 50 per cent (in South Africa), 62 per cent (in Thailand), 68 per cent (in the UK), 84–99.5 per cent (in Pakistan) and 91 per cent (in Germany).

References

Aziz, U.A., Fairbairn, T.I. and Ward, R.G. (1991) 'Report on the review of the University of the South Pacific', USP Council Paper C33/7/1.

Bhim, T. (Chair) (1990) 'Report of the University Grants Committee of the University of the South Pacific 1991–1993'.

Bolabola, C. and Wah, R. (eds) (1995) *South Pacific women in distance education: studies from countries of the University of the South Pacific*, Suva: USP University Extension, Vancouver: Commonwealth of Learning.

Cava, L. and Tuiloma, L. (1994) 'Distance education for nurses in Fiji', *On PIRADE*, 2, 4–5.

Commonwealth Youth Programme (1995) 'Interview', *South Pacific Centre News*, 9, 3, 11–12.

Distance Education Centre (1997) 'Distance education in Solomon Islands', submission to Solomon Islands New York Mission, Honiara: Solomon Islands College of Higher Education.

Douglas, N. and Douglas, N. (eds) (1994) *Pacific Islands Yearbook*, Suva: The Fiji Times Ltd.

El-Bushra, J. (1973) *Correspondence Teaching at University*, Cambridge: International Extension College.

Extension Services (1992) 'Extension Services and distance education: their future direction and place in the USP', USP Council Paper C35/5/1.

Fairbairn, T. (1992) *Report of the Seminar on South Pacific Post Secondary Education*, Suva: Institute of Social and Administrative Studies, USP.

Goldsmith, E. (1993) *The Way: An Ecological World View*, Boston: Shambhala.

Guernsey, L. (1998) 'Distance education for the not-so-distant', *The Chronicle of Higher Education*, XLIV, 29, A29–30.

Hau'ofa, E. (1993) 'Our sea of islands', in E. Waddell, V. Naidu and E. Hau'ofa (eds), *A New Oceania: Rediscovering Our Sea of Islands*, Suva: School of Social and Economic Development, USP.

Hendey, D. (1994) *Distance Education: Implications for NZODA – A Discussion Paper*, AEAS Report #75, Wellington: New Zealand Ministry of Foreign Affairs and Trade.

Kanaimawi, R.E. (Chair) (1993) *Report of the University Grants Committee of the University of the South Pacific*, Suva: USP Press.

Keegan, D. and Rumble, G. (1982) 'Distance teaching at university level', in G. Rumble and K. Harry (eds), *The Distance Teaching Universities*, London and Canberra: Croom Helm, New York: St Martin's Press.

Matthewson, C. (1996) *Practices and Resources in Distance Education: Pacific Islands (with Particular Reference to Pre-Tertiary Education)*, Vancouver: Commonwealth of Learning.

Matthewson, C. (forthcoming) 'The South Pacific: voyages of navigation in distance education', in R. Guy, T. Kosuge and R. Hayakawa (eds), *Distance Education in the South Pacific: Nets and Voyages*, Suva: USP Press.

Matthewson, C. and Thaman, K. (1998) 'Designing the rebblib: staff development in a Pacific multi-cultural environment', in C. Latchem and F. Lockwood (eds), *Staff Development in Open and Flexible Learning*, London: Routledge.

Matthewson, C., Cokanasiga, I., Wah, R. and Yerbury, C. (1995) *Distance Education*

Feasibility Study in the Republic of the Marshall Islands, Wellington: New Zealand Ministry of Foreign Affairs and Trade.

Matthewson, C., Fairbairn-Dunlop, P., Wah, R. and Wickham, A. (1996) *NZODA Assistance for Distance Education in the South Pacific 1996/7–2000/1: A Development Plan*, revised Matthewson (1997), Wellington: New Zealand Ministry of Foreign Affairs and Trade.

Padolina, M. (1998) 'Challenges in and to education', unpublished paper, University of the Philippines Open University.

Renwick, W.L., King, St C. and Shale, D.G. (1991) *Distance Education at the University of the South Pacific*, Vancouver: Commonwealth of Learning.

Runner, P. (1996) *Education Policy Options for Vanuatu*, Port Vila: Ministry of Education.

Thaman, K. (1997) 'Considerations of culture in distance education', in L. Rowan, L. Bartlett and T. Evans (eds), *Shifting Borders: Globalisation, Localisation and Open and Distance Education*, Geelong: Deakin University Press.

Treadaway, J. (1996) 'Providing primary and secondary education: can distance education help?', unpublished paper, Solomon Islands College of Higher Education.

University Extension (1997) *Annual Report 1996*, Suva: USP.

University of the South Pacific (1996) *USP Statistics 1996*, Suva: Planning and Development Office.

University of the South Pacific (1997) *USP Statistics 1997*, Suva: Planning and Development Office.

Va'a, R. (1997) 'Cultural accountability in the USP science courses at a distance', in L. Rowan, L. Bartlett and T. Evans (eds), *Shifting Borders: Globalisation, Localisation and Open and Distance Education*, Geelong: Deakin University Press.

Wah, R. (1997) 'Distance education in the South Pacific', in L. Rowan, L. Bartlett and T. Evans (eds), *Shifting Borders: Globalisation, Localisation and Open and Distance Education*, Geelong: Deakin University Press.

Open learning and/or distance education: which one for what purpose?

John Daniel

The preceding chapters in this book illustrate well the rich variety of activity that goes under the name of open and distance learning at the turn of the millennium. What else is left to say?

I fear that the very richness and variety of the projects and institutions described mask a problem. There is a conceptual fuzziness that is endemic in open and distance learning which has a number of origins. Confusion of ends and means is one, the search for simplicity in public policy is another, and enthusiasm for the potential contribution of information technology to education and training is a third. When any domain of human endeavour suddenly becomes fashionable it becomes difficult to sustain a clear and consistent framework for discourse about it. Some appropriate the topical descriptor 'open learning' with little concern for whether it really fits their particular activity. Others invent new terms, like 'distributed learning' in order to imply that their own approach is a novel form of distance education. In the early 1990s the European Commission introduced the term 'open distance learning' for its policies and programmes in this broad field. This expression, or its sister term 'open and distance learning', now has wide international currency. The problem with the term is not that it makes light of conceptual rigour but that it can easily mislead people about the educational and social purposes being pursued.

The term 'open learning' stands for the general aim of opening up education and training more widely. Openness has many dimensions and most projects that describe themselves as open learning concentrate on only a few of them. Two examples demonstrate this. For the UK Open University widening intake through open admission was a key dimension. For New York's Empire State College opening up the curriculum for students to design their own programme was the principal goal. Distance education, on the other hand, is one means of pursuing some dimensions of openness. In terms of our two examples it allows the Open University to widen its intake to include people wherever they live but contributes less to Empire State College's goal of letting students shape their own programmes. A simple way to summarise scholarly reflection on these terms is to say that open learning may or may not involve distance education whereas distance education may or may not contribute to open learning.

Today many people automatically associate the educational uses of the newer information and communication technologies with distance learning. This leads them to link three ideas and assume that technology-based teaching will foster distance learning and therefore show productivity gains over classroom methods. There will be widespread disappointment when this assumption proves false, as it usually will.

What are the aims?

The conflation of open learning and distance education into a single descriptor for a broad and diverse field has created confusion about the goals being targeted. It is helpful to list a variety of aims that individuals, institutions and governments may wish to pursue and match them with various approaches to open learning and distance education.

Important aims for the development of education and training may be grouped under five headings:

- *Access.* Where there is a desperate need, particularly in the developing world, to increase access to education at all levels;

- *Cost.* Since resources are finite the aim of increasing access is closely related to the need to reduce costs. This is notably the case for higher education in developing countries;

- *Quality.* When access is expanded and costs are cut there is a risk of loss of educational quality when traditional methods of classroom instruction are used;

- *Flexibility.* At all levels of education, and most particularly in higher education, students have increasingly diverse backgrounds and needs. As the concept of lifelong learning becomes a reality there are demands for education and training to be offered in more convenient ways so that people can fit study around their work and other obligations;

- *Innovation.* This has in some quarters become an aim in its own right. However, the emphasis on innovation implicitly assumes that new techniques will help achieve some of the more concrete aims listed above. The failure to make these secondary aims explicit is responsible for much of the confusion surrounding the use of new technology.

these aims being achieved?

..- nay ask how successful the approaches of open and distance learning have been in achieving these five salient aims, and what are their key features that can claim success in meeting them? In answering these questions I shall focus on applications in higher education and look at the records of four institutional approaches to open and distance learning: the large distance-teaching universities, other distance-teaching universities, dual-mode institutions, and more *ad hoc* applications of technology-based teaching.

The mega universities

Elsewhere (Daniel 1996) I have defined a mega university as a distance-teaching university with a unitary management structure that enrols over 100,000 students annually. There were ten such institutions when I reviewed their activities in 1996 and several others (in India, Iran and Pakistan) have since passed the (arbitrary) threshold of 100,000. How have these mega universities performed against the five criteria of access, cost, quality, flexibility and innovation?

In terms of access the mega universities are clearly a success story. It is not simply that they enrol large numbers of students and account for significant proportions of the university enrolments in their countries. They have also, in most cases, broadened the socio-economic profile of the student body and given special opportunities to students with disabilities and certain other disadvantaged groups. The performance of the mega-universities on cost is also impressive. The cost per full-time equivalent student at these universities lies in a range between 10 and 60 per cent of the average cost per full-time equivalent student at the conventional universities in their own countries.

The quality of the mega universities varies in ways that seem to reflect the ambitions of their founders. The clearest case of demonstrably high quality is the UK Open University, which in 1998 was ranked tenth out of more than 100 UK universities in national assessments of teaching quality. The graduates of Sukhothai Thammathirat Open University in Thailand have the nation's highest acceptance rate for applications to graduate school in other universities. India's University Grants Commission has declared the programmes of the Indira Gandhi National Open University to be of equivalent quality to those in other universities.

Flexibility is a multi-dimensional concept. The mega universities score highly on some dimensions and poorly on others. Most offer students considerable flexibility as regards place of study, reducing to a minimum requirements for students to attend meetings in person. Time of study is also flexible within the constraints of paced systems with a schedule of assignment deadlines. The mega universities are much less flexible in their curricular offerings. Each course tends to be presented as a carefully developed standard package although students usually have considerable flexibility in combining courses to make up their programmes of study.

Technological innovation is also complex. The mega universities have been innovative in the technology of processes but less so in the technology of equipment. Their fundamental innovation was to introduce into higher education the industrial technology of division of labour. By separating the tasks of course development, course presentation, student support and assessment they have created the revolution in approach that underpins their success in achieving other aims. However, although the mega universities must use communications media to reach their students, they are reliant on technologies that are readily accessible to students. This means that they tend to use trailing-edge rather than leading-edge technologies. Nevertheless, because of the scale of their operations they often find themselves pioneering the mass use of new technologies in higher education. An example of this is the UK Open University which, with 40,000 students networked from computers at home in 1998, must be one of the world's most networked universities.

Other distance-teaching universities

Although the criterion of 100,000 enrolments is arbitrary, it does represent some real differences. There are at least twenty universities that operate wholly or mainly through distance teaching but have not achieved the scale of the mega universities.

These institutions share the same access goals as the mega universities and have been successful in achieving them. Being smaller, they are often well integrated with national networks of conventional universities. Perhaps because they are perceived as less different from campus institutions than the mega universities some of them (e.g. Athabasca University and the Télé-université in Canada) attract up to 40 per cent of their enrolments from students who are also enrolled in campus universities. This is an interesting contribution to widening access.

The smaller distance-teaching universities, being deprived of the large economies of scale of the mega universities, do not enjoy the same cost advantage. Nevertheless, by tailoring their curricular diversity and production methods, even institutions with less than 10,000 full-time equivalent students can make themselves cost-competitive with campus universities.

Because they do not seek massive enrolments and are well integrated with national higher education systems, the smaller distance-teaching universities are usually perceived as quality institutions. The Alberta government rates Athabasca University as providing the best student services in the province. Furthermore it seems to be generally the case that students who take distance and campus courses at different universities simultaneously say that the distance courses are more demanding and of higher quality. Their size gives the smaller institutions some advantages on various dimensions of flexibility. The Open University of Hong Kong, for example, uses a variety of courses from other universities which it offers within its own degree programmes. This allows it to expand its curriculum with courses of quality at low cost. The smaller distance-teaching universities are also well placed to innovate intelligently with technology as they can afford to take somewhat bigger risks than the mega universities in trying new approaches with students.

Dual-mode institutions

Australia was a pioneer of the dual-mode approach and remains a leader in its development. Broadly speaking individual faculty members are responsible for teaching the same course in the classroom and at a distance. However, because distance teaching is an integral part of the university's mission it is underpinned by solid infrastructural support. What are the achievements of this approach?

Offering a distance version of some or all courses gives access to the university to students who, for various reasons, cannot come to campus. However, it is not a suitable approach for addressing the high-volume access demands of developing countries. This is because, notwithstanding the infrastructural support provided by the institution, it is difficult to scale up enrolments beyond what an individual academic can cope with.

No one claims that serving students at a distance in dual-mode universities is cheaper than having them as additional students in the classroom. However, when numbers are reasonably small this is a cost-effective means of serving additional students since the same faculty member handles both modes. The involvement of the same individuals in both modes of instruction should also ensure comparable quality. The common outcome of many studies of student achievement is that those taking the distance version of the course perform as well or better than those on campus. Often the discipline of preparing materials for distance students means that the teacher is also more systematic in the classroom.

Dual-mode operation shares much of the curricular flexibility of classroom teaching while providing the desired convenience for the off-campus students. Its potential for technological innovation depends crucially on the tastes and initiatives of the individual faculty members.

Ad hoc technology-based teaching

Today most universities claim to be engaged in some distance education activity. I use the term 'ad hoc technology-based teaching' to describe such activities where the institution has not – or not yet – made the commitment to provide the consistency of infrastructural and systems support that would make it a dual-mode university.

Two common forms of technology-based teaching are remote classroom instruction through telecommunications and, more recently, Internet and Web-based courses. Indeed, the latter are so recent that any assessment can only be preliminary. Practitioners of these forms of technology-based teaching do not claim that they widen access in any significant way. Remote classroom teaching provides a measure of convenience to students away from the campus but is not an approach that lends itself to scale. Web-based teaching is scaleable in terms of sheer numbers if it is thought of as one-way transmission of information. However, by restricting access to those with a networked computer it narrows rather than broadens the clientele served.

Equally, few claim that these forms of technology-based teaching lower the costs of higher education. At best remote classroom instruction allows the inclusion of relatively small numbers of additional students within an acceptable increment in overall cost. The economics of Web-based teaching depend entirely on the scale on which they are used. The quality of remote classroom instruction mirrors that in the classroom but may be slightly better because of the extra effort and preparation required of the instructor. Since Web-based teaching is in its infancy it would be unfair to make quality judgements. Remote classroom teaching provides some flexibility of place but is otherwise similar to regular classes. Web-based teaching appears to be flexible in both place and time, but it is too early to say whether it will be more successful as a stand-alone learning medium or as one element in a multiple-media learning system.

Finally, both forms of technology-based teaching achieve the aim of technological innovation. Because of their appetite for bandwidth, remote classroom teaching systems have been vigorously promoted by the telecommunications industry. The Web has a much wider appeal to the academic community and various projects are under way to provide systems, standards and structures for its use in formal teaching and learning.

Conclusions

We have summarised the achievements of various manifestations of open learning and distance education against five important educational aims: to increase access, cut costs, improve quality, enhance flexibility and innovate intelligently. What can we conclude?

It is clear that the approaches to open and distance learning that have proved most successful in meeting these objectives are the mega universities and the smaller distance-teaching universities. Dual-mode universities and *ad hoc* applications of technology to teaching are making useful and interesting contributions in particular contexts but appear to have limited potential for addressing the crucial issues of access and cost.

What are the features of the large and small distance-teaching universities that have made them able to make such an important contribution to wider access, lower costs and greater flexibility? Essentially it is because they have first reorganised the teaching–learning process and then used particular technologies and media within the context of the learning systems they have created. The key element in the design of their learning systems is that they start with the student and arrange an effective learning environment for individual study. This contrasts with the other approaches we examined which start from the situation of the teachers instructing in a conventional manner and attempt to multiply their impact by using technology.

This book has illustrated well the variety of purposes and the richness of applications that are being pursued in the names of open learning and distance education in the last part of the twentieth century. The diversity of the field is now so great, however, that these terms, when used without qualification, are of limited usefulness for our professional discourse. I conclude with the plea that we discipline ourselves to specify more clearly the particular dimensions of openness we seek to develop through open learning and the educational objectives that we wish to achieve by distance education. There are many challenges facing education and training that open learning and distance education can help us to meet. However, there are no panaceas and we should make clear in each case how we are trying to match solutions and problems.

Reference

Daniel, J.S. (1996) *Mega-Universities and Knowledge Media: Technology Strategies for Higher Education*, London: Kogan Page.

Index